GEOFFREY CHAUCER

THE PROLOGUE

OUR BOOKS ON LITERATURE

Geoffrey Chaucer

THE PROLOGUE

[Including Introduction to the Author and His Times, Complete Text and Paraphrase, Study Questions and Critical Essays.]

Anshu Mallika Sawhney
M.A. English, Delhi University
M. Phil., Himachal Pradesh University

ANMOL PUBLICATIONS PVT. LTD.
NEW DELHI - 110 002 (INDIA)

ANMOL PUBLICATIONS PVT. LTD.

H.O.: 4374/4B, Ansari Road, Darya Ganj,
New Delhi-110 002 (India)
Ph.: 23278000, 23261597

B.O.: No. 1015, Ist Main Road, BSK IIIrd Stage
IIIrd Phase, IIIrd Block
Bangalore - 560 085 (India)
Visit us at: www.anmolpublications.com

First Published, 2009

PRINTED IN INDIA

Printed at Mehra Offset Press, Delhi.

Contents

Preface ix

1. Biography: Geoffrey Chaucer 1
2. A Brief Chronology of Chaucer's Life and Times 17
3. Major Works 22
4. Chaucer's Contemporaries 25
5. Some Important Events in the Fourteenth Century 32
6. The Echo of Black Death in Chaucer's Age 38
7. An Introduction to Middle English 53
8. Introduction: The Canterbury Tales 66
9. List of Characters: The Canterbury Tales 74
10. The Canterbury Tales: Plot Overveiw 87
11. The General Prologue 97
12. General Prologue: Text and Paraphrase 102
13. Summary and Analysis of General Prologue 152
14. Study Questions 157

Q. Crtically Analyse Chaucer's General Prologue. ?
Or
Q. Discuss Chaucer's General Prologue as an Epic Poem.?
Or
Q. Discuss the Genral Prologue placing it in its Historical Context. ?
Or
Q. Discuss Chaucer's use of Irony and Satire in General Prologue. ? 157

Q. Discuss The Narrator as Writer and Pilgrim in General Prologue.
Or
Q. Discuss the role of narrator in General Prologue.
Or
Q. Does narrator in General Prologue acts as a Pilgrim? Elucidate 177

Q. Discuss the presence of Carnival Imagery in General Prologue.
Or
Q. How does Chaucer implements imagery in Genral Prologue. 196

Q. Comment on The Nun Prioress of the General Prologue.
Or
Q. Chaucer describes the nun in the opposite way. Does he do it intentionally? Discuss 202

Q. Draft a Character Sketch of Chaucer's Knight in General Prologue.
Or
Q. Why is Knight an important character in Chaucer's General Prologue? 205

Q. Discuss The Canterbury Tales as Framed Narratives.
Or
Q. Explanations of the function of the Prologue and frame of the Canterbury Tales which fall back on the Gothic nature of the late medieval period may to some extent are right. Do you agree? Discuss
Or
Q. We can, if we wish, look upon two narrative levels—the level of the world of fact and the level of imaginative creation—as an imitation of life itself as it is lived. Elucidate. 206

Q. What is The Role of Women in The Canterbery Tales?
Or
Q. Chaucer, in his female pilgrimage thought of women as having an evil-like quality that they always tempt and take from men. Discuss 220

Q. Analyse the Characters of The Canterbury Tales
Or
Q. An interesting aspect of the famous literary work, "The Canterbury Tales," is the contrast of realistic and exaggerated qualities that Chaucer entitles to each of his characters. Discuss 228

Q. Discuss The General Prologue's Development of the Dream Vision.
Or
Q. Throughout the works of Chaucer, a steady perversion of courtly/romantic tradition shows itself. Do you agree? Discuss
Or
Q. The idea of a dream vision had definite pseudoscientific significance in those times and so in Chaucer's work. Discuss 235

Q. Analyse the Structural Techniques and Devices in The Prologue to the Canterbury Tales. 240

Q. Discuss Contradiction and Corruption in the Canterbury Tales. 241

15. Critical Essays 245

Bibliography 296

Preface

Geoffrey Chaucer (1343 - 1400), popularly known as Chaucer was a writer, official and bureaucrat. He was one of the most remarkable and outstanding poets before William Shakespeare. In the world of literature Canterbury Tales hold special mention, as it is one of the greatest epics created by Geoffrey Chaucer. Meaning of the name of this London born poet in French is shoemaker. His father was an immensely prosperous and rich wine merchant as well as butler of king.

Canterbury Tales was a story of pilgrimage with 30 people. They were going on a shrine of the martyr, St. Thomas on a spring day in April. In order to amuse them, they were telling stories. All these stories were interlinked. But, the book was left unfinished as the author died.

Author

Chapter 1

Biography: Geoffrey Chaucer

Geoffrey Chaucer, English poet. The name Chaucer, a French form of the Latin calcearius, a shoemaker, is found in London and the eastern counties as early as the second half of the 13th century. Some of the London Chaucers lived in Cordwainer Street, in the shoemakers' quarter; several of them, however, were vintners, and among others the poet's father John, and probably also his grandfather Robert. Legal pleadings inform us that in December 1324 John Chaucer was not much over twelve years old, and that he was still unmarried in 1328, the year which used to be considered that of Geoffrey's birth. The poet was probably born from eight to twelve years later, since in 1386, when giving evidence in Sir Richard le Scrope's suit against Sir Robert Grosvenor as to the right to bear certain arms, he was set down as "del age de xl ans et plus, armeez par xxvij ans." At a later date, and probably at the time of the poet's birth, his father lived in Thames Street, and had to wife a certain Agnes, niece of Hamo de Compton, whom we may regard as Geoffrey Chaucer's mother.

In 1357 Geoffrey is found, apparently as a lad, in the service of Elizabeth, countess of Ulster, wife of Lionel, Duke of Clarence, entries in two leaves of her household accounts, accidentally preserved, showing that she paid in April, May and December various small sums for his clothing and expenses. In 1359, as we learn from his deposition in the Scrope suit, Chaucer went to the war in France. At some period of the campaign he was at "Retters," i.e. Rethel, near Reims, and subsequently had the ill luck to be taken prisoner. On the 1st of March 1360 the King [Edward III] contributed £16 to his ransom, and by a year or two later Chaucer must have entered the royal service, since on the 10th of June 1367 Edward granted him a pension of twenty marks for his past and future services. A pension of ten marks had been granted by the king the previous September to a Philippa Chaucer for services to the queen as one of her "domicellae" or "damoiselles," and it seems probable that at this date Chaucer was already married and this Philippa his wife, a conclusion which used to be resisted on the ground of allusions in his early poems to a hopeless love-affair, now reckoned part of his poetical outfit. Philippa is usually said to have been one of two daughters of a Sir Payne Roet, the other being Katherine, who after the death of her first husband, Sir Hugh de Swynford, in 1372, became governess to John of Gaunt's children, and subsequently his mistress and (in 1396) his wife. It is possible that Philippa was sister to Sir Hugh and sister-in-law to Katherine. In either case the marriage helps to account for the favour subsequently shown to Chaucer by John of Gaunt.

In the grant of his pension Chaucer is called "dilectus vallectus noster," our beloved yeoman; before the end of 1368 he had risen to be one of the king's esquires. In September of the following year John of Gaunt's wife, the duchess Blanche, died at the age of twenty-nine, and Chaucer wrote in her honour The Book of the Duchesse, a poem of 1334 lines in octosyllabic couplets, the first of his undoubtedly genuine works which can be connected with a definite date. In June 1370 he went abroad on the king's service, though on what errand, or whither it took him, is not known.

He was back probably some time before Michaelmas, and seems to have remained in England till the 1st of December 1372, when he started, with an advance of 100 marks in his pocket, for Italy, as one of the three commissioners to treat with the Genoese as to an English port where they might have special facilities for trade. The accounts which he delivered on his return on the 23rd of May 1373 show that he had also visited Florence on the king's business, and he probably went also to Padua and there made the acquaintance of Petrarch.

In the second quarter of 1374 Chaucer lived in a whirl of prosperity. On the 23rd of April the king granted him a pitcher of wine daily, subsequently commuted for an annuity of 20 marks. From John of Gaunt, who in August 1372 had granted Philippa Chaucer £10 a year, he himself now received (June 13) a like annuity in reward for his own and his wife's services. On the 8th of June he was appointed Comptroller of the Custom and Subsidy of Wools, Hides and Woodfells and also of the Petty Customs of Wine in the Port of London. A month before this appointment, and probably in anticipation of it, he took (May 10, 1374) a lease for life from the city of London of the dwelling-house above the gate of Aldgate, and here he lived for the next twelve years.

His own and his wife's income now amounted to over £60, the equivalent of upwards of £1000 in modern money. In the next two years large windfalls came to him in the form of two wardships of Kentish heirs, one of whom paid him £104, and a grant of £71,4s,6p; the value of some confiscated wool. In December 1376 he was sent abroad on the king's service in the retinue of Sir John Burley; in February 1377 he was sent to Paris and Montreuil in connexion probably with the peace negotiations between England and France, and at the end of April (after a reward of £20 for his good services) he was again despatched to France.

On the accession of Richard II Chaucer was confirmed in his offices and pensions. In January 1378 he seems to have been in France in connexion with a proposed marriage between Richard and the daughter of the French king; and on the 28th of May of the same year he was sent with Sir Edward de Berkeley to the lord of Milan and Sir John Hawkwood to treat for help in the king's wars, returning on the 19th of September. This was his last diplomatic journey, and the close of a period of his life generally considered to have been so unprolific of poetry that little beyond the Clerk's "Tale of Grisilde," one or two other of the stories afterwards included in the Canterbury Tales, and a few short poems, are attributed to it, though the poet's actual absences from England during the eight years amount to little more than eighteen months. During the next twelve or fifteen years there is no question that Chaucer was constantly engaged in literary work, though for the first half of them he had no lack of official employment. Abundant favour was shown him by the new king. He was paid £22 as a reward for his later missions in Edward III's reign, and was allowed an annual gratuity of 10 marks in addition to his pay of £10 as comptroller of the customs of wool. In April 1382 a new comptrollership, that of the petty customs in the Port of London, was given him, and shortly after he was allowed to exercise it by deputy, a similar licence being given him in February 1385, at the instance of the earl of Oxford, as regards the comptrollership of wool.

In October 1385 Chaucer was made a justice of the peace for Kent. In February 1386 we catch a glimpse of his wife Philippa being admitted to the fraternity of Lincoln cathedral in the company of Henry, Earl of Derby (afterwards Henry IV), Sir Thomas de Swynford and other distinguished persons. In August 1386 he was elected one of the two knights of the shire for Kent, and with this dignity, though it was one not much appreciated in those days, his good fortune reached its climax. In December of the same year he was superseded in both his comptrollerships, almost certainly as a result of the absence of his patron, John of Gaunt, in Spain, and the supremacy of the Duke of Gloucester. In the following year the cessation of Philippa's pension suggests that she died between Midsummer and Michaelmas. In May 1388 Chaucer surrendered to the king his two pensions of 20 marks each, and they were re-granted at his request to one John Scalby. The transaction was unusual and probably points to a pressing need for ready money, nor for the next fourteen months do we know of any source of income possessed by Chaucer beyond his annuity of £10 from John of Gaunt.

In July 1389, after John of Gaunt had returned to England, and the king had taken the government into his own hands,

Chaucer was appointed clerk of the works at various royal palaces at a salary of two shillings a day, or over £31 a year, worth upwards of £500 present value. To this post was subsequently added the charge of some repairs at St George's Chapel, Windsor. He was also made a commissioner to maintain the banks of the Thames between Woolwich and Greenwich, and was given by the Earl of March (grandson of Lionel, Duke of Clarence, his old patron) a sub-forestership at North Petherton, Devon, obviously a sinecure. While on the king's business, in September 1390, Chaucer was twice robbed by highwaymen, losing £20 of the king's money. In June 1391 he was superseded in his office of clerk of the works, and seems to have suffered another spell of misfortune, of which the first alleviation came in January 1393 when the king made him a present of £10. In February 1394 he was granted a new pension of £20. It is possible, also, that about this time, or a little later, he was in the service of the Earl of Derby. In 1397 he received from King Richard a grant of a butt of wine yearly. For this he appears to have asked in terms that suggest poverty, and in May 1398 he obtained letters of protection against his creditors, a step perhaps rendered necessary by an action for debt taken against him earlier in the year.

On the accession of Henry IV a new pension of 40 marks was conferred on Chaucer (13th of October 1399) and Richard II's grants were formally confirmed. Henry himself, however, was probably straitened for ready money, and no instalment of the new pension was paid during the few months of his reign that the poet lived.

Nevertheless, on the strength of his expectations, on the 24th of December 1399 he leased a tenement in the garden of St Mary's Chapel, Westminster, and it was probably here that he died, on the 25th of the following October. He was buried in Westminster Abbey, and his tomb became the nucleus of what is now known as Poets' Corner.

The portrait of Chaucer, which the affection of his disciple, Thomas Hoccleve, caused to be painted in a copy of the latter's Regement of Princes (now Harleian MS. 4866 in the British

Museum), shows him an old man with white hair; he has a fresh complexion, grey eyes, a straight nose, a grey moustache and a small double-pointed beard. His dress and hood are black, and he carries in his hands a string of beads. We may imagine that it was thus that during the last months of his life he used to walk about the precincts of the Abbey.

Henry IV's promise of an additional pension was doubtless elicited by the Compleynt to his Purs, in the envoy to which Chaucer addresses him as the "conquerour of Brutes Albioun." Thus within the last year of his life the poet was still writing. Nevertheless, as early as 1393-1394, in lines to his friend Scogan, he had written as if his day for poetry were past, and it seems probable that his longer poems were all composed before this date. In the preceding fifteen — or, if another view be taken, twenty - years, his literary activity was very great, and with the aid of the lists of his works which he gives in the Legende of Good Women (lines 414-431), and the talk on the road which precedes the "Man of Law's Tale" (Canterbury Tales, B. 46-76), the order in which his main works were written can be traced with approximate certainty,[1] while a few, both of these and of the minor poems, can be connected with definite dates.

The development of his genius has been attractively summed up as comprised in three stages, French, Italian and English, and there is a rough approximation to the truth in this formula, since his earliest poems are translated from the French or based on French models, and the two great works of his middle period are borrowed from the Italian, while his latest stories have no such obvious and direct originals and in their humour and freedom anticipate the typically English temper of Henry Fielding. But Chaucer's indebtedness to French poetry was no passing phase. For various reasons — a not very remote French origin of his own family may be one of them — he was in no way interested in older English literature or in the work of his English contemporaries, save possibly that of "the moral Gower." On the other hand he knew the Roman de la rose as modern English poets know

Shakespeare, and the full extent of his debt to his French contemporaries, not merely in 1369, but in 1385 and in 1393 (the dates are approximate), is only gradually being discovered.

To be in touch throughout his life with the best French poets of the day was much for Chaucer. Even with their stimulus alone he might have developed no small part of his genius. But it was his great good fortune to add to this continuing French influence, lessons in plot and construction derived from Boccaccio's Filostrato and Teseide, as well as some glimpses of the higher art of the Divina Commedia. He shows acquaintance also with one of Petrarch's sonnets, and though, when all is said, the Italian books with which he can be proved to have been intimate are but few, they sufficed.

His study of them was but an episode in his literary life, but it was an episode of unique importance. Before it began he had already been making his own artistic experiments, and it is noteworthy that while he learnt so much from Boccaccio he improved on his originals as he translated them. Doubtless his busy life in the service of the crown had taught him self-confidence, and he uses his Italian models in his own way and with the most triumphant and assured success. When he had no more Italian poems to adapt he had learnt his lesson. The art of weaving a plot out of his own imagination was never his, but he could take what might be little more than an anecdote and lend it body and life and colour with a skill which has never been surpassed.

The most direct example of Chaucer's French studies is his translation of Le Roman de la rose, a poem written in some 4000 lines by Guillaume Lorris about 1237 and extended to over 22,000 by Jean Clopinel, better known as Jean de Meun, forty years later. We know from Chaucer himself that he translated this poem, and the extant English fragment of 7698 lines was generally assigned to him from 1532, when it was first printed, till its authorship was challenged in the early years of the Chaucer Society. The ground of this challenge was its wide divergence from Chaucer's practice in his undoubtedly genuine works as to certain niceties of rhyme, notable as to not rhyming words ending in -y with others ending -ye. It was subsequently discovered, however, that the whole fragment was divisible linguistically into three portions, of which the first and second end respectively at lines 1705 and 5810, and that in the first of these three sections the variations from Chaucer's accepted practice are insignificant. Lines 1-1705 have therefore been provisionally accepted as Chaucer's, and the other two fragments as the work of unknown translators (James I of Scotland has been suggested as one of them), which somehow came to be pieced together. If, however, the difficulties in the way of this theory are less than those which confront any other, they are still considerable, and the question can hardly be treated as closed.

While our knowledge of Chaucer's Romaunt of the Rose is in this unsatisfactory state, another translation of his from the French, the Book of the Lyon (alluded to in the "Retraction" found, in some manuscripts, at the end of the Canterbury Tales), which must certainly have been taken from Guillaume Machault's Le Dit du lion, has perished altogether. The strength of French influence on Chaucer's early work may, however, be amply illustrated from the first of his poems with which we are on sure ground, the Book of the Duchesse, or, as it is alternatively called, the Deth of Blaunche. Here not only are individual passages closely imitated from Machault and Froissart, but the dream, the May morning, and the whole machinery of the poem are taken over from contemporary French conventions. But even at this stage Chaucer could prove his right to borrow by the skill with which he makes his materials serve his own purpose, and some of the lines in the Deth of Blaunche are among the most tender and charming he ever wrote.

Chaucer's A.B.C., a poem in honour of the Blessed Virgin, of which the stanzas begin with the successive letters of the alphabet, is another early example of French influence. It is taken from the Pelerinage de la vie humaine, written by Guillaume de Deguilleville about 1330. The occurrence of some magnificent lines in Chaucer's version, combined with evidence that he did not yet possess the skill to translate at all literally as soon as rhymes had to be considered, accounts for this poem having been dated sometimes earlier than the Book of the Duchesse, and sometimes several years later. With it is usually moved up and down, though it should surely be placed in the 'seventies, the Compleynt to Pity, a fine poem which yet, from its slight obscurity and absence of Chaucer's usual ease, may very well some day prove to be a translation from the French.

While Chaucer thus sought to reproduce both the matter and the style of French poetry in England, he found other materials in popular Latin books. Among his lost works are renderings of "Origenes upon the Maudeleyne," and of Pope Innocent III on "The Wreced Engendring of Mankinde" (De miseria conditionis humanae). He must have begun his attempts at straightforward narrative with the Lyf of Seynt Cecyle (the weakest of all his works, the second Nun's Tale in the Canterbury series) from the Legenda Aurea of Jacobus de Voragine, and the story of the patience of Grisilde, taken from Petrarch's Latin version of a tale by Boccaccio. In both of these he condenses a little, but ventures on very few changes, though he lets his readers see his impatience with his originals.

In his story of Constance (afterwards ascribed to the Man of Law), taken from the Anglo-Norman chronicle of Nicholas Trivet, written about 1334, we find him struggling to put some substance into another weak tale, but still without the courage to remedy its radical faults, though here, as with Grisilde, he does as much for his heroine as the conventional exaltation of one virtue at a time permitted. It is possible that other tales which now stand in the Canterbury series were written originally at this period. What is certain is that at some time in the 'seventies three or four Italian poems passed into Chaucer's possession, and that he set to work busily to make use of them. One of the most interesting of the poems reclaimed for him by Professor Skeat is a fragmentary "Compleynt," part of which is written in terza rima. While he thus experimented with the metre of the Divina Commedia, he made his first attempt to use the material provided by

Boccaccio's Teseide in another fragment of great interest, that of Quene Anelida and Fals Arcyte. More than a third of this is taken up with another, and quite successful, metrical experiment in Anelida's "compleynt," but in the introduction of Anelida herself Chaucer made the first of his three unsuccessful efforts to construct a plot for an important poem out of his own head, and the fragment which begins so well breaks off abruptly at line 357.

For a time the Teseide seems to have been laid aside, and it was perhaps at this moment, in despondency at his failure, that Chaucer wrote his most important prose work, the translation of the De Consolatione Philosophiae of Boethius. Reminiscences of this helped to enrich many of his subsequent poems, and inspired five of his shorter pieces (The Former Age, Fortune, Truth, Gentilesse and Lak of Stedfastnesse), but the translation itself was only a partial success. To borrow his own phrase, his "Englysh was insufficient" to reproduce such difficult Latin. The translation is often barely intelligible without the original, and it is only here and there that it flows with any ease or rhythm.

If Chaucer felt this himself he must have been speedily consoled by achieving in Troilus and Criseyde his greatest artistic triumph. Warned by his failure in Anelida and Arcyte, he was content this time to take his plot unaltered from the Filostrato, and to follow Boccaccio step by step through the poem. But he did not follow him as a mere translator. He had done his duty manfully for the saints "of other holinesse" in Cecyle, Grisilde and Constance, whom he was forbidden by the rules of the game to clothe with complete flesh and blood. In this great love-story there were no such restrictions, and the characters which Boccaccio's treatment left thin and conventional became in Chaucer's hands convincingly human. No other English poem is so instinct with the glory and tragedy of youth, and in the details of the story Chaucer's gifts of vivid colouring, of humour and pity, are all at their highest.

An unfortunate theory that the reference in the Legende of Good Women to "al the love of Palamon and Arcyte" is to a hypothetical poem in seven-line stanzas on this theme, which Chaucer is imagined, when he came to plan the Canterbury Tales, to have suppressed in favour of a new version in heroic couplets, has obscured the close connexion in temper and power between what we know as the "Knight's Tale" and the Troilus. The poem may have been more or less extensively revised before, with admirable fitness, it was assigned to the Knight, but that its main composition can be separated by several years from that of Troilus is aesthetically incredible. Chaucer's art here again is at its highest.

He takes the plot of Boccaccio's Teseide, but only as much of it as he wants, and what he takes he heightens and humanizes with the same skill which he had shown in transforming the Filostrato. Of the individual characters Theseus himself, the arbiter of the plot, is most notably developed; Emilie and her two lovers receive just as much individuality as they will bear without disturbing the atmosphere of romance.

The whole story is pulled together and made more rapid and effective. A comparison of almost any scene as told by the two poets suffices to show Chaucer's immense superiority. At some subsequent period the "Squire's Tale" of Cambuscan, the fair Canacee and the Horse of Brass, was gallantly begun in something of the same key, but Chaucer took for it more materials than he could use, and for lack of the help of a leader like Boccaccio he was obliged to leave the story, in Milton's phrase, "half-told," though the fragment written certainly takes us very much less than half-way.

Meanwhile, in connexion (as is reasonably believed) with the betrothal or marriage of Anne of Bohemia to Richard II (i.e. about 1381-1382), Chaucer had brought to a successful completion the Parlement of Foules, a charming sketch of 699 lines, in which the other birds, on Saint Valentine's day, counsel the "Formel Egle" on her choice of a mate. His success here, as in the case of the Deth of Blaunche the Duchesse, was due to the absence of any need for a climax; and though the materials which he borrowed were mainly Latin (with some help from passages of the Teseide not fully needed for Palamon and Arcyte) his method of handling them would have been quite approved by his friends among the French poets.

A more ambitious venture, the Hous of Fame, in which Chaucer imagines himself borne aloft by an eagle to Fame's temple, describes what he sees and hears there, and then breaks off in apparent inability to get home, shows a curious mixture of the poetic ideals of the Roman de la rose and reminiscences of the Divina Commedia. As the Hous of Fame is most often remembered and quoted for the personal touches and humour of Chaucer's conversation with the eagle, so the most-quoted passages in the Prologue to the Legende of Good Women are those in which Chaucer professes his affection for the daisy, and the attack on his loyalty by Cupid and its defence by Alceste.

Recent discoveries have shown, however, that (besides obligations to Machault) some of the touches about the daisy and the controversy between the partisans of the Flower and of the Leaf are snatches from poems by his friends Froissart and Deschamps, which Chaucer takes up and returns to them with pretty compliments, and that he was indebted to Froissart for some of the framework of his poem. Both of the two versions of the Prologue to the Legende are charming, and some of the tales, notably that of Cleopatra, rank with Chaucer's best work. When, however, he had written eight and part of the ninth he tired of his scheme, which was planned to celebrate nineteen of Cupid's faithful "saints," with Alcestis as their queen. With his usual hopefulness he had overlooked the risk of monotony, which obviously weighed heavily on him ere he broke off, and the loss of the other ten stories is less to be regretted than that of the celebration of Alceste, and a possible epilogue which might have exceeded in charm the Prologue itself.

Chaucer's failure to complete the scheme of the Legende of Good Women may have been partly due to the attractions of the Canterbury Tales, which were probably taken up in immediate succession to it. His guardianship of two Kentish wards, his justiceship of the peace, his representing the county in the parliament of 1386, his commissionership of the river-bank between Greenwich and Woolwich, all make it easy to understand his dramatic use of the merry crowds he saw on the Canterbury road, without supposing him to have had recourse to Boccaccio's Decamerone, a book which there is no proof of his having seen.

The pilgrims whom he imagines to have assembled at the Tabard Inn in Southwark, where Harry Bailey was host, are said to have numbered "wel nyne and twenty in a company," and the Prologue gives full-length sketches of a Knight, a Squire (his son), and their Yeoman; of a Prioress, Monk, Friar, Oxford Clerk, and Parson, with two disreputable hangers-on of the church, a Summoner and Pardoner; of a Serjeant-at-Law and a Doctor of Physic, and of a Franklin, or country gentleman, Merchant, Shipman, Miller, Cook, Manciple, Reeve, Ploughman (the Parson's brother) and the ever-famous Wife of Bath. Five London burgesses are described in a group, and a Nun and Priest[3] are mentioned as in attendance on the Prioress.

Each of these, with Chaucer himself making the twenty-ninth, was pledged to tell two tales, but including one second attempt and a tale told by the Yeoman of a Canon, who overtakes the pilgrims on the road, we have only twenty finished stories, two unfinished and two interrupted ones. As in the case of the Legende of Good Women, our loss is not so much that of the additional stories as of the completed framework.

The wonderful character sketches of the Prologue are carried yet farther by the Talks on the Road which link the different tales, and two of these Talks, in which the Wife of Bath and the Pardoner respectively edify the company, have the importance of separate Tales, but between the Tales that have come down to us there are seven links missing,[4] and it was left to a later and weaker hand to narrate, in the "Tale of Beryn," the adventures of the pilgrims at Canterbury.

The reference to the Lyf of Seynt Cecyle in the Prologue to the Legende of Good Women gives external proof that Chaucer included earlier work in the scheme of the Canterbury Tales, and mention has been made of other stories which are indisputably early. In the absence of any such metrical tests as have proved useful in the case of Shakespeare, the dates at which several of the Tales were composed remain doubtful, while in the case of at least two, the Clerk's tale of Grisilde and the Monk's tragedies, there is evidence of early work being revised and supplemented. It is fortunately impossible to separate the prologue to the charmingly told story of "yonge Hugh of Lincoln" from the tale itself, and, with the "quod sche" in the second line as proof that Chaucer was here writing specially for his Prioress, we are forbidden to limit the new stories to any one metre or tone.

There can be no doubt, however, that what may be called the Tales of the Churls (Miller, Reeve, Summoner, Friar, &c.), and the conversational outpourings of the Pardoner and Wife of Bath, form, with the immortal Prologue, the most important and distinctive additions to the older work. In these, and in the Pardoner's story of Death and the Three Revellers, and the Nun's Priest's masterly handling of the fable of the Cock and Fox, both of them free from the grossness which marks the others, Chaucer takes stories which could have been told in a short page of prose and elabourates them with all the skill in narration which he had sedulously cultivated. The conjugal reminiscences of the Wife of Bath and the Reeve's Tale with its abominable climax (lightened a little by Aleyn's farewell, lines 316-319) are among the great things in Chaucer, as surely as Troilus, and Palamon and Arcyte and the Prologue. They help notably to give him the width of range which may certainly be claimed for him.

In or soon after 1391 Chaucer wrote in prose for an elevenyear-old reader, whom he addresses as "Litel Lowis my son," a treatise on the use of the Astrolabe, its short prologue being the prettiest specimen of his prose. The wearisome tale of "Melibee and his wyf Prudence," which was perhaps as much admired in English as it had been in Latin and French, may have been translated at any time. The sermon on Penitence, used as the Parson's Tale, was probably the work of his old age. "Envoys" to his friends Scogan and Bukton, a translation of some balades by Sir Otes de Granson, and the Compleynt to his Purs complete the record of his minor poetry. We have his own statement that in his youth he had written many Balades, Roundels and Virelayes in honour of Love, and the two songs embedded respectively in the Parlement of Foules and the Prologue to the Legende of Good Women are charming and musical.

His extant shorter poems, however, whether early or late, offer no excuse for claiming high rank for him as a lyrist. He had very little sheer singing power, and though there are fine lines in his short poems, witness the famous "Flee fro the prees and dwell with soothfastnesse," they lack the sustained concentration of great work. From the drama, again, Chaucer was cut off, and it is idle to argue from the innumerable dramatic touches in his poems and his gift of characterization as to what he might have done had he lived two centuries later. His own age delighted in stories, and he gave it the stories it demanded, invested with a humanity, a grace and strength which place him among the world's greatest narrative poets, and which bring the England of his own day, with all the colour and warmth of life, wonderfully near to all his readers.

The part played by Chaucer in the development of the English language has often been overrated. He neither corrupted it, as used to be said, by introducing French words which it would otherwise have avoided, nor bore any such part in fixing it as was afterwards played by the translators of the Bible. When he was growing up, educated society in England was still bilingual, and the changes in vocabulary and pronunciation which took place during his life were the natural results of a society, which had been bilingual with a bias towards French, giving an exclusive preference to English. The practical identity of Chaucer's language with that of Gower shows that both merely used the best English of their day with the care and slightly conservative tendency which befitted poets. Chaucer's service to the English language lies in his decisive success having made it impossible for any later

English poet to attain fame, as Gower had done, by writing alternatively in Latin and French. The claim which should be made for him is that, at least as regards poetry, he proved that English was "sufficient."

Chaucer borrowed both his stanza forms and his "decasyllabic" couplets (mostly with an extra syllable at the end of the line) from Guillaume Machault, and his music, like that of his French master and his successors, depends very largely on assigning to every syllable its full value, and more especially on the due pronunciation of the final -e. The slower movement of change in Scotland allowed time for Chaucer to exercise a potent influence on Scottish poetry, but in England this final -e, to which most of the earlier grammatical forms by Chaucer's time had been reduced, itself fell rapidly into disuse during the 15th century, and a serious barrier was thus raised to the appreciation of the artistic value of his verse.

His disciples, Hoccleve and Lydgate, who at first had caught some echoes of his rhythms, gradually yielded to the change in pronunciation, so that there was no living tradition to hand down his secret, while successive copyists reduced his text to a state in which it was only by accident that lines could be scanned correctly. For fully three centuries his reputation was sustained solely by his narrative power, his warmest panegyrists betraying no consciousness that they were praising one of the greatest technical masters of poetry. Even when thus maimed, however, his works found readers and lovers in every generation, and every improvement in his text has set his fame on a surer basis.

Chapter 2

A Brief Chronology of Chaucer's Life and Times

1300	Dante's Divine Comedy.
1300	Birth of Guillaume de Machaut, French musician and poet (died 1377).
1304	Birth of Francis Petrarch (died 1374).
1313	Birth of Giovanni Boccaccio (died 1375).
1321	Death of Dante Alighieri (b.1265).
1330	Birth of John Gower (died 1408).
1335	Boccaccio's Filostrato (source of Troilus).
1336-38	Boccaccio's Filocolo (possible source of The Franklin's Tale).
1337	Hundred Years War begins (ends 1453).
1339	Boccaccio begins Il Teseida delle Nozze d'Emilia (source of The Knight's Tale).
1340-45	Birth of Chaucer.
1346	Birth of Eustache Deschamps, French poet (died c. 1406).
1346	English victory at Crecy; see Jean Froissart, on the Hundred Years War (1337-1453).
1348-50	The Black Death; see the chilling description of the Plague in Boccaccio's Decameron, the introduction to the First Day.
1349-51	Boccaccio's Decameron.
1356	English victory at Poitiers; see Jean Froissart, on the Hundred Years War (1337-1453).
1357	Chaucer a page in the household of the Countess of Ulster.

1359-60 Chaucer serves in the war in France.
1360 Chaucer, captured by the French, is ransomed (for 16 pounds).
1360 Peace with France, Treaty of Bretigny (lull in Hundred Years War; resumes in 1369).
1361-62 Severe recurrence of the Plague.
1360's Langland's Piers Plowman (The "A text").
1361-67 Jean Froissart, French poet and chronicler (c. 1337-1404) serves in the household of Queen Phillippa.
1366 Chaucer marries Philippa Roet, a lady-in-waiting in the Queen's household.
1366 Chaucer travels to Spain.
1366 Death of John Chaucer, Chaucer's father.
1367 Birth of Chaucer's son, Thomas.
1367 Chaucer serves as a "valettus" and later as a squire in the court of Edward III; granted a payment of 20 marks per annum for life.
1368 Chaucer travels to the continent (France probably) on "the King's service."
1368 Birth of Thomas Hoccleve (died 1450), who wrote poems as a "disciple" of Chaucer.
1368-72 Chaucer writes "Fragment A" of the Romaunt of the Rose, The Book of the Duchess, probably a good many lyrics in French and English, now lost, and such lyrics as The Complaint unto Pity and The Complaint to His Lady.
1369 Chaucer serves with John of Gaunt's army in France.
1370 Birth of John Lydgate, admirer and imitator of Chaucer (died 1450).
1370 Chaucer again serves with the army in France.
1372 Chaucer's wife Philippa in the household of John of Gaunt's wife.
1372 Chaucer travels to Italy (Genoa and Florence) on a diplomatic mission.
1374 Death of Petrarch.
1374 Chaucer granted a gallon pitcher of wine daily for life.
1374 Chaucer is appointed controller of the customs; granted a lease on a dwelling over Aldgate.
1375 Death of Boccaccio.
1375 Chaucer and Otho de Graunson (French knight and

poet on whose poems Chaucer drew for his "Complaint of Venus") both receive grants from John of Gaunt.

1376-77 Several trips to France, negotiating for peace and the marriage of Richard.

1377 Edward III died; Richard II becomes king.

1377 Pope Gregory XI condemns doctrines of John Wycliffe (1335/38-1384); Lollard movement grows.

1378 The "Great Schism" — rival Popes in Rome (Urban) and Avignon (Clement); See Deliberations of the University of Paris. The schism ends 1409.

1378 Chaucer travels to Italy (Milan) on diplomatic mission.

1378 John Gower and Richard Forester have Chaucer's power of attorney while he travels abroad. Late 1370's Chaucer writes Saint Cecelia (possibly later); The House of Fame, Anelida and Arcite.

1380 Cecily Chaumpaigne signs a document, releasing Chaucer from all actions in the case of my rape ("de raptu meo").

1380 Birth of Chaucer's second son, Lewis.

1380 Chaucer writes The Parliament of Fowls.

1381 The Peasants' Revolt; see the accounts in Gray's Scalacronica and the Anonimalle Chronicle.

1381 Death of Chaucer's mother, Agnes Chaucer.

1382-86 Chaucer writes Boece, Troilus and Criseyede.

1382 Chaucer's controllorship of the customs is renewed, with permission to have a deputy.

1382 The Bible is translated into English (The "Wyclifite Bible"; a later versions is made in 1388).

1385 Chaucer is granted a permanent deputy in the customs.

1385 Eustache Deschamps sends Chaucer a poem of praise, hailing him as "great translator, noble Geoffrey Chaucer." See Chaucer's Reputation.

1385-87 Chaucer writes "Palamoun and Arcite" (later used as The Knight's Tale); " The Legend of Good Women (though some parts are probably earlier and the prologue was later revised).

1385-89 Chaucer serves as justice of peace for Kent.

1386 Chaucer gives up the house in Aldgate; resigns from customs.

1386 Chaucer serves as member of Parliament for Kent (where he now probably lives).

1386/87 (Perhaps earlier) Chaucer is praised as a poet of Love and Philosophy by Thomas Usk, a younger contemporary (1350-88), author of The Testament of Love.

1387-90 John Gower's Confessio amantis (first "published" 1390; later revised).

1387-92 Chaucer begins The Canterbury Tales.

1388 Some of Richard's closest supporters removed by the Lords Appellant; some (including Thomas Usk, an admirer and imitator of Chaucer) are executed.

1389 Chaucer is appointed clerk of the works at Westminster, Tower of London, and other royal estates.

1390 As clerk of the works, Chaucer has scaffolds built for jousts in Smithfield.

1390 Chaucer is robbed of horse, goods, 20 pounds, 6 shillings, 8 pence at Hacham, Surrey (perhaps robbed again a bit later).

1391-92 Chaucer writes Treatise of the Astrolabe (with additions 1393 and later).

1392-95 Chaucer writes most of The Canterbury Tales, including probably "The Marriage Group."

1394 King Richard II grants Chaucer an annuity of 20 pounds a year,

1396 Chaucer writes "The Envoy to Bukton," in which the addressee is urged to read "The Wife of Bath."

1396-00 Chaucer writes the latest of the Tales, including probably The Nun's Priest's Tale, The Canon's Yeoman's Tale (though part is probably earlier), the Parson's Tale, and several short poems, including the envoys to Scogan and Bukton and the "Complaint to His Purse."

1398 Chaucer is granted a tun of wine a year.

1399 Richard II is deposed; Henry IV becomes king.

1399 Chaucer leases a tenement, for 53 years, in the garden of the Lady Chapel at Westminster Abbey.

1399	King Henry IV confirms, and adds to, Chaucer's royal annuities.
1400	"The Complaint of Chaucer to His Purse."
1400	Chaucer's death (on 25 October, according to tradition).

Chapter 3

Major Works

- Translation of Roman de la Rose, possibly extant as The Romance of the Rose
- The Book of the Duchess
- The House of Fame
- Anelida and Arcite
- Parlement of Foules
- Translation of Boethius' Consolation of Philosophy as Boece
- Troilus and Criseyde
- The Legend of Good Women
- The Canterbury Tales
- Treatise on the Astrolabe

Short Poems

- An ABC
- Chaucers Wordes unto Adam, His Owne Scriveyn
- The Complaint unto Pity
- The Complaint of Chaucer to his Purse
- The Complaint of Mars
- The Complaint of Venus
- A Complaint to His Lady
- The Former Age
- Fortune
- Gentilesse
- Lak of Stedfastnesse
- Lenvoy de Chaucer a Scogan
- Lenvoy de Chaucer a Bukton

- Proverbs
- To Rosemounde
- Truth
- Womanly Noblesse

Poems Dubiously Ascribed to Chaucer

- Against Women Unconstant
- A Balade of Complaint
- Complaynt D'Amours
- Merciles Beaute
- The Visioner's Tale
- The Equatorie of the Planets - A rough translation of a Latin work derived from an Arab work of the same title. It is a description of the construction and use of what is called an 'equatorium planetarum', and was used in calculating planetary orbits and positions (at the time it was believed the sun orbited the Earth). The similar Treatise on the Astrolabe, not usually doubted as Chaucer's work, plus Chaucer's name as a gloss to the manuscript are the main pieces of evidence for the ascription to Chaucer. However, the evidence Chaucer wrote such a work is questionable, and as such is not included in The Riverside Chaucer. If Chaucer did not compose this work, it was probably written by a contemporary.

Works Mentioned by Chaucer, Presumed Lost

- Of the Wreched Engendrynge of Mankynde, possible translation of Innocent III's De miseria conditionis humanae
- Origenes upon the Maudeleyne
- The book of the Leoun - The Book of the Leon is mentioned in Chaucer's retraction at the end of The Canterbury Tales. It is likely he wrote such a work; one suggestion is that the work was such a bad piece of writing it was lost, but if so, Chaucer would not have included it in the middle of his retraction. Indeed, he would not have included it at all. A likely

source dictates it was probably a 'redaction of Guillaume de Machaut's 'Dit dou lyon,' a story about courtly love, a subject which Chaucer scholars agree he frequently wrote about (Le Romaunt de Rose).

Pseudepigraphies and Works Plagiarizing Chaucer

- The Pilgrim's Tale — Written in the sixteenth-century with many Chaucerian allusions
- The Plowman's Tale AKA The Complaint of the Ploughman — A Lollard satire later appropriated as a Protestant text
- Pierce the Ploughman's Crede — A Lollard satire later appropriated by Protestants
- The Ploughman's Tale — Its body is largely a version of Thomas Hoccleve's "Item de Beata Virgine"
- "La Belle Dame Sans Merci" — Richard Roos' translation of a poem of the same name by Alain Chartier
- The Testament of Love — Actually by Thomas Usk
- Jack Upland — A Lollard satire
- God Spede the Plow — Borrows parts of Chaucer's Monk's Tale

Chapter 4

Chaucer's Contemporaries

O moral Gower, this book I directe
To the and to the, philosophical Strode,
To vouchen sauf, ther nede is, to correcte,
Of youre benignites and zeles goode.
Troilus and Criseyde (Book 5, l. 1856-1859)

Richard II was a great patron of the arts and a literary culture flourished at his court in the second half of the Fourteenth Century. Chaucer was widely known amongst the literati of the day, and his circle included influential figures such as Sir Lewis Clifford, Sir Richard Stury and Sir John Montagu. He was also friendly with other contemporary writers, including Thomas Hoccleve, Henry Scogan, Ralph Strode and John Gower. He seems to have been particularly close to 'Moral' Gower, as he dubs him in Troilus and Criseyde, giving him power of attorney when he left for Italy in 1378. In the first version of his Confessio Amantis, Gower makes a flattering reference to Chaucer as composing 'ditees and songes glad' in the flower of his youth.

Often referred to as the 'Father of the English Language' Chaucer's poetry and use of English inspired a whole generation of poets. The dominance of French following the Norman conquest of 1066 had impeded the growth of English as a literary language for hundreds of years, and it was not until the Fourteenth Century that the vernacular came once more to be used as the language of choice in all areas of society, including at court and in business. Nonetheless, most writers

– such as Gower – still wrote fluently in French and Latin, as well as in their native tongue. Chaucer proved that English could be written with elegance and power and it is thanks to his works that its prestige grew as a medium for serious literature. His poetry naturally inspired praise and imitation from his contemporaries.

Of these admirers, the prolific John Lydgate is probably one of the best known today. A monk at the great Benedictine Abbey of St Edmund at Bury, he emulated Chaucer's style, and in the prologue to his Siege of Thebes even portrayed himself as meeting Chaucer's pilgrims at their inn in Canterbury. Although Lydgate's work has suffered from adverse criticism (the antiquarian Joseph Ritson famously dismissing him as a 'voluminous, prosaick, and drivelling monk') he played a crucial role in ensuring Chaucer's popularity throughout the Fifteenth Century.

John Gower Confessio Amantis

England: c.1425-1450
MS Hunter 7 (S.1.7)

The Confessio Amantis is Gower's most acclaimed English work. Completed in its first version in 1390, when Gower was about sixty, it is a lover's account of his confession to Genius, the priest of Venus, under headings supplied by the seven deadly sins. Like The Canterbury Tales, Gower uses this narrative framework to tell a series of tales which in this work explore the general nature of each sin together with the particular forms it may take in a lover. Chaucer undoubtedly knew the work well. According to the original prologue, Gower wrote the book for Richard II after the king asked him for a poem on the theme of love. Two or three years later, the reference to Richard was cut out, presumably because of his growing unpopularity. Gower then wrote another version of the prologue in which he says that the work was written for 'Engelondes sake'.

The decorative scheme in this manuscript was for the beginning of each book to be marked by an illuminated and decorated page. The opening of the third book is displayed to the left; it is adorned by a spraywork border incorporating floral and leaf motifs. Several of these pages (including the beginnings of books one, two, six, seven and eight) are missing, and this may suggest that they originally included miniatures as well. There is a seventeenth century inscription in the book indicating that it was owned by the Benedictine Abbey of Bury St Edmonds: if this is correct, then this copy is likely to have been read by John Lydgate.

Ranulf Higden Polychronicon (translated by John of Trevisa)

England: c.1470
MS Hunter 367 (V.1.4)

Originally composed in Latin, this universal history is a chronicle of the period from the Creation to 1357. Its author was a Benedictine monk who arranged the work into seven books, in imitation of the seven days of Genesis. This translation was made by John of Trevisa (c.1330-1412) and completed in 1387. There was an increasing interest in history throughout the late medieval period, and Trevisa's version was just one of several standard vernacular histories available. His translation is interesting for the additional comments that he makes to update the original text.

Where Higden, for example, discusses the fact that children learn their lessons in French, Trevisa comments that the situation has changed by the time he is writing, and that lessons are now conducted in English. He acknowledges that this has its advantages for speed of learning, but points out rather disapprovingly that now children 'know no more French than their left heel, and that is harmful for them if they should pass the sea and work in strange lands'.

This copy is one of some fourteen surviving manuscripts of the translation. It also includes Higden's preface to the work, the Dialogue of the Lord and the Clerk. The manuscript is well written on vellum and is skilfully decorated with illuminated initials and floreated pages. To the left is the opening of the first chapter of Book Five which deals with the reign of Vortigern in Britain and the arrival of the Saxons Hengist and Horsa.

John Gower Vox Clamantis

England: c.1400
MS Hunter 59 (T.2.17)

Gower used the Peasants' Revolt of 1381 in this long Latin poem to describe the faults of government and the various classes of society. Caused by a complex interaction of social discontents, the Revolt was a brief but horrific episode of anarchic insurrection. The rebels (not all of them peasants) plundered London, massacred a group of Flemings, and murdered the Archbishop of Canterbury.

The earlier portion of the Vox Clamantis contains a vivid account of this uprising in the form of an allegory, with a somewhat hysterical portrayal of the rebels as domestic animals reverting to bestiality. Chaucer himself only makes one passing reference to the Revolt in a facetious remark about Jack Straw, one of its main leaders, in the Nun's Priest's Tale. Nonetheless, as a member of the upper class, he probably shared Gower's view of the rebels as being a lawless rabble. In this copy of the revised version of the Vox Clamantis and Chronica Tripertita, the text is preceded by a full page representation of the author firing his shafts at the world. This globe is composed of the elements of air, earth and water in three compartments.

There is a second illustration (found towards the end of the text) of the Gower arms supported by two flying angels, with a cloth-covered bier below. This does not depict Gower's coffin, as the manuscript was actually made before his death in 1408. In fact, the text has been revised and corrected by means of extensive erasure and substitution, possibly under the supervision of Gower himself. There seems originally to have been another illustration on folio 131v, but this has also been erased and only survives as a shadowy palimpsest beneath the text.

John Lydgate Fall of Princes

England: c.1470-1480
MS Hunter 5 (S.1.5)

Lydgate is credited with some 145,000 lines of verse, almost a quarter of which is contained in the Fall of Princes, his longest single work. The poem is a greatly amplified version of Laurent de Premierfait's translation of Boccaccio's De Casibus Virorum Illustrium, with additions from a variety of sources including the Bible, Ovid and other works by Boccaccio. The result is a universal encyclopaedia of history and mythology, somewhat ponderous in tone and exhaustively fleshed out with moral teaching. The work was commissioned from Lydgate in 1431 by Humphrey, Duke of Gloucester, younger brother of Henry V and Protector of England during the minority of Henry VI, and it occupied the following eight years of his life.

This is an imposing de-luxe copy of the work, written out in a very neat hand. Its major decoration is found in six full page borders, filled with delicate sprays of penwork in a foreign style. Like our copy of Gower's Confessio Amantis, this copy is incomplete, the pages at the beginning of books three and four having been cut out, probably for their decoration. One of the quires has also been misbound, and several notes in an early seventeenth century hand (including the instruction on one folio to 'Turne forwards eight leaves') attempt to make this explicit to any reader. Another interesting feature is a number of crossed out lines on folio 197r obliterating references to the female 'Pope Joan'. There are several early ownership inscriptions at the end of the volume, including records of the births of some members of the Lumner and Calthorpe families in the Sixteenth Century.

John Lydgate Life of Our Lady

England: c.1450-1500
MS Hunter 232 (U.3.5)

Lydgate wrote religious poetry throughout his career. The quasi-liturgical Life of Our Lady was probably composed for Henry V in about 1415-16. A genuinely devout composition written in the 'high style', the work draws upon the Apocryphal Gospel of Pseudo-Matthew, as well as other devotional texts such as the Meditationes Vitae Christi. It has been praised for its religious intensity and luminous rhetoric.

The manuscript is incomplete, missing the final part of the poem. It is a fairly standard fifteenth-century production, well written with penwork initials throughout, but lacking any illumination. It is interesting for its copious early sixteenth-century marginalia. As well as numerous signatures, doodles and pen trials, it bears fragments of administrative type annotations relating to indentures, scraps of doggerel verse, and lines of quotations from the Gospels. The opening on the left is typical: in the lower margin of the left hand page, the beginning of the verse at the top of the page is repeated, while if the book is turned upside down, a fragment of a poem may be read ('Mussynge in my mynde grete / mervell that I heve that ever / so fayer a mayde shoulde heve ...'), along with some practise letter 'h's and what might be a monogram. Many of the names found in the margins are connected to the Goldings, an important Essex family of the Tudor period.

Nicholas Love Mirror of the Blessed Life of Jesus Christ

England: 1475

MS Hunter 77 (T.3.15)

The Meditationes Vitae Christi, a devotional life of Christ originally written in Latin, was extremely popular throughout medieval Europe. The Mirror is a free translation of the work. It was made by Nicholas Love (d. 1424), a prior of the Carthusian Priory of Mount Grace in Yorkshire. Concentrating on the Passion, the Mirror dispenses meditative and doctrinal comment on the Bible. Its sixty three chapters are each split into seven sections, every section representing a day of the week.

This is a finely produced manuscript written in an expert script on good quality vellum. It boasts several floreated pages, with illuminated initials and decorative penwork throughout. Stephen Dodesham (d. 1481/82), its scribe, is identified from a contemporary inscription on a flyleaf. He was a monk of

Witham Charterhouse near Frome, Somerset; he later moved to Sheen Charterhouse in Richmond, Surrey, founded by Henry V in 1414. Dodesham was a prolific scribe whose career began in the late 1420s; over twenty of his manuscripts survive, including two others in the Hunterian collection.

Chapter 5

Some Important Events in the Fourteenth Century

1338 The Beginning of the 100 Years' War

Isabella of France Received at Paris

England and France had been complexly interwoven ever since the Conquest of England by William I, who set a precedent by leaving his French holdings to his eldest son, Robert, and his English holdings to his second son, William II. English dominion of French territories reached a high point under Henry II, but from the thirteenth century, France began to be successful in restoring French sovereignty to French lands, first during the reign of John, who managed to lose Normandy, and then with the division of the two aristocracies from 1244 with the Decree of the Two Masters. The situation was re-complicated however during the reign of Edward II, who, like his predecessors, married a French princess, Isabelle, daughter of Philip IV.

Edward's reign was a troubled one. His magnates became alarmed at the influence of Edward's lover, Piers Gaveston, and exiled Gaveston in 1311, but he was later executed when he attempted to return the following year. Under Edward's rule the English suffered a decisive defeat by the Scots at Bannockburn in 1314, and later languished under the oppressive rule of Edward and a new favourite, Hugh Despencer. Isabelle in the meantime became the lover of Roger

Mortimer, and together the two plotted to overthrow Edward, leading an invasion of England in 1326. Edward was imprisoned and no doubt executed.

The Coronation of Edward III

Edward III was only 15 when he succeeded to the throne, yet he managed to avenge his father by executing Roger Mortimer in 1330. He won an important battle against the Scots in 1333 at Halidon Hill and began a lifelong a career of military aggression. In 1338, after the death of his mother's brother, Philip IV, he declared himself king of France, on the basis of his mother's claims, thus beginning the Hundred Year's war. The English had held land in France ever since the reigns of William I's sons, but John had lost Normandy in 1204 (by unwisely divorcing his English wife to marry Isabelle of Angouleme, betrothed to a member of the powerful Lusignan family, and thus giving the French king an excuse to attack Normandy when John refused a summons to appear before him). Edward's ambition was to recover the territories that England had once held in France.

The Battle of Crecy

In 1346, thanks in part to the use of the longbow, the English defeated a much larger mounted French force at Crecy, introducing a period of peace.

The Battle of Poitiers

In 1355 Edward, the Black Prince, captured Bordeaux which he used as a base to raid and plunder the south of France. In 1356, the English scored their second major victory at Poitiers, where they succeeded in capturing the French king, John. Afterwards, the peace of Bretigny was signed, which was generally favorable to the English. In the 1370's after the accession of King Charles V, the tide of war began to turn in favor of the French. The Black Prince died in 1376, followed by his father in 1377, who was succeeded by his 10-year-old grandson, Richard II. The problem of peace with France was one that dogged Richard's reign, complicated by the fact that wealth from spoil and plunder was an incentive for the military class to keep war alive. Richard's uncle, Thomas of Gloucester, was one of the most determined advocates of war.

The Battle of Nicropoli

Throughout the fourteenth century, the Western Church was in profound crisis. In 1309, Pope Clement V moved the seat of the Church from Rome to Avignon, France, where the Church came under the influence of the French monarchs. In 1378, the cardinals who had elected Pope Urban VI became dissatisfied with his behavior and sought to annul his election, claiming that it had been made under duress.

They withdrew their obedience and elected a new Pope, Clement VII. Urban excommunicated Clement, who returned to Avignon. One result of the crisis in the Western Church was to encourage Muslim aggression in Eastern Europe. The French historian Froissart reports that the Turkish leader Bajazet, who defeated the French at the Battle of Nicropoli, had declared that the Western Church was corrupted by those who should have been its guardians and he was born to accomplish its ruin. He would, he boasted, march to Rome and feed his horse on the altar of St. Peter.

1381 The Peasants' Revolt

The Death of Wat Tyler

Although the immediate cause of the Rebellion was the imposition of an unpopular poll (head) tax, contributing factors were neglect of administration and justice for warfare, corruption of justice, the recurrent breakdown of law and order. The Rebellion of 1381 began in South-West Essex when a tax commissioner, John Bampton, arrived at Brentwood in Barstable Hundred and was driven from the village. Neighbouring villagers also panicked when they heard what had happened and when news spread that the government intended an exemplary punishment, a full-scale revolt ensued. The revolt's most effective leader was Wat Tyler, who led the rebels to Canterbury where Archbishop Sudbury was executed, the sheriff seized, and judicial records burned.

The rebels reached London June 10 and requested a meeting with King Richard on June 11. Richard (age 14) met with Wat Tyler on June 14 at Mile End, London and granted collective charters of pardon and freedom from serfdom to the men of Essex and Hertfordshire. On June 14 and 15 the so-called Anonymous Chronicle speaks of 140-160 Flemish textile workers killed. The king met with Wat Tyler again on June 15 at Smithfield who made a series of fantastic demands, including that all lordship be abolished save that of the king, that the goods of the church be given to the parishoners and that there be only one bishop. A scuffle ensued, Tyler was killed, and the king stepped forward, and spoke at the age of fourteen, the culminating speech of his political career. "Your leader is dead. Follow me; I am your leader."

The Battle of Radcot Bridge

In 1386, a group of nobles, jealous of the influence on Richard of certain advisors who were outside the royal circle, forced themselves on the king as a governing council. The following year, however, encouraged by Michael de la Pole, Robert de Vere and others, Richard managed to reassert his prerogative, but afterwards there was an armed uprising by the Duke of Gloucester, the Earl of Arundel, the Earl of Warwick and others who appealed of treason these same advisors. There was a military encounter, known as the Battle of Radcot Bridge, between these forces and Robert de Vere, who had determined to escape to Ireland.

The Flight of Robert de Vere

1387-8 The Merciless Parliament

In 1388, at the initiative of Thomas of Gloucester, Henry, Earl of Derby, Richard of Arundel, Thomas of Warwick, and others, the so-called Merciless Parliament convicted of treason a number of Richard's advisors (many of whom had ties to Chaucer): Simon Burley, John Beauchamp, John Salisbury, Robert de Vere, Michael de la Pole, Nicholas Brembre, James Berners, and Robert Tresilian. Burley, Beauchamp, Salisbury,

Berners, Tresilian and others were executed.

The Marriage of Richard to Isabel of France

In 1396, in order to bring an end to the French wars, Richard married Isabel of France, daughter of King Phillip the VI, who was only 8 years old at the time. The marriage was opposed by Richard's old enemy, Thomas of Gloucester, and indirectly led to Richard's death after he was informed of a plot by Gloucester and others to remove and imprison him. In retaliation, Richard had Gloucester imprisoned and murdered, exiled Henry Bolingbroke, and seized Henry's property when he was out of the way. It was was this course of action that furnished the pretext for the charges of tyranny against Richard and led to his deposition and murder.

The Death of Gloucester

Gloucester was arrested and put in Mowbray's charge and taken to Calais where he died in mysterious circumstances, by some reports strangled with his bedding as he is portrayed here. Richard called a Parliament and accused those involved in the plot against him of treason, using as a pretext the actions of the Merciless Parliament that had taken place some eleven years previously.

The Challenge of Derby and Mowbray

According to some French chronicles, the Earl of Arundel, Thomas Mowbray, the Earl of Derby and the Duke of Gloucester met in August of 1397 at Arundel on the invitation of the Duke of Gloucester. There they plotted to seize Richard, along with John of Gaunt, and the Duke of York and imprison them forever. Mowbray informed Richard of their intentions, and Richard responded with the arrest of Gloucester and others. Mowbray and Henry Percy, Earl of Derby, mutually accused each other of treason. Henry accused Mowbray of the death of Gloucester and of appropriating money destined to pay the soldiers at Calais while Mowbray accused Derby of treason against the king. Richard banished Derby for ten years and exiled Mowbray forever. Mowbray later died in Venice.

1399 The Arrest of Richard II

Shortly after the exile of Henry Percy, his father, John of Gaunt died, and Richard seized all his properties. Richard also neglected to inform Henry of his father's death. Henry, raised an army, returned to England, and had Richard arrested and imprisoned.

The Abdication of Richard II

Richard supposedly abdicated voluntarily to Henry, although Richard was never seen alive again after his imprisonment.

Chapter 6

The Echo of Black Death in Chaucer's Age

W.H. Hudson has rightly said, "Every man belongs to his race and age; no matter how marked his personality, the spirit of his race and age finds expression through him." For a comprehensive study of an author's literary works, what is also required (among other things) is the social background of that period – the kind of society the author was living in.

Apart from many other changes in the English society in the age of Chaucer, the most dramatic change was a demographic one – the occurrence of the most devastating plague called Black Death. It erupted first of all in Dorset in 1348 and was at its peak in 1349. This epidemic wrought havoc and around one-third of the population of England perished in it. The true medical causes of this plague could not be established but the effects of this devastation were long-term as well as social, political and religious in nature.

The socio-economic system of England was paralyzed. The Black Death led to an acute shortage of labour. This aggravated the social tensions between the workers and landlords and other employers. This was also one of the causes of the traumatic Peasants' Revolt of 1381, under the rule of Richard II. The Kentish priest, John Ball, who preached the dignity of labour, raised the question:

"When Adam delved and Eve span
Who was then a gentilman?"

There was a demand for higher wages by the workers, which according to Compton-Rickett was "a dim foreshadowing of those industrial troubles that lay in the distant future."

The Church too was deeply affected by the unstable nature of the society and its medieval beliefs. The Parish clergy suffered a decline not only in numbers but also in quality, both morally and intellectually. This inadequacy of the parish clergy proved a recurrent theme in Langland's poetry. In his 'Prologue to Canterbury Tales' Chaucer says:

That if gold ruste what shal iren doo?

(This means: If gold rusts what shall iron do?)

The theologian and reformer, John Wycliffe criticized the misuse of papal powers and revenues. Thus, we can see that the influence of Black Death was not limited to a single sphere of life, rather it was manifold and engulfed the whole society.

The Black Death

"Oh happy posterity who will not experience such abysmal woe and who will look upon our testimony as fable." -Petrarch, Florentine humanist "Buried with my own hands five of my children in a single grave... No bells. No tears. This is the end of the world." -Agniola di Tura, Siena, 1347 Once upon a time, Death came to a faerie tale land. Europe in the 14th century was a place rich in its own magic, a land of purported enchanted forests and witches. It was in this world that the stories of my childhood were born: Hansel and Gretel, Rapunzel, Sleeping Beauty, the Pied Piper. And while these stories seemingly romanticize the world their characters inhabit, hidden within them are tales of danger and horror: wolves, cutthroats, diseases. These last, the great illnesses of the century, intrigue me the most.

The Middle Ages have always enchanted me, but my fascination did not take obvious form until I read another faerie tale, the Doomsday Book by Connie Willis. Kivrin, the main character, is sent back in time to Oxfordshire in the Christmas of 1348 by mistake, and finds herself caught in the

Black Death. In this novel of loss and hope, the author skillfully demonstrates what it means to be human through the suffering of her characters. The book dragged me into its dark waters of narrative and suddenly I had found a moment in the 14th century that intrigued me more than any other. What was this obsession, just morbid captivation? Did I really want to look back through the mainly objective eyes of history and see the memory of such misery dissected by scholarly examination? Why examine any history, least of all a time so horrible? Remembrances of the past allow us to open a mirror into the past, and see a reflection of our own soul.

Those things that we are drawn to in history are an accurate image of what we care about in life. I realised that the Black Death was my favourite moment in history because it is about the humanity within us all. The reactions of the people of that time link them to us, in the present, because of our similar responses to catastrophe. Events like the Black Death link us to our ancestors by providing a common thread of suffering and salvation. I see these themes all throughout history and even in our world today, and I enjoy finding commonality between all humans. There will be differences, of course, in beliefs and practices, but the emotions will be the same. Through the erasure of differences, we reach a point of enlightenment where we all share the human experience. Therefore, I decided to write a comprehensive report on the events surrounding the Black Death, this single moment in history that demonstrated all aspects of humanity, good and bad, and altered the course of history irrevocably.

The Black Death: A Little Background

The 14th century was, according to the contemporary historian Barbara Tuchman, "born to woe" (A Distant Mirror, pg. 24). It began in the clutches of feudalism, where most of the people were desperately poor and malnourished. According to the Malthusian principle, the population was about to reach a critical mass where demand would overstep supply and create an economic crisis. The century had begun with a chill in which the Baltic Sea froze twice and the years that followed would be filled with horrible storms and unseasonable cold. The weather cycle of the planet was entering what would later be known as the Little Ice Age. This odd climactic change provided a perfect opportunity for the germs that caused the Plague to enter the human population by disrupting the feeding cycles of the fleas who carried the disease. At the time, however, the contemporaries could know little of this. What they worried about was the loss of certain crops in Scandinavia, the closing trade channels with Greenland due to the freezing of the ocean, and the shorter growing season.

The food crisis became ever greater. Crops failed all over Europe, resulting in widespread famine. Tuchman records, "Reports spread of people eating their own children, or the poor in Poland feeding on hanged bodies taken down from the gibbet" (A Distant Mirror, pg. 24). The Cambridge Illustrated History of the Middle Ages tells us that, "The ninety years from 1340-1430 share with the tenth and twentieth centuries the dubious honour of being one of the most violent periods in the history of Europe. Violent not so much due to the bloodshed, the blind cruelty, or the reigning injustice, which were indeed present, but to the harshness of daily existence, the complete uncertainty about the future. 'I never knew a single year in my village without troubles, war or death,' an old man would say on his deathbed in Charles VII's reign" (Fossier, pg. 52). Next, throw into the mix a plague of unrivaled proportions, a pandemic to end all others: the Black Death.

The Black Death: A Description of the Disease

What exactly was the Black Death? Although medical historians argue about what disease it really was, the symptoms described by medieval chroniclers generally point to the black plague. This disease comes in four strains: the choleric, the septicemic, the enteric, and the bubonic. The first involved a horrible hacking cough while the lungs filled with fluid. Eventually the victim would drown in his or her own bodily fluid, but not before affecting everyone that they came into contact with. They would die within two days of contracting this strain. The second was the most painless and the most deadly, a silent sweep through the bloodstream that left the victim insane as it poisoned the brain. It had a 98% mortality rate, and the few survivors that were left severely brain damaged. The third was extremely rare, but just as deadly as the septicemic, and infected the intestinal tract.

The fourth was the most physically horrible. Symptoms were a swelling of the lymph nodes and the formation of buboes filled with gangrenous black pus. This was the longest, most painful version of the Black Death. The tongue would swell so that the victim could no longer swallow. Blood vessels would burst under the slightest touch, causing horrible bruising. Often before the body entirely ruptured, a fever of such high temperatures that a person would literally seem to be burning from within would bring on death by dehydration. Oddly, this was the least deadly strain, with only about a 60% mortality rate. Yet all of these statistics tell nothing about what the disease really was, or how it really destroyed the people infected by it. For a more personal picture, I turned to historical fiction.

In Doomsday Book, a child who has just died of the plague is described like this: Kivrin washed her little body, which was nearly covered with purplish-blue bruises. Where Eliwys had held her hand, the skin was completely black. She looked like she had been beaten. As she had been, Kivrin thought, beaten and tortured. And murdered. The slaughter of the innocents (Willis, pgs. 494-495).

The Black Death: The Path of the Disease

Tracing the path of the plague as it wrapped its deadly coils around Europe in the 14th century is easy. Simply follow the path of the traders. By 1346, rumors of a horrifying plague in the Orient were spreading over Europe, but they caused no alarm. The laws of infection were unknown. A plague in the Orient in 1346 was like a plague on Mars would be today. Too soon, the disease came across Asia. It raced through India, leaving behind cities of dead, then swept up into the Middle East. In the spring of 1347 it became a terrifying ritual of dehumanization in the massive cities of Constantinople and Cairo, where as many as 7000 people were buried in mass graves daily during the height of the plague (Ziegler, pg. 39).

Traditionally the story of the movement of the Black Death into Europe starts with a siege of the island-city of Caffa by a Tartar khan. Supposedly his forces became so depleted by the plague that he began to launch infected bodies over the walls of the city to counteract his losses. Although the residents of Caffa threw the bodies into the ocean as soon as they sailed over the walls, they still became infected and attempted to flee by boat. They sailed to Italy and thus set off a chain of events that would lead to the deaths of over 20 million people. This story is not very likely true, because of the etiology of the disease (in which it cannot be spread by dead bodies without extreme close contact in enclosed spaces) (Tuchman, pg. 92).

Yet, as the Dictionary of the Middle Ages says, "...however accurate the particulars of the Caffa account, the story tells a great deal about the mechanism of the plague's spread. It moved overland until it reached the terminus of European sea travel. Once there, like an invading army it followed major routes of trade and communication, traveling across the open seas, up rivers, and along major highways..." (Volume II, pg. 258). In reality, the Black Death came through hundreds of tiny ports all along the Mediterranean. Here the new technologies of the age contributed to the massive effect of the disease: by this time, all of Christendom was connected by an elabourate series of trade routes and communication lines along which thousands of possibly infected traders traversed daily. Italy, the most urbanized, economically sophisticated country at the time, was the hardest hit because of its trade connections.

The Black Death: Italy

By the winter of 1348, the Black Death had reached Florence, the most populous city in Italy. In that city lived Boccaccio, the author of Decameron. This famous work is the story of travellers in an inn telling their stories of the plague. In the preface, Boccaccio provides his readers with a graphic description: Whether through the operation of the heavenly bodies or because of our own iniquities, which the just wrath of God sought to correct, the plague had arisen in the East some years before, causing the death of countless human beings. It spread without stop from one place to another until, unfortunately, it swept over the West. Neither knowledge nor human foresight availed against it, although the city was cleansed of much filth by chosen officers in charge and sick persons were forbidden to enter it, while advice was broadcast for the preservation of health.

Nor did humble supplication serve. Not once but many times these were ordained in the form of processions and other ways for the propitiation of God by the faithful, but, in spite of everything, toward the spring of the year that plague began to show its ravages in a way just short of miraculous (Boccaccio, n. pg.). Indeed the Black Death seemed almost miraculous to the people of Italy, simply because the sheer level of catastrophe could not be blamed on anything earthly. As they attempted to stop the dread disease through quarantine, their actions only seemed more and more futile. It seemed that the massive catacombs beneath Rome would need to be reopened to accommodate all of the newly deceased.

Cities were filled constantly with the stench of the dead and dying. Because Italy had been the most civilized of the European countries devastated by the plague, the disorder to follow seemed even worse. With most of its population living in rat-filled, unclean urban areas, the disease could cling to cities for several months on end, killing in waves. Although the doors to deserted shops and homes stood open, no one dared to enter and rob. Criminals were released from jail to throw the dead in common pits, while ships at sea manned only by dead sailors drifted aimlessly. Government broke down as officials died and laws could no longer be enforced (Bishop, pg. 307).

The Black Death: France and the British Isles

Soon after entering Italy the plague spread to France, the most populous country in Europe at the time. Despite the fact that it was highly rural, the disease spread rapidly. At one point, 400 people were dying a day in Avignon, the residence of the pope. In one six week period one out of every three cardinals died, and 11,000 people were buried in a single graveyard. In one village with a 1340 population of 1,200, parish records from 1348 show 615 deaths in fourteen weeks, as opposed to 30 over the past ten years. In Paris, 800 people a day were said to have died. New laws were passed to keep panic to a minimum?such as one ordering that only widows may wear black and another so that there was a limit of two grievers to a funeral.

Black flags were hung from the church towers of Normandy either in mourning or warning. As more and more villages were left deserted, those who had fled brought the disease to new locations. The pestilence continued on its relentless march to the English Channel. The Black Death swept into the British Isles across the Channel and up the rivers. By November of 1348 the plague had begun to cause massive social disorder throughout southern England. Think of how terrifying it must have been to live during this time. Religion dictated virtually everything. There was an elabourate bell-ringing ritual for a dead soul to get into heaven: 10 rings for a man, 3 for a woman, and 1 for a child. During the plague, the bells rang constantly across England, pealing morbidly all through the night. Eventually, the bishops ordered that the bells stopped because the constant ringing was terrifying people. The messengers who proclaimed the order were often infected themselves and the plague was spread that way too.

There weren?t enough priests to give the last rites to all the dying. After people died, there wasn?t enough space in the consecrated church graveyards to bury them all, and there weren?t enough healthy people left to dig the graves.

In Doomsday Book, Kivrin witnesses a healthy man bury himself alive. The village priest, Father Roche, is at first hesitant about finishing the burial in the consecrated church ground because the deceased committed suicide, but Kivrin explains that he was out of his mind (implying that he was suffering from the septicemic strain). "She helped Roche straighten the steward's body a little, though he was already stiff.

They did not attempt to move him or wrap him in a shroud. Roche laid a black cloth over his face and they took turns shoveling the dirt in on him.

The frozen earth clattered like stones. "Roche did not go to the church for his vestments or the missal. He stood first beside Lefric's grave and then the steward's and said the prayers for the dead. Kivrin, standing beside him, her hands folded, thought, He wasn't in his right mind. He had buried his wife and six children, he had buried almost everyone he knew, and even if he hadn't been feverish, if he had crawled into the grave and waited to freeze to death, the plague had still killed him" (Willis, pgs. 506-507).

The disease traveled through the British Isles in much the same way as it traveled through the rest of Europe. It stopped a Scottish army preparing to attack its ill southern brethren. According to the chronicler Henry Knighton, there were five thousand dead sheep rotting in a pasture, creating such a horrible stench that people were terrified to go near the site for almost a year (Bishop, pg. 308).

In one of the most famous quotes from the Black Death, monk John Clyn of Kilkenny recorded: Sensing the whole world, as it were, placed within the grasp of the Evil One and I, as if among the dead, waiting till death do come, have put into writing truthfully what I have heard and verified.

And that the writing many not perish with the scribe and the work fail with the labourer, I add parchment to continue it, if by chance anyone may be left in the future, and any child of Adam may escape this pestilence and continue the work thus commenced (Tuchman, pg. 105). At this point the monk's spidery handwriting ends and is replaced by the hand of another chronicler: "Here it seems that the author died."

The Black Death: The Rest of Europe

The rest of continental Europe was equally devastated. At times it seemed that civilization would not continue. "The country of Holland, one of the most rural and least densely settled parts of the Netherlands, suffered losses of 30% to 35%—losses so great that reclamation of lands along the Zuider Zee came to a halt after 300 years of diking, draining, and damming" (Bishop, pg. 180). Odd reports of wolves descending from the Alps and devouring entire villages pepper the chronicles of the time, betraying the highly superstitious nature of the people.

Perhaps the most interesting (and tragic) social phenomenon of the entire disease comes from Germany. During the plague, a cult of the 5th and 6th centuries was revived. Hundreds of people calling themselves flagellants would snake through towns in long chains, whipping themselves and crying out prayers in frenzied supplication for God's mercy.

Women following the processions would wipe up the flagellants' blood and call the cloths holy. The Pope quickly condemned this violence, especially when the flagellants began to blame the Jews for the plague and burn Jewish villages. Yet he couldn?t stop the rising tide of violence, and this was the beginning of the ghetto culture that would come to a head during the Holocaust. Scandinavia remained isolated until the summer of 1349, when the plague sailed in on a ship of dead men. A British ship had been seen floating in the harbor, and was pulled in by some fishermen. It was full of plague victims and the disease spread outward from the dock. In Scandinavia, the plague would kill over 45% of the population because of climactic conditions conducive to the septicemic strain. In Iceland over 50% died. Perhaps most terrifying is the story of Greenland's colonists.

The plague was probably carried in on a transport ship sometime in 1350. This was the last of the transports to the island until the early fifteenth century when a Norwegian ship came into the dock (due to the freezing of the sea). Sailors got out to investigate and found only cattle wandering through deserted villages. Not a single person remained alive.

The Black Death: The Contemporary Response to the Plague

The contemporary European of 1348 was a peasant, a man who understood little about what was happening to him. He did not use the phrase "Black Death" but instead called the disease "the Pestilence" or "the Great Mortality." He saw only God's desertion in the face of a disaster so horrible. One historian describes,

The European, in the face of the Black Death, was in general overwhelmed by a sense of inevitable doom. If the plague was decreed by God and the inexorable movement of the planets, then how could frail man seek to oppose it? The preacher might counsel hope, but only with the proviso that the sins of man must first be washed away by the immensity of his suffering.

The doctor might proscribe remedies, but with the tepid enthusiasm of a civil-defence expert advising those threatened by imminent nuclear attack to adopt a crouching posture and clasp their hands behind their necks. The Black Death descended on a people who were drilled by their theological and their scientific training into a reaction of apathy and fatalistic resignation. Nothing could have provided more promising material on which a plague might feed (Ziegler, pg. 25).

The flight from cities, the abandonment of the sick, the sordid burials in communal ditches, crops withering in empty fields while livestock ran free?all of these are common in chronicles of the time. The general sense of doom and desperation that overtook the people was completely understandable yet, sometimes it seems that the emotions must have been worn down, dulled by horrors, as in the words of an unknown chronicler: "And in these days was burying without sorrowe and wedding without friendschippe" (Tuchman, pg. 96). But all emotion could not be wiped away. The prevailing tone of the years 1347-1351 is that of a grief beyond words.

The Black Death: Medicine in the 14th Century

Today a disease can be investigated by medicine. In the 14th century medicine seemed like it had advanced as far as it could. For instance, each city had a municipal surgeon, a municipal physician, and about twenty private doctors. There were also hospitals and sanitation systems to remove industrial waste. The system seemed novel, but it immediately fell prey to the complexities of the Black Death and quickly proved useless. It did not, for instance, take into account the spread of the disease, through a bacterium in the stomachs of fleas traveling on rats. The doctors of the time never suspected that the disease could be transferred from an animal to a human, and therefore did not take measures to kill the rats or even keep them out of kitchens.

Medicine at that time was dictated by astrology, to which physicians believed all physiology was subject. Bleeding was the most common cure for every sort of disease. There was a rudimentary knowledge of quarantine, which may have helped to some degree, as Tuchman reports: Stern measures of quarantine were ordered by many cities? Poland established a quarantine at its frontiers which succeeded in giving it relative immunity. Draconian means were adopted by the despot of Milan, Archbishop Giovanni Visconti, head of the most uninhibited ruling family of the 14th century.

He ordered that the first three houses in which the plague was discovered were to be walled up with their occupants inside, enclosing the well, the sick, and the dead in a common tomb (Tuchman, pg. 108). However, the Black Death would revolutionize the medical system. In the High Middle Ages, where there were no major epidemics, the doctors could rely upon ancient teachings and astrology. Because of the plague, doctors were forced to evolve. Eventually this would lead to modern clinical medicine.

The Black Death: Religion

The central part of life in the 14th century was the Church. As soon as the first victims succumbed, God immediately became both the cause and the cure of this plague. Prayers were called out, lamentations wailed, processions marched down streets filled with the dead.

For, in the words of a Florentine chronicler, the living would "...drag the corpses out of the houses with their own hands... and to lay them in front of doors, where anyone who made the rounds might see them, especially in the morning, more of them than he could count; afterwards they would have the biers brought up..." The dehumanizing effects of the Black Death are highly evident later in the chronicle: "Nor was it once or twice only that one and the same bier carried two or three corpses at once, but quite a considerable number of such cases occurred... as two priests bearing the cross were on their way to perform the last office for someone, three or four biers were brought up... whereas the priests supposed that they had but one corpse to bury, they discovered that there were six to eight, or sometimes more.

Nor for all their number were their obsequies honoured by either tears or lights or crowds of mourners; rather, it was come to this, that a dead man was then of no more account than a dead goat would be today." As a result, many of the survivors began to adopt Epicurean attitudes, reveling and gambling with wild abandon.

Religion was left along the wayside by many. When the plague hit Siena, an Italian city, it interrupted the construction of a cathedral. The plague killed off so many workers that the cathedral was never finished. Cathedrals had once been a sign of the greatness of a city, but the Sienan one became nothing more than a crumbling nave after the plague swept through. In England, the Bishop of Bath and Wells issued this proclamation: "The Sacrament of the Eucharist, when no priest is available, may be administered by a deacon. If, however, there is no priest to administer the Sacrament of Extreme Unction, then, as in other matters, faith must suffice...

(Therefore)... persuade all men, in particular, those who are now sick or should feel sick in the future, that, if they are on the point of death and cannot secure the services of a priest, then they should make confession to each other... or if no man is present, then even to a woman." (n. pg.). Today, one copy of this faded message resides in the Bodleian library at Oxford University. Its words seem like they must have been pompous and irrelevant today, in light of the magnitude of the plague, but at the time it was a desperate measure made by desperate men attempting to cling to their faith. Never before had anyone but a priest been able to perform any of these duties. Yet, because so many of the clergy had died, and because faith was so needed at that dark time, something had to be done.

Ziegler Remarks,

Yet, perhaps even more than this, the frenzied charity in which the rich of Europe indulged during and after the Black Death demonstrated their faith in the one institution where it seemed a proper sense of social discipline survived. Discredited the Church might be in the eyes of many but, to the nobles and the monied elite, it was still the dyke which held back the flood of anarchic insurrection. Unless it were shored up then everything, it seemed, might be swept away. The rich gave eagerly so that the clergy might beautify their buildings and enhance their standing in the world. Their own position severely threatened, they felt sustained by the assertion in art of the authority of the Church and the representation of a stable, enduring hierarchy (Ziegler,pg. 236).

Religion in art was also affected. For the first time, Christ was portrayed as angry, while a personified Death dominated most paintings. In contrast, the Virgin became a protector for all people, instead of just monks and nuns.

The Black Death: The Aftermath

The aftermath of the Black Death, the fallout of one of the most massive tragedies in the history of mankind, was the genesis of a new era in human history. Education was stimulated by a spurt of university founding. Charles IV explained that he felt he needed to further the cause of "precious knowledge which the mad rage of pestilential death has stifled throughout the wide realms of the world" (n. pg.). Not all were founded for this love of learning however; Corpus Christi College was founded at Cambridge for solely monetary purposes. Fees for celebrating masses for the dead were so high that the college was established to educate clerics who would be required to pray for the dead.

The economy was jumpstarted by the loss of so many lives. Suddenly workers could break free of the feudal system and demand any wages they wanted. A middle class began to emerge; the rigors of the two class system that had dominated the Middle Ages were slowly broken down as former peasants moved into deserted manors. The fact that the plague had not discriminated in the slightest when choosing who to kill, leaving as many rich as poor dead, changed the way that the common man viewed his economic superiors.

Perhaps the greatest change brought on by the plague was the loss of religion. Once the dust had settled, and the people saw that there was seemingly no Divine purpose in their pain, they began to question God. If their God could be so cruel so wantonly, they wanted no part of him. According to Tuchman, "Once people envisioned the possibility of change in a fixed order, the end of an age of submission came in sight; the turn to individual conscience lay ahead. To that extent the Black Death may have been the unrecognized beginning of modern man" (Tuchman, pg. 123). That sole ruling institution of the Middle Ages, the Church, was called into question. This could have been the spark for the Protestant Reformation.

Chapter 7

An Introduction to Middle English

What Is Middle English?

The English language has changed continually throughout history. In the early Middle Ages these changes were often the result of invasions or migrations; as people from other countries settled in the British Isles they brought their own languages, which combined with or even superceded the native languages.

Old English

If you were to travel back in time to the tenth century, you probably wouldn't be able to understand a word that anyone said to you. They'd be speaking Old English (or Anglo-Saxon, as it's sometimes called), a language very different from the English that we speak today. For a start, the grammar was entirely different – more like Latin or Russian than modern English. Words were inflected – that is to say, rather than using a preposition like 'of' or 'from' to show what is happening in the sentence, a suffix would be attached to the word. For example, a word like 'stow', meaning 'place', would have the suffix 'um' attached to it to mean 'in'. And, as you can see, not only the grammar but the vocabulary was very different. Talking to a tenth-century Englishman, you'd probably only be able to recognize a few words like 'a' or 'the'. Only about one-sixth of current English vocabulary has an Old English root, with the rest being foreign influences – but these are often the most important and commonly used words – such as 'to be'. Other old words still exist in place names – you may not recognize that the word 'stow' means 'place', but there are plenty of towns called Stowe or which include it in their name. And even if you could understand a word when it was written down, Old English pronounciation was very different to today. Even the alphabet was different – there are extra letters taken from the Norse runes.

Take a look at this piece of Old English poetry and see if you can understand any of it: Wæs se grimma gæst Grendel haten, mære mearcstapa, se þe moras heold, fen ond fæsten Choose what you think this is about –

- A monster living on a moor
- The arrival of an unwelcome guest at a house
- A sheep-shearing contest

In fact, these lines are from Beowulf, a great poem from the 11th century, and this description is the first time that Grendel, a monster, is described. This is how it might run in modern English: Grendel this monster grim was called, march-riever mighty, in moorland living, in fen and fastness (trans R.I.Altman).

There are a few words you might recognize – 'grimma' is 'grim', 'moras' is 'moorland' and 'fen' is 'fen'. A 'march-riever' is someone who sneaks over a border to steal from and harass the inhabitants. Some words make sense if you think about them a little more – 'gaest' is an evil spirit or monster, and our word 'ghost' is its descendent. Other words you might guess from your knowledge of foreign languages – 'haten' does not mean 'hate', but 'called' or 'named', like the German 'heissen'. (Beowulf is a wonderful poem – try to get hold of the translation by Seamus Heaney if you can).

The Changing Language

So why did the language change? There are a number of reasons, but a major factor was the Norman invasion of Britain in 1066. The Normans spoke an early form of French, which quickly became the 'official' language of England, overtaking the native language for governmental administration and legal matters. But the Normans and the English had to communicate somehow, and their struggles to speak changed the English language. New French vocabulary was introduced to Old English, and the English grammar gradually became simplified as the Normans struggled with it. (As well as French and English, Latin was also an important language in the Middle Ages. It was used for some government business, for education and during religious worship in church.)

Gradually Old English turned into the Middle English that Chaucer writes in – but still the official language of England was French! It was only in 1362, during Chaucer's lifetime, that English was used at the opening of Parliament for the first time. During the same year a law called the 'Statute of Pleading' was passed, making English the official language of the courts and in Parliament (and even then, it took a while to get everyone to speak English). In 1399, King Henry IV became the first king of England since the Norman Conquest whose mother tongue was English. However, English was a still a language of low status – especially when it came to writing poetry and literature. During the 14th century, the Italians and French were experiencing an explosion of creativity – great poets like Dante, Petrach and Boccaccio were writing in entirely new ways. But English had no such great writers. This was where Chaucer made a difference – he took the language of the man in the street and turned it into a series of masterpieces. Chaucer proved that poetry written in English could be every bit as good as books in Latin or French.

Chaucer's Middle English and Regional Dialects

To see how different Middle English is from Old English, take a look at this passage from Chaucer's famous book The Canterbury Tales. Unlike Beowulf, you shouldn't have any problems understanding it, even though it still looks a bit odd compared with Modern English.

A Knight there was, and that a worthy man,
That fro the tyme that he first bigan
To riden out, he loved chivalrie,
Trouthe and honour, fredom and curteisie.

This is the description of the Knight, one of the group of pilgrims described in The Canterbury Tales; later we'll look at this passage more closely as we work through some ways of understanding Middle English. But if you compare this with the extract from Beowulf, you can see how English had changed between the 11th and the 14th centuries.

However, this is only one Middle English dialect; The Canterbury Tales were written in the English spoken by Londoners. In fourteenth-century England, it was far more difficult to travel around than it was today, since the only way to travel was by horse, boat, or on foot. With little contact between people from different regions, regional dialects became noticeably different. Someone from the North, for example, might find a Londoner almost incomprehensible. Caxton, the man who brought the printing press to Britian, tells a famous story about a man trying to buy eggs:

In my days it happened that certain merchants were in a ship in Thames for to have sailed over the sea into Zeland, and for lack of wind they tarried atte foreland, and went to land for to refresh them. And on of them named Sheffield, a mercer, in-to an house and asked for meat, and especially he asked after eggs. And the good wife answered, that she could speak no French. And the merchant was angry, for he also could speak no French, but would have eggs, and she undestood him not. And then at last another said that he would have eyren? Then the good wife said that she undestood him well. Lo, what should a man in these days now write, eggs or Eiern, certainly it is hard to please every man, by cause of diversity and change of language.

The English we speak today developed from the English that was spoken in London, so although we can understand most of Chaucer's language, Middle English from the north is much more difficult. Try taking a look at these lines (again, you'll see þ, which is 'th', so 'þe' is spelt 'the' today; ' is a sort of 'yuh' sound, like the 'gh' in 'night')

Þis kyng lay at Camylot vpon Krystmasse
With mony luflych lorde, ledez of þe best,
Rekenly of þe Rounde Table alle þo rich breþer,
With rych reuel ory't and rechles merþes.

The words 'Camylot' and the 'Rounde Table' should give you a clue as to this poem. These lines are taken from Sir Gawain and the Green Knight, written at about the same time as The Canterbury Tales, but by an author whose name is now forgotten. Here's a translation into modern English: King Arthur lay at Camelot upon a Christmas-tide, with many a gallant lord and lovely lady, and all the noble brotherhood of the Round Table. There they held rich revels with merry talk and jokes.

As you can see, the language of Gawain is half-way between Old English and Chaucer's English. The other thing you'll notice is that Chaucer writes rhyming poetry, as they did in Europe, whereas the Gawain poet uses alliteration, in the old English tradition that we also saw in Beowulf. We can get some idea of how important this different language was from Chaucer's own words - Chaucer ends his long poem Troilus and Criseyde (about the Trojan war) with a plea that his poem will be understood in different parts of Britian.

And for ther is so gret diversite [great diversity]
In English and in writyng of oure tonge, [tongue - i.e. language]
So prey I God that non, myswrite thee [miswrite - i.e. copy it out wrongly]
Ne thee mysmetre for defaute of tonge; [mismetre - i.e. get the rhythm wrong because their language isn't very good]
And red whereso thow be, [red = read; elles = else; or elles songe, songe = sung]
That thow be understonde, [understonde = God understool]
I beseche!

Of course, the English language has continued to change since Chaucer's day - for example, Shakespeare's English is quite different from Chaucer's - and is still changing now. Until just a few years ago, 'C U L8R' was just a string of letters and numbers, but now most people know what it means!

Reading Middle English - Woring out the Meaning

Although Middle English can look quite tricky to start with, it isn't difficult to work out what it means. In this section we'll take a look at an example of Chaucer's English, taken from the Prologue to The Canterbury Tales, and suggest some ways in which you can work through it to gain a clearer understanding of the language.

A knyght ther was, and that a worthy man,
That fro the tyme that he first bigan
To riden out, he loved chivalrie,
Trouthe and honour, fredom and curteisie.
Ful worthy was he in his lordes were,
And therto hadde he riden, no man ferre,
As wel in cristendom as in hethenesse,
And evere honoured for his worthynesse.

As you look at this, you will realise that you already recognise many of the words - most of the first line, for example, is made up of modern words, and you'll also recognise 'first', 'loved' and 'honour'.

Some other words look quite familiar, although the spelling isn't what you expect - 'knyght', for example, instead of 'knight', and 'fredom' instead of 'freedom'. But there are some words that look a bit trickier - 'bigan', 'riden' and 'trouthe', perhaps. So how can you work out what they mean?

Working Out the Meaning - reading Aloud

One of the best ways to understand Middle English is to try reading it aloud. Often a word will look strange, but will sound perfectly normal when spoken. So if you read these eight lines out, you'll find that 'bigan' actually sounds like the modern

English word 'began' - and in fact it is exactly the same word, just spelled differently.

Working out the Meaning - change the Spelling

This leads us to another way to work out Middle English. Often a Middle English word is very similar to a modern English word, but the spelling is different. So try thinking about the spelling - can you change or remove some letters from the Middle English word to make it more like modern English? The word 'trouthe' looks hard - but if you take away the 'o' and the 'e' it becomes 'truth'.

Working out the Meaning - context

There are also some Middle English words which don't really have a modern English equivalent - for example, 'cristendom' and 'hethenesse'. When you look at the first of these words you might notice that it begins with 'crist', which looks very much like 'Christ', and in fact 'cristendom' is an old-fashioned word meaning 'the countries where people are Christians'. This may help to provide some context for the other word, 'hethenesse'.

The poem says that the knight had 'riden' (ridden on horseback) 'As wel in cristendom as in hethenesse'. This seems to suggest that 'cristendom' and 'hethenesse' are contrasted in some way; are they opposites, perhaps? Could 'hethenesse' be the countries where people are not Christians? In fact, this is absolutely correct, and if you look again at the word, you may now think that 'hethen' looks like the modern word 'heathen'.

Working out the meaning - tricky words

Just occasionally there will be Middle English words that you can't work out at all, because the word has no modern English equivalent. In these cases you will need to use some other way of finding out the meaning. In books of Chaucer's poetry there is often a mini-dictionary or glossary in the back; this can help out with tricky words. If this doesn't help, you will need to look at a specialist dictionary of Middle English words, like the Middle English Dictionary. You can access this on the Internet at http://ets.umdl.umich.edu/m/med/ - the easiest way to use it is to click on 'Lookups' and then type in the word. There are also some other websites with Chaucer glossaries and dictionaries - see the Web Links and Resources section below.

Some Other Points

References to other texts, etc.

Chaucer's poetry can seem difficult because he sometimes mentions the names of people or places you haven't heard of. Often these are people from Greek mythology, or from history or literature. It doesn't always matter if you don't know exactly who he's talking about; you can usually enjoy the poetry anyway. In some cases, however, it can make the poem more enjoyable if you find out more about the person he mentions. The poem may have some notes attached to it, explaining - or you can do a search on the Internet.

The order of words

Chaucer often changes the usual order of words around, just as modern poets sometimes do. For example, he says 'A knyght ther was' instead of 'There was a knight'. Sometimes he uses very long sentences, spread over several lines, which can make it tricky to work out exactly what he's saying. But there's no need to worry; you can usually get the 'gist' of it quite easily, and it doesn't take very long to get used to unravelling Chaucer's long sentences.

Double negatives

Your teachers or parents may have told you that you shouldn't use the 'double negative'; in other words, you shouldn't say, for example, 'I don't want nothing', because 'don't' and 'nothing' are both negatives. They may have told you that these two negatives cancel each other out, making a positive - so 'I don't want nothing' really means 'I do want something'. This may be true as far as modern English is concerned, but in medieval times the opposite was true; poets and other writers used double negatives all the time to add emphasis to a negative statement. In fact, sometimes they used a triple negative, when they wanted to make a point really strongly! E.g. 'He nevere yet no vileynye ne sayde' means 'he very definitely never said anything bad at all'.

The Pronunciation of Chaucer's Middle English

English has never had a prettier sound than it had — apparently — in Chaucer's day, and every serious student of Chaucer's poetry will eventually want to master the fine details of its phonology. There are various readily available books which treat, among other things, pronunciation of Chaucer's dialect. For introductory purposes, the best are (for American readers) the standard American editions of Chaucer's work, that is, especially, the editions of F.N. Robinson, D.W. Robertson, Jr., and Albert C. Baugh. Another excellent, very brief introduction is that of E. Talbot Donaldson in the Norton Anthology of English Literature.

In all such introductions one repeatedly encounters such phrases as "It is important to maintain the distinction between such-and-such and so-and-so," for instance between "open o," as in broth (or aw, shucks), and "close o," as in note. Nothing could be truer, but when one listens to distinguished Chaucerians deliver scholarly papers at medieval conventions, or when one listens to the records made by great Chaucerians past and present, one discovers surprising differences of opinion about how things ought to be pronounced. For instance, some specialists make consonants sound much like consonants in modern English, except clearer, more precise, while other specialists speak consonants as they would in Danish or, God help us, German. For the beginner there's a valuable lesson in this: Chaucer's Middle English is relatively easy to fake. What follows here are some notes on how to fake it convincingly, so that one gets pretty clearly the sound of Chaucer's verse, making people who know the correct pronunciation believe momentarily that perhaps they've learned it wrong.

1. Read aloud or recite with authority, exactly as when speaking Hungarian — if you know no Hungarian — you speak with conviction and easy familiarity. (This, I'm told by Hungarians, is what Hungarians themselves do.) This easy authority, however fake, gets the tone of the language, its warmth and, loosely, outgoing character — not pushy like low-class German, not jaundiced or intimate-but-weary, like modern French, and not, above all, slurred to a mumble, like modern American. Make Middle English open-hearted, like Mark Twain's jokes.
2. Pronounce the vowels like vowels in modern European languages, especially French, German, or Italian (but resist the temptation to drag in the consonant sounds of those languages). Thus a is ah, as in "Ah, so there you are!"; e is ay, as in "Say there!"; I is ee, as in "Gee, it's Marie!"; o is Oh as in "O!"; and u is, for the most part, oo, as in "Who?" That is, the vowels, a e I o u are, basically, ah ey ee oh ooh. Make them long or short exactly as you would in modern English. To be extra expressive, add the following complications:
3. Distinguish between "close e" (e with the throat closed, like the sound of an oboe) and "open e" (e wide-throated, like the sound of a clarinet); that is,, distinguish between the tight e of "eek" or meet, and the easy, breathy e of there when there is pronounced with a touch of Irish, to rhyme with air. (In Middle English, any e followed by r rhymes with air.) For purposes of faking it is fair to say that if a word is spelled ea in modern English (as in sea or beast), it had and open e in Middle English; if spelled ee in modern English (as in see or sleet), it was a close e for Chaucer. And the same goes for close and open o; words now pronounced like note

or stone were open for Chaucer, like the o in our word cloth; words now pronounced like mood or good (modern o either long or short) were close o for Chaucer, like the o in our so. If this is too confusing, try to follow, in general, the pronunciation of the Cisco Kid: "Boot hombray, thees es nut yoor pesstol." For the sound al, very common in Chaucer, say ahl, as in "Ah'll be seeing you."

4. Final e: Many words in Chaucer have a pronounced final e, as in knowe, fewe, etc.... Pronounce the e like the a in sofa. In a line of verse, this e is silent if the word which follows it begins with a vowel but pronounced if the word which follows it begins with a consonant (except h and sometimes w or y). So that in the line, "That, by my trouthe, I take no kepe," the final e in trouthe is silent, the final e in take pronounced.
5. Diphthongs (that is, two vowels together, as in cause) can be a problem for the faker. For instance, for Chaucer fewe and newe are not quite rhymes. Short of learning Anglo-Saxon (which is behind the annoyance) or picking up the sounds by ear through listening to recordings, the faker can only depend on these two principles: (a) that au and aw are always ow, as in cow so that cause = cowzuh, drawe = drowwuh, daunger = downjer; and (b) when pronouncing any other diphthong, take the Middle English sounds of the words separately and squeeze them together, so that iu becomes ee + oo = yew. This works about have the time, which is good odds.
6. As for consonants, the rule is simple, pronounce every one of them except when you're positive the word is French (one can swallow the g in sign, for instance) or when the consonant is an initial h. With g or gg, pronounce the same word in modern English (e.g., juggen, modern judge, has the dj, but frogges, modern frogs, has the sound gg).

7. For consonant clusters like th or gh, all you really need is this: Like any consonant or consonant cluster that can be either voiced or unvoiced (z is voiced, sss is unvoiced), the th tends to be unvoiced at the beginning and ends of words but voiced in the middle (between vowels). (F in Middle English is always unvoiced, v always voiced.) Thus that is unvoiced (like the th in thin) but bathed is voiced (like the the in then). Similarly, s is unvoiced (or hissed) in saw and was but voiced in resoun (ray-zoon). The gh sound is slightly but not excessively German, as in ich or nach; and ch, even in French words like chivalrie, is almost always pronounced as in church.
8. Some words in Middle English are accented in peculiar places — for example, corâge or solémpnely — and some can be accented as the poet pleases, as in náture and natúre. Take the pronunciation that makes the rhythm feel right, not, of course, that every line has to be rigidly iambic. In most doubtful cases, no one can really prove you wrong. For instance one may read either, "For thére is phisícién but oón," or, "For there is phisícién but oón," or even, "For thére is phisicién but oón" (slightly hovering over the first two syllables of phisicien) and the solemnest phonologiest can only muse that he himself would read it somewhat differently. There are of course downright ridiculous readings, but it's comforting to notice that most of them have been urged, from time to time, by reputable scholars.
9. One last word about e's. Don't say nay for nuh (as in "I ne have," that is, "I haven't"), thay for thuh (as in "the cat"). Say thay when Middle English the means the pronoun thee (as in "thee, thou cat"). And watch for occasional long e's at the ends of words, as in beaute (bay-oh-tay, i.e., "beauty").

If you do all this, or some of it, and at the same time put

across the sense of the lines you read, only pedants and people of mean spirit will notice your errors. You will, of course, make errors. Practice, both alone and with sympathetic friends; list to records; if you feel desperate, take a good course and, thereafter, blame your teacher.

Chapter 8

Introduction: The Canterbury Tales

The Canterbury Tales is a collection of stories written by Geoffrey Chaucer in the 14th century (two of them in prose, the rest in verse). The tales, some of which are originals and others not, are contained inside a frame tale and told by a collection of pilgrims on a pilgrimage from Southwark to Canterbury to visit the shrine of Saint Thomas Becket at Canterbury Cathedral. The Canterbury Tales are written in Middle English. Although the tales are considered to be his magnum opus, some believe the structure of the tales are indebted to the works of The Decameron, which Chaucer is said to have read on an earlier visit to Italy.

The Prologue and Individual Tales

The characters, introduced in the General Prologue of the book, tell tales of great cultural relevance. The first part of the prologue begins with "Whan that Aprill with his shoures soote" indicating the start of spring and the end of a brutal winter. The themes of the tales vary, and include topics such as courtly love, treachery, and avarice. The genres also vary, and include romance, Breton lai, sermon, beast fable, and fabliaux. Though there is an overall frame, there is no single poetic structure to the work; Chaucer utilizes a variety of rhyme schemes and metrical patterns, and there are also two prose tales. The Tales include some of the tales are serious and others comical. Religious malpractice is a major theme as well as focusing on the division of the three estates. Most of the tales are interlinked with similar themes running through them and some are told in retaliation for other tales in the form of an argument. The work is incomplete, as it was originally intended that each character would tell four tales, two on the way to Canterbury and two on the return journey. This would have meant a possible one hundred and twenty tales which would have dwarfed the twenty-four tales actually written.

People have sought political overtones within the tales, particularly as Chaucer himself was a significant courtier and political figure at the time, close to the corridors of power. There are many hints at contemporary events, and the theme of marriage common in the tales has been presumed to refer to several different marriages, most often those of John of Gaunt. Aside from Chaucer himself, Harry Bailly of the Tabard Inn was a real person, and it is considered quite likely that the cook was Roger Knight de Ware, a contemporary London cook.

The Complete Work

The work began some time in the 1380s but Chaucer stopped working on it in the late 1390s. It was not written down fully conceived: it seems to have had many revisions with the addition of new tales at various times. The plan for one hundred and twenty tales is from the general prologue. It is announced by Harry Bailey, the host, that there will be four tales each (two on the way to Canterbury, two on the way back to the tavern). This is not necessarily the opinion of Chaucer himself, who appears as the only character to tell more than one tale. It has been suggested that the unfinished state was deliberate on Chaucer's part. It had a total of 646 pages!

The structure of The Canterbury Tales is a frame narrative and easy to find in other contemporary works, such as The Book of Good Love by Juan Ruiz and Boccaccio's Decameron, which may have been one of Chaucer's main sources of inspiration. Chaucer indeed adapted several of Boccaccio's stories to put in the mouths of his own pilgrims, but what sets Chaucer's work apart from his contemporaries' is his characters. Compared to Boccaccio's main characters - seven women and three men, all young, fresh and well-to-do, and given Classical names - the characters in Chaucer are of extremely varied stock, including representatives of most of the branches of the middle classes at that time. Not only are the participants very different, but they tell very different types of tales, with their personalities showing through both in their choices of tales and in the way they tell them.

The idea of a pilgrimage appears to have been mainly a useful device to get such a diverse collection of people together for literary purposes. In fact, the Monk would probably not be allowed to undertake the pilgrimageand some of the other characters would be unlikely ever to want to attend. Also all of the pilgrims ride horses, so there is no suggestion of them suffering for their religion. None of the popular shrines along the way are visited and there is no suggestion that anyone attends mass, so that it seems much more like a tourist's jaunt.

Chaucer does not pay much attention to the progress of the trip. He hints that the tales take several days but he does not detail any overnight stays. Although the journey could be done in one day this speed would make telling tales difficult and three to four days was the usual duration for such pilgrimages. The 18th of April is mentioned in the tales and Walter William Skeat, a 19th century editor, determined 17 April 1387 as the probable first day of the tales.

Scholars divide the tales into ten fragments. The tales that make up a fragment are directly connected, usually with one character speaking to and handing over to another character, but there is no connection between most of the other fragments. This means that there are several possible permutations for the order of the fragments and consequently the tales themselves. The above listing is perhaps the most common in modern times, with the fragments numbered I-X, but an alternative order lists them A-G, with the tales from the Physician's until the Nun's Priest's placed before the Wife of Bath's. The exception to the independence between fragments are the last two. The Manciple's tale is the last tale in IX but fragment X starts with the Parson's prologue by saying that the Manciple had finished his tale. The reason that they are kept as two different fragments is that the Manciple starts his short tale in the morning but the Parson's tale is told at four in the afternoon. It is assumed that Chaucer would have amended his manuscript or inserted more tales to fill the time.

In 2008 The Modern Library will publish a major new translation of the complete work by translator, Burton Raffel.

Significance

It is sometimes argued that the greatest contribution that this work made to English literature was in popularising the literary use of the vernacular, English, rather than French or Latin. English had, however, been used as a literary language for centuries before Chaucer's life, and several of Chaucer's contemporaries—John Gower, William Langland, and the Pearl Poet—also wrote major literary works in English. It is unclear to what extent Chaucer was responsible for starting a trend rather than simply being part of it. It is interesting to note that, although Chaucer had a powerful influence in poetic and artistic terms, which can be seen in the great number of forgeries and mistaken attributions (such as The Flower and the Leaf which was translated by John Dryden), modern English spelling and orthography owes much more to the innovations made by the Court of Chancery in the decades during and after his lifetime.

In 2004, Professor Linne Mooney was able to identify the scrivener who worked for Chaucer as an Adam Pinkhurst. Mooney, then a professor at the University of Maine and a visiting fellow at Corpus Christi College, Cambridge, was able to match Pinkhurst's signature, on an oath he signed, to his lettering on a copy of The Canterbury Tales that was transcribed from Chaucer's working copy.

The Canterbury Tales can also tell modern readers much about "the occult" during Chaucer's time, especially in regards to astrology and the astrological lore prevalent during Chaucer's era. There are hundreds if not thousands of astrological allusions found in this work; some are quite overt while others are more subtle in nature.

While some readers look to interpret the characters of "The Canterbury Tales" as historical figures, other readers choose to interpret its significance in less literal terms. After analysis of his diction and historical context, his work appears to develop a critique against society during his lifetime. Within a number of his descriptions, his comments can appear complimentary in nature, but through clever language, the statements are ultimately critical of the pilgrim's actions. It is unclear whether Chaucer would intend for the reader to link his characters with actual persons. Instead, it appears that Chaucer creates fictional characters to be general representations of people in such fields of work. With an understanding of medieval society, one can detect subtle satire at work.

Antisemitism

Edward I of England expelled all Jews from England in 1290, but antisemitism did not disappear in the absence of Jews. In 1385, Geoffrey Chaucer published his Canterbury Tales which included an account of Jews murdering a deeply pious and innocent Christian boy ('The Prioress's Tale'). This blood libel became a part of English literary tradition. Jeremy Cohen contends in this regard: "from Chaucer to Margery Kempe, from the cycles of Corpus Christi Day miracle plays to the poetry of the seventeenth century, European literature retained its picture of the Jewish Christ killer, who inflicted violence on that which was most sacred to the culture and society of Western Christianity."

The Pilgrims' Route and Real Locations

The City of Canterbury has a museum dedicated to The

Canterbury Tales. The postulated return journey has intrigued many and continuations have been written as well, often to the horror or (occasional) delight of Chaucerians everywhere, as tales written for the characters who are mentioned but not given a chance to speak. The Tale of Beryn is a story by an anonymous author within a 15th century manuscript of the work.

The tales are rearranged and there are some interludes in Canterbury, which they had finally reached, and Beryn is the first tale on the return journey, told by the Merchant. John Lydgate's Siege of Thebes is also a depiction of the return journey but the tales themselves are actually prequels to the tale of classical origin told by the Knight in Chaucer's work.

Influences

The title of the work has become an everyday phrase and been variously adapted and adopted; for example Margaret Atwood's The Handmaid's Tale, and others. Recently an animated version of some of the tales has been produced for British television. As well as versions with Modern English dialogue, there have been versions in the original Middle English and Welsh. Many literary works (both fiction and non-fiction alike) have used a similar frame narrative to the Canterbury Tales as an homage.

Science Fiction writer Dan Simmons wrote his Hugo Award winning novel Hyperion based around an extra-planetary group of pilgrims. Evolutionary biologist Richard Dawkins used The Canterbury Tales as a structure for his 2004 non-fiction book about evolution - The Ancestor's Tale: A Pilgrimage to the Dawn of Evolution. His animal pilgrims are on their way to find the common ancestor, each telling a tale about evolution.

Henry Dudeney's book The Canterbury Puzzles contains a part which is supposedly lost text from the Tales.

Stage and film Adaptations

The Two Noble Kinsmen, by William Shakespeare and

John Fletcher, a retelling of The Knight's Tale, was first published in 1613 or 1614 and published in 1634.

- 1944, A Canterbury Tale, a film jointly written and directed by Michael Powell and Emeric Pressburger, is based on the narrative frame of Chaucer's tales - that is, a group of strangers, each with his or her own story and in need of some kind of redemption, making their way to Canterbury together. The movie opens with a scene showing a group of medieval pilgrims journeying by foot and on horseback through the Kentish countryside as a narrator speaks the opening lines of the Tales' prologue. This scene makes a now-famous transition to the time of World War 2. The film's story takes place in an imaginary town in Kent and ends with the main characters arriving at Canterbury Cathedral, bells pealing and Chaucer's words again resounding. A Canterbury Tale is recognized as one of the Powell-Pressburger team's most poetic and artful films. It was produced as wartime propaganda, using Chaucer's poetry, referring to the famous pilgrimage, and offering stirring photography of Kent to remind the public of what made Britain so special and worth fighting for. One scene in the film centres on a local historian lecturing his audience of British soldiers about the pilgrims of Chaucer's time and the vibrant history of England.
- Pasolini, see The Canterbury Tales (film)
- 1961, Erik Chisholm completed his opera, The Canterbury Tales. The opera is in three acts: The Wyf of Bath's Tale, The Pardoner's Tale and The Nun's Priest's Tale.
- 2004, BBC, modern re-tellings of selected tales.[5]
- 2005, Royal Shakespeare Company, translation by Mike Poulton
- 2001, A Knight's Tale took its name from "The Knight's Tale," with a fictionalized Chaucer portrayed as a friend to the knight. At one point

Chaucer declares he will use his verse to vilify two church officials who cheated him; they are a summoner and a pardoner. However the film actually has very little to do with the tale. In a deleted scene included on the DVD release, Chaucer is also seen with his wife, who comments that his new companions are better than the pilgrims he befriended earlier.

Chapter 9

List of Characters: The Canterbury Tales

CHARACTER LIST

The Host

He is the proprietor of the Tabard Inn where the pilgrims to Canterbury stay and travels with them on their journey. It is the Host who devised the scheme of the tales, proposing that each tell two tales on the way to Canterbury, and he frequently mediates arguments between pilgrims and suggests who shall tell the next story.

The Knight

A noble fighter who served in the Crusades, he travels with his son, the Squire. The Knight tells the first tale, a romantic tale of a love triangle between two knights and a woman they both love.

The Squire

A 'lusty bachelor' of twenty, the Squire is the son of the Knight. He tells an incomplete tale concerning the gifts that a mysterious knight brings to the court of Tartary.

The Knight's Yeoman

The Yeoman is the second servant who travels with the

Knight. He does not tell a tale.

The Prioress

A delicate, sentimental woman, the Prioress weeps over any small tragedy such as the death of a mouse. She attempts to appear refined, but her refinement is superficial. Her tale concerns the murder of a small child at the hands of Jews who loathe the child for singing about the Virgin Mary.

The Second Nun

The secretary to the Prioress, the Second Nun tells as her tale the biography of Saint Cecilia.

The Monk

A robust and masculine man, the Monk travels with the Prioress and Second Nun. He tells the tale of a hen and her 'husband,' a rooster who prophesies misfortune.

The Friar (Hubert)

He is an immoral man concerned largely with profit rather than turning men away from sin. His tale is an attack on the wickedness of summoners.

The Merchant

He is an arrogant man obsessed with profit margins. His story is a comic tale concerning an elderly blind man who takes a young wife who proves unfaithful.

The Clerk

The Clerk is a student at Oxford, and his lack of an actual profession leaves him impoverished. Although educated, his intellectual pursuits have left him virtually unemployable. He tells a tale of the humble Griselde, who marries a man of high status who cruelly tests her devotion to him.

The Man of Law

The lawyer tells a religiously inspired tale concerning

Constance, a woman who suffers a number of tragedies but is at each turn saved by her devotion to her Christian beliefs.

The Franklin

He travels with the Man of Law. The Franklin is a man who takes delight in all simple pleasures, most prominently culinary ones. His story is that of a woman who promises to have an affair with a man if he can do something she deems impossible that would nevertheless save her husband.

The Weaver

One of the five guildsmen who travel with the pilgrims to Canterbury, he does not tell a tale.

The Dyer

One of the five guildsmen who travel with the pilgrims to Canterbury, he does not tell a tale.

The Carpenter

One of the five guildsmen who travel with the pilgrims to Canterbury, he does not tell a tale.

The Tapestry-Maker

One of the five guildsmen who travel with the pilgrims to Canterbury, he does not tell a tale.

The Haberdasher

One of the five guildsmen who travel with the pilgrims to Canterbury, he does not tell a tale.

The Cook

A lewd and vulgar man, the Cook often engages in violent and contentious behavior. He tells a tale that appears to be a fabliau. However, this tale does not exist in a completed form.

The Shipman

He tells the tale of a woman who agrees to have an affair

with a monk who will pay her so that she can repay a debt to her husband, but this monk borrows this money from the husband himself.

The Physician

The Physician tells a tale about a father who, in order to protect his daughter from scoundrels who contrive to rape her, murders his daughter.

The Wife of Bath

The most ostentatious of the travellers, the Wife of Bath has been married five times and is currently searching for another man to marry. The Wife of Bath is opinionated and boisterous, and her tale, which centres around the question "what do women want?," promotes her view that women wish to have authority over men.

The Parson

The Parson is a man devoted to his congregation, decent and principled. His tale is a long dissertation on the definition of sin and its various forms.

The Miller

A large man with an imposing physique, the Miller is rude and contemptuous of his fellow travellers. His tale is a comic story of a devious student who contrives to have an affair with the wife of a dimwitted carpenter.

The Manciple

Also trained in the law, the Manciple tells a fable that attributes the dark appearance and unpleasant sound of crows to the actions of a white crow who told the god Phoebus of his wife's infidelity.

The Reeve

A slender man with a fiery temper, he tells a tale in response to the Miller's Tale. His tale concerns a villainous Miller who is humiliated by two Oxford students.

The Summoner

The profession of the summoner is to issue summons for people to appear in front of the Church court, and in this the Summoner is quite unfair. He tells a tale in response to the Friar's diatribe against summoners that parodies the Friar's profession.

The Pardoner

An effeminate and shamelessly immoral man, the Pardoner is intensely self-loathing yet devoted to his task of defrauding people of their money by making them believe that they have sinned and need to buy pardons. His tale is an allegory about three rioters who find death through their avarice. The Pardoner uses this tale as an attempt to sell false relics to the travellers.

The Canon

A mysterious and threatening figure, he and his Yeoman are not original travellers with the pilgrims to Canterbury. They seek out the party when they learn about the tales that they have been telling. When the Canon's Yeoman reveals too much about his master's profession, the Canon suddenly disappears.

The Canon's Yeoman

The assistant to the Canon, he speaks openly about his master's tricks as an alchemist, prompting the Canon to leave the pilgrims. The Yeoman then admits that he regrets the deceptions of his master, and tells a tale that details the methods of a canon's fraud.

Arcite

Theban knight who is imprisoned in Athens but released on the intervention of his friend Pirithous, he and his friend Palamon both fall in love with Emelye. He prays to Mars for aid in his duel with Palamon for Emelye, and although he wins the battle, he suddenly is killed in an earthquake upon his victory.

Palamon

Theban knight who is imprisoned in Athens. Both he and Arcite fall in love with Emelye. Before the duel for her hand in marriage, Palamon prays to Venus, the goddess of love, to win Emelye as a wife. Although he loses the battle, he wins Emelye as a wife when Arcite dies.

Emelye

The sister of Hippolyta, she is a pawn within the struggle between Arcite and Palamon, both who have fallen in love with her. Although she wishes to remain chaste in honour of the goddess, Diana, she accepts that she must marry one of the two knights.

Theseus

The King of Athens, he wages war upon Thebes in response to the injustice of the Theban king, and imprisons Arcite and Palamon. He sets the rules and regulations of their duel for Emelye.

Hippolyta

The Queen of Scythia, she is the husband of Theseus, King of Athens, and the sister of Emelye.

Pirithous

A prince and childhood friend of Theseus, he intervenes to have Arcite released from prison on the condition that he never return to Athens.

Lycurgus

The king of Thrace, he fights with Palamon during his duel with Arcite.

Emetreus

The king of India, he fights with Arcite during his duel with Palamon.

John

An oafish carpenter, he is an older man who marries the much younger Alison. He foolishly believes Nicholas' prediction that a second great flood is coming, and hides in a kneading bucket on his roof in preparation for it.

Alison

The crafty wife of John the carpenter, Alison is much younger than her husband. She has an affair with Nicholas, a boarder who stays with her and her husband.

Nicholas

An Oxford student who boards with John and Alison, Nicholas claims to study astronomy. He has an affair with Alison and conspires to have a day of privacy with her, but proves himself less crafty than he believes when he falls prey to Absolon's prank.

Absolon

A delicate, courtly lover who pursues Alison, he is a skilled musician and an unabashed romantic. He suffers humiliation at the hands of Alison, but gets revenge on Nicholas.

Symkyn

A vulgar, dishonest and foolish miller, Symkyn repeatedly cheats his customers out of grain. He receives his comeuppance when two Cambridge students that he has cheated seduce his wife and daughter then steal their grain back from him.

Aleyn

A Cambridge student who seduces the miller's daughter, Molly, when he and John stay at the miller's house.

John (2)

A Cambridge student who seduces the miller's wife when

he and Aleyn stay at the Miller's house.

Molly

The daughter of the Miller, she is a somewhat unattractive young woman, yet Aleyn nevertheless seduces her when the two students stay at the miller's home.

Constance

The daughter of the Roman emperor, she is given to be married to the Sultan of Syria after he agrees to convert to Christianity, but when his mother opposes this, she narrowly escapes an assassination attempt and ends up in England, where she marries King Alla and, escaping treachery once more, is sent back to Rome. She is a devoted Christian whose faith aids her throughout all of her travails.

The Sultan

The King of Syria, he agrees to convert to Christianity to marry Constance, but his actions infuriate his mother, who has him assassinated.

The Sultana

Villainous mother of the Sultan, she refuses to convert from Islam on the orders of her son and plots his assassination.

Dame Hermengild

The wife of the Warden of the Northumberland region where Constance lands in England, she converts to Christianity through the influence of Constance. A devious knight murders her in an attempt to frame Constance.

The Warden

The husband of Dame Hermengild, he watches over the castle of Northumberland while King Alla is at war. He converts to Christianity along with his wife.

King Alla

The English king of Northumberland, he marries Constance but is separated from her because of the machinations of his mother, Lady Donegild.

Lady Donegild

The treacherous mother of King Alla, she contrives to have Constance and her child banished from England. King Alla murders her for her evil actions.

Mauritius

The son of King Alla and Constance, he becomes the emperor of Rome when Constance's father realises his royal lineage.

Jankin: The fifth husband of the Wife of Bath, he was much younger than she and prone to reading misogynist religious texts that offended his wife. When he hurt her out of anger, he realised his error and submitted to her authority, after which he and his wife had a perfectly happy marriage.

The Knight (2): After raping a young woman, the knight is sentenced to death, but spared by the queen, who decides that the knight will receive mercy if he can answer the question "what do women want?"

The Old Woman: This elderly woman tells the Knight what women really desire on the condition that he will marry her. When he grants her the authority in marriage, the old woman transforms into a beautiful young woman.

The Summoner (2): The summoner, who is given no proper name, is a typical representation of his profession, according to the Friar. He meets the devil and shares trade secrets, and is cast into hell for his sinful behavior.

Satan: Introducing himself as a yeoman, he and the summoner become compatriots until he finally casts the summoner into hell.

The Friar: This boorish friar is rude and presumptuous, oblivious to the conditions of Thomas and his wife, who take him in as a boarder. Although ostensibly polite and refined, the friar callously begs Thomas for money.

Thomas: Owner of a home where the Friar stays, his infant child had recently died and he himself has taken ill.

When the Friar begs him for money, Thomas pays him with the 'gift' of a fart.

Griselde: A woman of low status, she marries Walter, the marquis of Saluzzo, but is subjected to a number of trials that her husband devises to prove her worth. She handles each of these trials honourably, proving herself dedicated and steadfast in the face of any tragedy.

Walter: The marquis of Saluzzo, he is a dedicated bachelor until the people of his region insist that he takes a wife. When he marries Griselde, he subjects her to a number of trials meant to prove her worth, each of them cruel and heartless.

Janicula: The father of Griselde. She returns to him after she has been cast out of her home by Walter.

January: A wealthy knight and perpetual bachelor, at the age of sixty this blind man decides to take a young wife. When he marries May, he bores her with his insistent sexual desire, leading her to have an affair. He regains his sight when Pluto and Proserpina find May having sex with Damian in his presence.

May: The young wife of January, she soon tires of his persistent and monotonous sexual desire and has an affair with January's squire, Damian. When January regains his sight and sees her engaged in a tryst with Damian, she insists that he should not believe his eyes.

Damian: January's squire, he has an affair with May.

Placebo: The brother of January, he argues with his brother against the merits of marrying a young woman at such an elderly age, yet finally relents to his brother's wishes when January insists on finding a bride.

Pluto: The king of the fairies, he and his wife stumble upon January, May and Damian when the latter two have a sexual encounter. He restores January's sight.

Proserpina: She is the wife of Pluto.

Canacee: The daughter of the King of Tartary, she receives the gift of knowing the language of animals and the healing properties of every herb.

Cambyuskan: The King of Tartary. A mysterious knight

brings him a mechanical horse that can transport him anywhere across the globe.

Arviragus: A devoted knight and husband to Dorigen, he travels to Britain to engage in war, causing great grief to his wife. He gives up his wife so that she may preserve her honour.

Dorigen: The wife of Arviragus, she becomes intensely depressed when he leaves for Britain, fearing for his life. She promises to have an affair with Aurelius if he can make the rocks that obstruct the shore on which Arviragus will land disappear.

Aurelius: A young squire who falls in love with Dorigen, he pays the Orleans student to make the rocks off of the Brittany shore disappear so that Dorigen will have an affair with him, but gives her up when he realises the pain that it would cause her.

The Orleans Student: A law student skilled in creating apparitions, he contrives to have the rocks off of the Brittany shore disappear, but when Aurelius does not engage in an affair with Dorigen, he forgives Aurelius of his debt for creating the apparition.

Virginius: An honourable and well-loved knight, he murders his daughter when Appius and Claudius scheme to have her raped.

Virginia: The daughter of Virginius, her incomparable beauty leads Appius to lust after her and scheme to have her raped.

Appius: A corrupt judge who governs the town where Virginius resides, he contrives to have Claudius claim that Virginius had stolen his slave from him, and claims that that slave is Virginia. When his scheme is revealed, he is taken to jail where he commits suicide.

Claudius: A churl who schemes with Appius, he claims that Virginia is his slave and that Virginius stole her from him. When his treachery is revealed, he is banished.

The Three Rioters: Three indistinguishable troublemakers who engage in all sorts of lewd behavior, they go on a search for Death and end up finding it in the form of gold coins.

The Old Man: An aged man who cannot die, he wishes to trade his body with a younger man. He tells the three rioters where they may find Death.

The Merchant (2): A devoted entrepreneur, he is somewhat stingy but dedicated to his business and to thrifty behavior. He insists that his wife repay one hundred francs that he lent her, leading her to seek the sum from Dan John.

Dan John: This monk claims to be a cousin of the merchant. He agrees to lend the merchant's life one hundred francs if she has an affair with him, then borrows the sum from the husband that she intends to repay.

The Wife: A dissatisfied wife, she claims that her husband, the merchant, is a stingy man who does not satisfy her. Displeased that her husband wants her to repay a one hundred franc debt, she agrees to an affair with Dan John for that sum. When the merchant offers that he has been repaid in his own money, she tells him that she will repay him through sex.

Melibee: A mighty and rich ruler, his enemies rape his wife and attack his daughter, leading him to strive for a war of retribution, yet his wife implores him to be merciful.

Prudence: The wife of Melibee, she is raped by his enemies, but wishes to grant them mercy.

Sophie: The young daughter of Melibee, she is left for dead by his enemies when they wound her in five places, but nevertheless barely survives.

Chanticleer: This rooster, peerless in his crowing, has seven companions, the most honoured of which is Pertelote. He dreams that he will be chased by a fox, a prophesy that comes true, and is a strong believer in this prophetic power of dreams.

Pertelote: The most favored of Chanticleer's companions, this hen is essential his 'wife.' She dismisses his idea that dreams predict future events, claiming that his ill temper stems from stomach maladies, but her advice to find healing herbs leads to the fulfillment of his prophecy.

Cecilia: Devout elite Roman woman who dies for her adherence to Christianity.

Valerian: Eventual husband of Cecilia who converts to Christianity upon the influence of Pope Urban. He is executed for his beliefs.

Pope Urban: Christian leader who baptizes Valerian and Tibertius and claims that Cecilia is a saint.

Tibertius: The brother of Cecilia, he converts to Christianity, but is executed with Valerian for his Christian beliefs.

Almachius: Roman prefect who ordered the deaths of Cecilia, Valerian and Tibertius for their Christian beliefs.

Maximus: Roman sergeant who claimed to see the spirits of Valerian and Tibertius ascending to heaven when they are executed, prompting many to convert to Christianity.

Phoebus: Deity who, when he lived on earth, took a wife who was unfaithful to him, despite his insistence on watching her. He teaches his prized white crow to speak the language of humans.

The Crow: This beautiful white crow can speak the language of humans, having been taught by Phoebus, but when he tells Phoebus that his wife had an affair, Phoebus plucks him and curses him, condemning all crows to be forever black and harsh of voice.

Chapter 10

The Canterbury Tales: Plot Overveiw

The Canterbury Tales begins with the introduction of each of the pilgrims making their journey to Canterbury to the shrine of Thomas a Becket. These pilgrims include a Knight, his son the Squire, the Knight's Yeoman, a Prioress, a Second Nun, a Monk, a Friar, a Merchant, a Clerk, a Man of Law, a Franklin, a Weaver, a Dyer, a Carpenter, a Tapestry-Maker, a Haberdasher, a Cook, a Shipman, a Physician, a Parson, a Miller, a Manciple, a Reeve, a Summoner, a Pardoner, the Wife of Bath, and Chaucer himself. These travellers, who stop at the Tabard Inn, decide to tell stories to pass their time on the way to Canterbury. The Host of the Tabard Inn sets the rules for the tales. Each of the pilgrims will tell two stories on the way to Canterbury, and two stories on the return trip. The Host will decide the best of the tales. They decide to draw lots to see who will tell the first tale, and the Knight receives the honour.

The Knight's Tale is a tale about two knights, Arcite and Palamon, who are captured in battle and imprisoned in Athens under the order of King Theseus. While imprisoned in a tower, both see Emelye, the sister of Queen Hippolyta, and fall instantly in love with her. Both knights eventually leave prison separately: a friend of Arcite begs Theseus to release him, while Palamon later escapes. Arcite returns to the Athenian court disguised as a servant, and when Palamon escapes he suddenly finds Arcite. They fight over Emelye, but their fight is stopped when Theseus finds them. Theseus sets the rules for a duel between the two knights for Emelye's affection, and each raise an army for a battle a year from that date. Before the battle, Arcite prays to Mars for victory in battle, Emelye prays to Diana that she may marry happily, and Palamon prays to Venus to have Emelye as his wife. All three gods hear their prayers and argue over whose should get precedence, but Saturn decides to mediate. During their battle, Arcite indeed is victorious, but as soon as he is crowned victor, an earthquake occurs that kills him. Before he dies, he reconciles with Palamon and tells him that he deserves to marry Emelye. Palamon and Emelye marry.

When the Knight finishes his tale, everybody is pleased with its honourable qualities, but the drunken Miller insists that he shall tell the next tale. The Miller's Tale is a comic table in which Nicholas, a student who lives with John the carpenter and his much younger wife, Alison, begins an affair with Alison. Another man, the courtly romantic Absolon, also falls in love with Alison. Nicholas contrives to spend a day with Alison by telling John that a flood equal to Noah's flood will come soon, and the only way that he, Nicholas and Alison will survive is by staying in separate kneading tubs placed on the roof of houses, out of sight of all.

While John remained in this kneading tub, Nicholas and Alison left to have sex, but were interrupted by Absolon, who demanded a kiss from Alison. She told him to close his eyes and he would receive a kiss. He did so, and she pulled down her pants so that he could kiss her nether region. The humiliated Absolon got a hot iron from a blacksmith and returned to Alison. This time, Nicholas tried the same trick, and Absolon burned him on the ass. Nicholas shouted for water, awakening John, who was asleep on the roof. He fell off the roof, hurting himself, and all were humiliated.

The pilgrims laughed heartily at this tale, but Oswald the Reeve took offense, thinking that the Miller meant to disparage older men. In response, The Reeve's Tale told the story of a dishonest Miller, Symkyn, who repeatedly cheated his clients, which included the college at Cambridge. Two Cambridge students, Aleyn and John, went to the miller to buy meal and corn, but while they were occupied Symkyn let their horses run free and stole their corn. They were forced to stay with Symkyn for the night. That night, Aleyn seduced the miller's daughter, Molly, while John seduced the miller's wife. When Aleyn told John of his exploits, Symkyn overheard and fought with him. The miller's wife hit Symkyn over the head with a staff, knocking him unconscious, and the two students escaped with the corn that Symkyn had stolen.

The Cook's Tale was intended to follow the Reeve's Tale, but this tale only exists as an incomplete fragment of no more than fifty lines. Following this tale is the Man of Law's Tale. The Man of Law's Tale tells the story of Constance, the daughter of a Roman emperor who becomes engaged to the Sultan of Syria on the condition that he converts to Christianity. Angered by his order to convert his country from Islam, the mother of the Sultan assassinates her son and Constance barely escapes. She is sent on a ship that lands in Britain, where she is taken in by the warden of a nearby castle and his wife, Dame Hermengild. Both of them soon convert to Christianity upon meeting her.

A young knight fell in love with Constance, but when she refused him, he murdered Dame Hermengild and attempted to frame Constance. However, when King Alla made the knight swear on the Bible that Constance murdered Hermengild, his eyes burst. Constance marries King Alla and they have a son, Mauritius, who is born when Alla is at war in Scotland. Lady Donegild contrives to have Constance banished by intercepting the letters between Alla and Constance and replacing them with false ones. Constance is thus sent away again, and on her voyage her ship comes across a Roman ship. A senator returns her to Rome, where nobody realises that she is the daughter of the emperor. Eventually, King Alla makes a pilgrimage to Rome, where he meets Constance once more, and the Roman emperor realises that Mauritius is his grandson and names him heir to the throne.

The Wife of Bath begins her tale with a long dissertation on marriage in which she recounts each of her five husbands. Her first several husbands were old men whom she would hector into providing for her, using guilt and refusal of sexual favors. However, the final two husbands were younger men, more difficult to handle. The final husband, Jankin, was a twenty-year-old, half the Wife of Bath's age. He was more difficult to handle, for he refused to let the Wife of Bath dominate him and read literature that proposed that women be submissive. When she tore a page out of one of his books, Jankin struck her, causing her to be deaf in one ear. However, he felt so guilty at his actions that from that point in the marriage, he was totally submissive to her and the two remained happy.

The Wife of Bath's Tale is itself a story of marriage dynamic. It tells the tale of a knight who, as punishment for raping a young woman, is sentenced to death. However, he is spared by the queen, who will grant him freedom if he can answer the question "what do women want?" The knight cannot find a satisfactory answer until he meets an old crone, who promises to tell him the answer if he marries her. He agrees, and receives his freedom when he tells the queen that women want sovereignty over their husbands. However, the knight is dissatisfied that he must marry the old, low-born hag. She therefore tells him that he can have her as a wife either old and ugly yet submissive, or young and beautiful yet dominant. He chooses to have her as a young woman, and although she had authority in marriage the two were completely happy from that point.

The Friar asks to tell the next tale, and asks for pardon from the Summoner, for he will tell a tale that exposes the fraud of that profession. The Friar's Tale tells about a wicked summoner who, while delivering summons for the church court, comes across a traveling yeoman who eventually reveals himself to be the devil himself. The two share trade secrets, and the devil tells him that they will meet again in hell if the summoner continues to pursue his trade. The summoner visits an old woman and issues her a summons, then offers to accept a bribe as a payment to prevent her excommunication. The old woman believes that she is without sin and curses the summoner. The devil then appears and casts the summoner into hell.

The Summoner was enraged by the Friar's Tale. Before he begins his tale, he tells a short anecdote: a friar visited hell and was surprised to see that there were no other friars. The angel who was with him then lifted up Satan's tail and thousands of friars swarmed out from his ass. The Summoner's Tale is an equally vitriolic attack on friars. It tells of a friar who stays with an innkeeper and his wife and bothers them about not contributing enough to the church and not attending recently. When the innkeeper tells him that he was not recently in church because he has been ill and his infant daughter recently died, the friar attempted to placate him and then asked for donations once more. Thomas the innkeeper promised to give the friar a 'gift,' and gives him a loud fart.

The Clerk, an Oxford student who has remained quiet throughout the journey, tells the next tale on the orders of the Host. The Clerk's Tale tells about Walter, an Italian marquis who finally decides to take a wife after the people of his province object to his longtime status as a bachelor. Walter marries Griselde, a low-born but amazingly virtuous woman whom everybody loves. However, Walter decides to test her devotion. When their first child, a daughter, is born, Walter tells her that his people are unhappy and wish for the child's death. He takes away the child, presumably to be murdered, but instead sends it to his sister to be raised. He does the same with their next child, a son.

Finally, Walter tells Griselde that the pope demands that he divorce her. He sends her away from his home completely naked, for she had no belongings when she entered his house. Each of these tragedies Griselde accepts with great patience. Walter soon decides to make amends, and sends for his two children. He tells Griselde that he will marry again, and introduces her to the presumed bride, whom he then reveals is their daughter. The family is reunited once more. The Clerk ends with the advice that women should strive to be as steadfast as Griselde, even if facing such adversity is unlikely and perhaps impossible.

The Merchant praises Griselde for her steadfast character, but claims that his wife is far different from the virtuous woman of the Clerk's story. He instead tells a tale of an unfaithful wife. The Merchant's Tale tells a story of January, an elderly blind knight who decides to marry a young woman, despite the objections of his brother, Placebo. January marries the young and beautiful May, who soon becomes dissatisfied with his constant sexual attention to her and decides to have an affair with his squire, Damian. When January and May are in their garden, May sneaks away to have sex with Damian. The gods Pluto and Proserpina come upon Damian and May and restore January's sight so that he may see what his wife is doing. When January sees what is occurring, May tells him not to believe his eyes, and he believes her.

The Squire tells the next tale, which is incomplete. The Squire's Tale begins with a mysterious knight arriving at the court of Tartary. This knight gives King Cambyuskan a mechanical horse that can transport him anywhere around the globe and return him within a day and gives Canacee, the daughter of Cambyuskan, a mirror that can discern honesty and a ring that allows the wearer to know the language of animals and the healing properties of all herbs. Canacee uses this ring to aid a bird who has been rejected in love, but the abruptly ends.

The Franklin's Tale that follows tells of the marriage between the knight Arviragus and his wife, Dorigen. When Arviragus travels on a military expedition, Dorigen laments his absence and fears that, when he returns, his ship will be wrecked upon the rocks off the shore. A young man, Aurelius, falls in love with her, but she refuses to return his favors. She agrees to have an affair with Aurelius only on the condition that he find a way to remove the rocks from the shore, a task she believes impossible. Aurelius pays a scholar who creates the illusion that the rocks have disappeared, while Arviragus returns. Dorigen admits to her husband the promise that she has made, and Arviragus tells her that she must fulfill that promise. He sends her to have an affair with Aurelius, but he realises the pain that it would cause Dorigen and does not make her fulfill the promise. The student in turn absolves Aurelius of his debt. The tale ends with the question: which of these men behaved most honourably?

The Physician's Tale that follows tells of Virginius, a respected Roman knight whose daughter, Virginia, was an incomparable beauty. Appius, the judge who governed his town, lusted after Virginia and collabourated with Claudius, who claimed in court that Virginia was his slave and Virginius had stolen her. Appius orders that Virginia be handed over to him. Virginius, knowing that Appius and Claudius did this in order to rape his daughter, instead gave her a choice between death or dishonour. She chooses death, and Virginius chops off his daughter's head, which he brings to Appius and Claudius. The people were so shocked by this that they realised that Appius and Claudius were frauds. Appius was jailed and committed suicide, while Claudius was banished.

The Pardoner prefaces his tale with an elabourate confession about the nature of his profession. He tells the secrets of his trade, including the sale of useless items as saints' relics, and admits that his job is not to turn people away from sin, but rather to frighten them to such a degree that they pay for pardons. The Pardoner's Tale concerns three rioters who search for Death to vanquish him. They find an old man who tells them that they may find Death under a nearby tree, but under this tree they only find a large fortune. Two of the rioters send the third into town to purchase food and drink for the night, for they intend to escape with their fortune, and while he is gone they plan to murder him.

The third rioter poisons the drink, intending to take all of the money for himself. When he returns, the two rioters stab him, then drink the poisoned wine and die themselves.

The three rioters thus find Death in the form of avarice. The Pardoner ends his tale with a diatribe against sin, imploring the travellers to pay him for pardons, but the Host confronts him.

The next story, The Shipman's Tale, is the story of a thrifty merchant who demands that his wife repay a one hundred franc debt that she owed him. The dissatisfied wife complained about this to Dan John, a monk who stayed with him, and he agrees to pay her the sum if she has an affair with him. She consents to this, and Dan John procures the one hundred francs by borrowing it from the merchant himself. However, the merchant realises that he has been paid with money that he had lent to the monk. The wife therefore tells him that she can repay the debt to her husband in bed.

The Prioress' Tale tells the story of a young Christian child who lived in a town in Asia that was dominated by a vicious Jewish population. When the child learned Alma redemptoris, a song praising the Virgin Mary, he traveled home from school singing this. The Jews, angry at his behavior, took the child and slit his throat, leaving him in a cesspool to die. The boy's mother searched frantically for her son. When she found him, he was not yet dead, for the Virgin Mary had placed a grain on his tongue that would allow him to speak until it was removed. When this was removed, the boy passed on to heaven. The story ends with a lament for the young boy and a curse for the Jews who perpetrated the heinous crime.

Chaucer himself tells the next tape, The Tale of Sir Thopas, a florid and fantastical poem in rhyming couplets that serves only to annoy the other pilgrims. The Host interrupts Chaucer shortly into this tale, and tells him to tell another. Chaucer then tells The Tale of Melibee, one of the few tales that is in prose format. This tale tells about Melibee, a powerful ruler whose enemies rape his wife, Prudence, and nearly murder his daughter, Sophie. When deciding whether to declare war on his enemies, Prudence advises him to remain merciful, and they engage in a long debate over the appropriate course of action. Melibee finally gives his enemies the option: they can receive a sentence either from him or from his wife. They submit to Melibee's judgment, and he intends to disinherit and banish the perpetrators. However, he submits to his wife's plea for mercy.

The Monk's Tale is not a narrative tale at all, but instead an account of various historical and literary figures who experience a fall from grace. These include Adam, Samson, Hercules, King Pedro of Spain, Bernabo Visconti, Nero, Julius Caesar, and Croesus. The Knights interrupts the Monk's Tale, finding his listing of historical tragedies monotonous and depressing.

The Nun's Priest's Tale tells the story of the rooster Chanticleer and the hen Pertelote. Chanticleer was ill one night and had a disturbing dream that he was chased by a fox. He feared this dream was prophetic, but Pertelote assured him that his dream merely stemmed from his illness and that he should find herbs to cure himself. Chanticleer insists that dreams are signifiers, but finally agrees with his wife. When he searches for herbs, Chanticleer is indeed chased by a fox, but is saved when Pertelote squawks, alerting the woman who owns the farm where the two fowl live and causing her to chase the fox away.

Chaucer follows this with The Second Nun's Tale. This tale is a biography of Saint Cecilia, who converts her husband and brother to Christianity during the time of the Roman empire, when Christian beliefs were illegal. Her brother and husband are executed for their beliefs, and she herself is cut three times with a sword during her execution, but does not immediately die. Rather, she lingers on for several more days, during which time she orders that her property be distributed to the poor. Upon her death Pope Urban declared her a saint.

After the Second Nun finishes her tale, a Canon (alchemist) and his Yeoman join the band of travellers. The Canon had heard how they were telling tales, and wished to join them. The Yeoman speaks incessantly about the Canon, telling fantastical stories about his work, but this annoys the

Canon, who suddenly departs. The Yeoman therefore decides to tell a tale himself. The Canon's Yeoman's Tale is a story of the work of a canon and the means by which they defraud people by making them think that they can duplicate money.

The Host tells the Cook to tell the next tale, but he is too drunk to coherently tell one. The Manciple therefore tells his story. The Manciple's Tale is the story of how Phoebus, when he assumed mortal form, was a jealous husband. He monitored his wife closely, fearing that she would be unfaithful. Phoebus had a white crow that could speak the language of humans and could sing beautiful. When the white crow learns that Phoebus' wife was unfaithful, Phoebus plucks him and curses the crow. According to the Manciple, this explains why crows are black and can only sing in an unpleasant tone.

The Parson tells the final tale. The Parson's Tale is not a narrative tale at all, however, but rather an extended sermon on the nature of sin and the three parts necessary for forgiveness: contrition, confession, and satisfaction. The tale gives examples of the seven deadly sins and explains them, and also details what is necessary for redemption. Chaucer ends the tales with a retraction, asking those who were offended by the tales to blame his rough manner and lack of education, for his intentions were not immoral, while asking those who found something redeemable in the tales to give credit to Christ.

Chapter 11

The General Prologue

The General Prologue

The most popular part of the Canterbury Tales is the General Prologue, which has long been admired for the lively, individualized portraits it offers. More recent criticism has reacted against this approach, claiming that the portraits are indicative of social types, part of a tradition of social satire, "estates satire", and insisting that they should not be read as individualized character portraits like those in a novel. Yet it is sure that Chaucer's capacity of human sympathy, like Shakespeare's, enabled him to go beyond the conventions of his time and create images of individualized human subjects that have been found not merely credible but endearing in every period from his own until now.

It is the General Prologue that serves to establish firmly the framework for the entire story-collection: the pilgrimage that risks being turned into a tale-telling competition. The title "General Prologue" is a modern invention, although a few manuscripts call it prologus. There are very few major textual differences between the various manuscripts. The structure of the General Prologue is a simple one. After an elabourate introduction in lines 1 - 34, the narrator begins the series of portraits (lines 35 - 719). These are followed by a report of the Host's suggestion of a tale-telling contest and its acceptance (lines 720 - 821). On the following morning the pilgrims assemble and it is decided that the Knight shall tell the first tale (lines 822 - 858).

Nothing indicates when Chaucer began to compose the

General Prologue and there are no variations between manuscripts that might suggest that he revised it after making an initial version. It is sometimes felt that the last two portraits, of Pardoner and Summoner, may have been added later but there is no evidence to support this. The portraits do not follow any particular order after the first few pilgrims have been introduced; the Knight who comes first is socially the highest person present (the Host calls him 'my mayster and my lord' in line 837).

The Knight is the picture of a professional soldier, come straight from foreign wars with clothes all stained from his armour. His travels are remarkably vast; he has fought in Prussia, Lithuania, Russia, Spain, North Africa, and Turkey against pagans, Moors, and Saracens, killing many. The variety of lords for whom he has fought suggests that he is some kind of mercenary, but it seems that Chaucer may have known people at the English court with similar records. The narrator insists: "He was a verray, parfit, gentil knight," but some modern readers, ill at ease with idealized warriors, and doubtful about the value of the narrator's enthusiasms, have questioned this evaluation.

His son, the Squire, is by contrast an elegant young man about court, with fashionable clothes and romantic skills of singing and dancing.

Their Yeoman is a skilled servant in charge of the knight's land, his dress is described in detail, but not his character.

The Prioress is one of the most fully described pilgrims, and it is with her that we first notice the narrator's refusal to judge the value of what he sees. Her portrait is more concerned with how she eats than how she prays. She is rather too kind to animals, while there is no mention of her kindness to people. Finally, she has a costly set of beads around her arm, which should be used for prayer, but end in a brooch inscribed ambiguously Amor vincit omnia (Virgil's "Love conquers all"). She has a Nun with her, and "three" priests. This is a problem in counting the total number of pilgrims as twenty-nine: the word 'three' must have been added later on account of the rhyme, while only one Nun's Priest is in fact given a Tale and he is not the subject of a portrait here.

The Monk continues the series of incongruous church-people; in this description the narratorial voice often seems to be echoing the monk's comments in indirect quotation. He has many horses at home; he does not respect his monastic rule, but goes hunting instead of praying. The narrator expresses surprisingly strong support for the Monk's chosen style of living.

The Friar follows, and by now it seems clear that Chaucer has a special interest in church-people who so confidently live in contradiction with what is expected of them; the narrator, though, gives no sign of feeling any problem, as when he reports that the "worthy" Friar avoided the company of lepers and beggars. By this point the alert reader is alert to the narrator's too-ready use of 'worthy' but critics are still unsure of what Chaucer's intended strategy was here.

The Merchant is briefly described, and is followed by the Clerk of Oxenford (Oxford) who is as sincere a student as could be wished: poor, skinny like his horse, and book-loving.

The Sergeant at Law is an expert lawyer, and with him is the Franklin, a gentleman from the country whose main interest is food: "It snowed in his house of meat and drink." Then Chaucer adds a brief list of five tradesmen belonging to the same fraternity, dressed in its uniform: a Haberdasher, a Carpenter, a Weaver, a Dyer and a Tapestry-maker. None of these is described here or given a Tale to tell later. They have brought their Cook with them, he is an expert, his skills are listed, as well as some unexpected personal details. The Shipman who is described next is expert at sailing and at stealing the wine his passengers bring with them; he is also a dangerous character, perhaps a pirate.

The Doctor of Physic is praised by the narrator, "He was a verray parfit praktisour," and there follows a list of the fifteen main masters of medieval medicine; the fact that he, like most doctors in satire, "loved gold in special" is added at the end.

The Wife of Bath is the only woman, beside the Prioress and her companion Nun, on this pilgrimage. Again the narrator is positive: "She was a worthy womman al hir live" and he glides quickly over the five husbands that later figure in such detail in her Prologue, where also we may read how she became deaf. She is a business woman of strong self-importance, and her elabourate dress is a sign of her character as well as her wealth.

From her, we pass to the most clearly idealized portrait in the Prologue, the Parson. While the previous churchmen were all interested in things of this world more than in true christianity, the Parson represents the opposite pole.

He is accompanied by his equally idealized brother, the Plowman, "a true swinker" (hard-working man) "Living in peace and perfect charity." If the Parson is the model churchman, the Plowman is the model lay christian, as in Piers Plowman, one who is always ready to help the poor. It is sometimes suggested that the choice of a Plowman shows that Chaucer had read a version of Piers Plowman.

The series then ends with a mixed group of people of whom most are quite terrible: the Miller is a kind of ugly thug without charm. The Manciple is praised as a skillful steward in a household of lawyers; they are clever men but he is cleverest, since he cheats them all, the narrator cheerfully tells us. The Reeve is the manager of a farm, and he too is lining his own pocket.

Last we learn of the Summoner and the Pardoner, two grotesque figures on the edge of the church, living by it without being priests; one administers the church courts, the other sells pardons (indulgences). Children are afraid of the Summoner's face, he is suffering from some kind of skin disease; he is corrupt, as the narrator tells us after naively saying "A better fellow should men not find." But it is the Pardoner who is really odd, and modern critics have enjoyed discussing just what Chaucer meant by saying: "I trowe he were a gelding or a mare". With his collection of pigs' bones in a glass, that he uses as relics of saints to delude simple poor people, he is a monster in every way, and he concludes the list of pilgrims.

The narrator of this Prologue is Chaucer, but this pilgrim Chaucer is not to be too simply identified with the author Chaucer. He explains that in what follows, he is only acting as the faithful reporter of what others have said, without adding or omitting anything; he must not then be blamed for what he reports. Neither must he be blamed if he does not put people in the order of their social rank, "My wit is short, ye may well understand." This persona continues to profess the utter naivety that we have already noted in his uncritical descriptions of the pilgrims.

It is in this way, too, that we should approach the conclusion of the Prologue. Here the Host of the Tabard Inn (Harry Bailey, a historical figure) decides to go with them and ironically it is he, not Chaucer, who proposes the story-telling contest that gives the framework of the Tales. He will also be the ultimate judge of which is the best: "of best sentence and most solas." He is, after all, well prepared by his job to know about the tales people tell! One model for the literary competition would seem to be the meetings of people interested in poetry, known in French as puys, with which Chaucer would have been familiar.

Chapter 12

General Prologue: Text and Paraphrase

1 Whan that Aprill with his shoures soote
When April with its sweet-smelling showers
2 The droghte of March hath perced to the roote,
Has pierced the drought of March to the root,
3 And bathed every veyne in swich licour
And bathed every vein (of the plants) in such liquid
4 Of which vertu engendred is the flour;
By which power the flower is created;
5 Whan Zephirus eek with his sweete breeth
When the West Wind also with its sweet breath,
6 Inspired hath in every holt and heeth
In every wood and field has breathed life into
7 The tendre croppes, and the yonge sonne
The tender new leaves, and the young sun
8 Hath in the Ram his half cours yronne,
Has run half its course in Aries,
9 And smale foweles maken melodye,
And small fowls make melody,
10 That slepen al the nyght with open ye
Those that sleep all the night with open eyes
11 (So priketh hem Nature in hir corages),
(So Nature incites them in their hearts),
12 Thanne longen folk to goon on pilgrimages,
Then folk long to go on pilgrimages,

13 And palmeres for to seken straunge strondes,
And professional pilgrims to seek foreign shores,
14 To ferne halwes, kowthe in sondry londes;
To distant shrines, known in various lands;
15 And specially from every shires ende
And specially from every shire's end
16 Of Engelond to Caunterbury they wende,
Of England to Canterbury they travel,
17 The hooly blisful martir for to seke,
To seek the holy blessed martyr,
18 That hem hath holpen whan that they were seeke.
Who helped them when they were sick.
19 Bifil that in that seson on a day,
It happened that in that season on one day,
20 In Southwerk at the Tabard as I lay
In Southwark at the Tabard Inn as I lay
21 Redy to wenden on my pilgrymage
Ready to go on my pilgrimage
22 To Caunterbury with ful devout corage,
To Canterbury with a very devout spirit,
23 At nyght was come into that hostelrye
At night had come into that hostelry
24 Wel nyne and twenty in a compaignye
Well nine and twenty in a company
25 Of sondry folk, by aventure yfalle
Of various sorts of people, by chance fallen
26 In felaweshipe, and pilgrimes were they alle,
In fellowship, and they were all pilgrims,
27 That toward Caunterbury wolden ryde.
Who intended to ride toward Canterbury.
28 The chambres and the stables weren wyde,
The bedrooms and the stables were spacious,
29 And wel we weren esed atte beste.
And we were well accommodated in the best way.
30 And shortly, whan the sonne was to reste,
And in brief, when the sun was (gone) to rest,
31 So hadde I spoken with hem everichon

I had so spoken with everyone of them
32 That I was of hir felaweshipe anon,
That I was of their fellowship straightway,
33 And made forward erly for to ryse,
And made agreement to rise early,
34 To take oure wey ther as I yow devyse.
To take our way where I (will) tell you.
35 But nathelees, whil I have tyme and space,
But nonetheless, while I have time and opportunity,
36 Er that I ferther in this tale pace,
Before I proceed further in this tale,
37 Me thynketh it acordaunt to resoun
It seems to me in accord with reason
38 To telle yow al the condicioun
To tell you all the circumstances
39 Of ech of hem, so as it semed me,
Of each of them, as it seemed to me,
40 And whiche they weren, and of what degree,
And who they were, and of what social rank,
41 And eek in what array that they were inne;
And also what clothing that they were in;
42 And at a knyght than wol I first bigynne.
And at a knight then will I first begin.
43 A KNYGHT ther was, and that a worthy man,
A KNIGHT there was, and that (one was) a worthy man,
44 That fro the tyme that he first bigan
Who from the time that he first began
45 To riden out, he loved chivalrie,
To ride out, he loved chivalry,
46 Trouthe and honour, fredom and curteisie.
Fidelity and good reputation, generosity and courtesy.
47 Ful worthy was he in his lordes werre,
He was very worthy in his lord's war,
48 And therto hadde he riden, no man ferre,
And for that he had ridden, no man farther,

49 As wel in cristendom as in hethenesse,
As well in Christendom as in heathen lands,
50 And evere honoured for his worthynesse;
And (was) ever honoured for his worthiness;
51 At Alisaundre he was whan it was wonne.
He was at Alexandria when it was won.
52 Ful ofte tyme he hadde the bord bigonne
He had sat very many times in the place of honour,
53 Aboven alle nacions in Pruce;
Above (knights of) all nations in Prussia;
54 In Lettow hadde he reysed and in Ruce,
He had campaigned in Lithuania and in Russia,
55 No Cristen man so ofte of his degree.
No Christian man of his rank so often.
56 In Gernade at the seege eek hadde he be
Also he had been in Grenada at the siege
57 Of Algezir, and riden in Belmarye.
Of Algeciras, and had ridden in Morocco.
58 At Lyeys was he and at Satalye,
He was at Ayash and at Atalia,
59 Whan they were wonne, and in the Grete See
When they were won, and in the Mediterranean
60 At many a noble armee hadde he be.
He had been at many a noble expedition.
61 At mortal batailles hadde he been fiftene,
He had been at fifteen mortal battles,
62 And foughten for oure feith at Tramyssene
And fought for our faith at Tlemcen
63 In lystes thries, and ay slayn his foo.
Three times in formal duels, and each time slain his foe.
64 This ilke worthy knyght hadde been also
This same worthy knight had also been
65 Somtyme with the lord of Palatye
At one time with the lord of Balat
66 Agayn another hethen in Turkye;
Against another heathen in Turkey;
67 And everemoore he hadde a sovereyn prys.

And evermore he had an outstanding reputation
68 And though that he were worthy, he was wys,
And although he was brave, he was prudent,
69 And of his port as meeke as is a mayde.
And of his deportment as meek as is a maid.
70 He nevere yet no vileynye ne sayde
He never yet said any rude word
71 In al his lyf unto no maner wight.
In all his life unto any sort of person.
72 He was a verray, parfit gentil knyght.
He was a truly perfect, noble knight.
73 But for to tellen yow of his array,
But to tell you of his clothing,
74 His hors were goode, but he was nat gay.
His horses were good, but he was not gaily dressed.
75 Of fustian he wered a gypon
He wore a tunic of coarse cloth
76 Al bismotered with his habergeon,
All stained (with rust) by his coat of mail,
77 For he was late ycome from his viage,
For he was recently come (back) from his expedition,
78 And wente for to doon his pilgrymage.
And went to do his pilgrimage.
79 With hym ther was his sone, a yong SQUIER,
With him there was his son, a young SQUIRE,
80 A lovyere and a lusty bacheler,
A lover and a lively bachelor,
81 With lokkes crulle as they were leyd in presse.
With locks curled as if they had been laid in a curler.
82 Of twenty yeer of age he was, I gesse.
He was twenty years of age, I guess.
83 Of his stature he was of evene lengthe,
Of his stature he was of moderate height,
84 And wonderly delyvere, and of greet strengthe.
And wonderfully agile, and of great strength.
85 And he hadde been somtyme in chyvachie
And he had been for a time on a cavalry expedition

86 In Flaundres, in Artoys, and Pycardie,
In Flanders, in Artois, and Picardy,
87 And born hym weel, as of so litel space,
And conducted himself well, for so little a space of time,
88 In hope to stonden in his lady grace.
In hope to stand in his lady's good graces.
89 Embrouded was he, as it were a meede
He was embroidered, as if it were a mead
90 Al ful of fresshe floures, whyte and reede.
All full of fresh flowers, white and red.
91 Syngynge he was, or floytynge, al the day;
Singing he was, or fluting, all the day;
92 He was as fressh as is the month of May.
He was as fresh as is the month of May.
93 Short was his gowne, with sleves longe and wyde.
His gown was short, with long and wide sleeves.
94 Wel koude he sitte on hors and faire ryde.
He well knew how to sit on horse and handsomely ride.
95 He koude songes make and wel endite,
He knew how to make songs and well compose (the words),
96 Juste and eek daunce, and weel purtreye and write.
Joust and also dance, and well draw and write.
97 So hoote he lovede that by nyghtertale
He loved so passionately that at nighttime
98 He sleep namoore than dooth a nyghtyngale.
He slept no more than does a nightingale.
99 Curteis he was, lowely, and servysable,
Courteous he was, humble, and willing to serve,
100 And carf biforn his fader at the table.
And carved before his father at the table.
101 A YEMAN hadde he and servantz namo
He (the Knight) had A YEOMAN and no more servants
102 At that tyme, for hym liste ride so,
At that time, for it pleased him so to travel,

103 And he was clad in cote and hood of grene.
And he (the yeoman) was clad in coat and hood of green.
104 A sheef of pecok arwes, bright and kene,
A sheaf of peacock arrows, bright and keen,
105 Under his belt he bar ful thriftily
He carried under his belt very properly
106 (Wel koude he dresse his takel yemanly;
(He well knew how to care for his equipment as a yeoman should;
107 His arwes drouped noght with fetheres lowe),
His arrows did not fall short because of drooping feathers),
108 And in his hand he baar a myghty bowe.
And in his hand he carried a mighty bow.
109 A not heed hadde he, with a broun visage.
He had a close-cropped head, with a brown face.
110 Of wodecraft wel koude he al the usage.
He well knew all the practice of woodcraft.
111 Upon his arm he baar a gay bracer,
He wore an elegant archer's wrist-guard upon his arm,
112 And by his syde a swerd and a bokeler,
And by his side a sword and a small shield,
113 And on that oother syde a gay daggere
And on that other side an elegant dagger
114 Harneised wel and sharp as point of spere;
Well ornamented and sharp as the point of a spear;
115 A Cristopher on his brest of silver sheene.
A Christopher-medal of bright silver on his breast.
116 An horn he bar, the bawdryk was of grene;
He carried a horn, the shoulder strap was green;
117 A forster was he, soothly, as I gesse.
He was a forester, truly, as I guess.
118 Ther was also a Nonne, a PRIORESSE,
There was also a Nun, a PRIORESS,

119 That of hir smylyng was ful symple and coy;
Who was very simple and modest in her smiling;
120 Hire gretteste ooth was but by Seinte Loy;
Her greatest oath was but by Saint Loy;
121 And she was cleped madame Eglentyne.
And she was called Madam Eglantine.
122 Ful weel she soong the service dyvyne,
She sang the divine service very well,
123 Entuned in hir nose ful semely;
Intoned in her nose in a very polite manner;
124 And Frenssh she spak ful faire and fetisly,
And she spoke French very well and elegantly,
125 After the scole of Stratford atte Bowe,
In the manner of Stratford at the Bow,
126 For Frenssh of Parys was to hire unknowe.
For French of Paris was to her unknown.
127 At mete wel ytaught was she with alle;
At meals she was well taught indeed;
128 She leet no morsel from hir lippes falle,
She let no morsel fall from her lips,
129 Ne wette hir fyngres in hir sauce depe;
Nor wet her fingers deep in her sauce;
130 Wel koude she carie a morsel and wel kepe
She well knew how to carry a morsel (to her mouth)
and take good care
131 That no drope ne fille upon hire brest.
That no drop fell upon her breast.
132 In curteisie was set ful muchel hir lest.
Her greatest pleasure was in good manners.
133 Hir over-lippe wyped she so clene
She wiped her upper lip so clean
134 That in hir coppe ther was no ferthyng sene
That in her cup there was seen no tiny bit
135 Of grece, whan she dronken hadde hir draughte.
Of grease, when she had drunk her drink.
136 Ful semely after hir mete she raughte.
She reached for her food in a very seemly manner.

137 And sikerly she was of greet desport,
And surely she was of excellent deportment,
138 And ful plesaunt, and amyable of port,
And very pleasant, and amiable in demeanor,
139 And peyned hire to countrefete cheere
And she took pains to imitate the manners
140 Of court, and to been estatlich of manere,
Of court, and to be dignified in behavior,
141 And to ben holden digne of reverence.
And to be considered worthy of reverence.
142 But for to speken of hire conscience,
But to speak of her moral sense,
143 She was so charitable and so pitous
She was so charitable and so compassionate
144 She wolde wepe, if that she saugh a mous
She would weep, if she saw a mouse
145 Kaught in a trappe, if it were deed or bledde.
Caught in a trap, if it were dead or bled.
146 Of smale houndes hadde she that she fedde
She had some small hounds that she fed
147 With rosted flessh, or milk and wastel-breed.
With roasted meat, or milk and fine white bread.
148 But soore wepte she if oon of hem were deed,
But sorely she wept if one of them were dead,
149 Or if men smoot it with a yerde smerte;
Or if someone smote it smartly with a stick;
150 And al was conscience and tendre herte.
And all was feeling and tender heart.
151 Ful semyly hir wympul pynched was,
Her wimple was pleated in a very seemly manner,
152 Hir nose tretys, hir eyen greye as glas,
Her nose well formed, her eyes gray as glass,
153 Hir mouth ful smal, and therto softe and reed.
Her mouth very small, and moreover soft and red.
154 But sikerly she hadde a fair forheed;
But surely she had a fair forehead;
155 It was almoost a spanne brood, I trowe;

It was almost nine inches broad, I believe;
156 For, hardily, she was nat undergrowe.
For, certainly, she was not undergrown.
157 Ful fetys was hir cloke, as I was war.
Her cloak was very well made, as I was aware.
158 Of smal coral aboute hire arm she bar
About her arm she bore of small coral
159 A peire of bedes, gauded al with grene,
A set of beads, adorned with large green beads,
160 And theron heng a brooch of gold ful sheene,
And thereon hung a brooch of very bright gold,
161 On which ther was first write a crowned A,
On which there was first written an A with a crown,
162 And after Amor vincit omnia.
And after "Love conquers all."
163 Another NONNE with hire hadde she,
She had another NUN with her,
164 That was hir chapeleyne, and preestes thre.
Who was her secretary, and three priests.
165 A MONK ther was, a fair for the maistrie,
There was a MONK, an extremely fine one,
166 An outridere, that lovede venerie,
An outrider (a monk with business outside the monastery), who loved hunting,
167 A manly man, to been an abbot able.
A virile man, qualified to be an abbot.
168 Ful many a deyntee hors hadde he in stable,
He had very many fine horses in his stable,
169 And whan he rood, men myghte his brydel heere
And when he rode, one could hear his bridle
170 Gynglen in a whistlynge wynd als cleere
Jingle in a whistling wind as clear
171 And eek as loude as dooth the chapel belle
And also as loud as does the chapel belle
172 Ther as this lord was kepere of the celle.
Where this lord was prior of the subordinate monastery.

173 The reule of Seint Maure or of Seint Beneit —
The rule of Saint Maurus or of Saint Benedict —
174 By cause that it was old and somdel streit
Because it was old and somewhat strict
175 This ilke Monk leet olde thynges pace,
This same Monk let old things pass away,
176 And heeld after the newe world the space.
And followed the broader customs of modern times.
177 He yaf nat of that text a pulled hen,
He gave not a plucked hen for that text
178 That seith that hunters ben nat hooly men,
That says that hunters are not holy men,
179 Ne that a monk, whan he is recchelees,
Nor that a monk, when he is heedless of rules,
180 Is likned til a fissh that is waterlees —
Is like a fish that is out of water —
181 This is to seyn, a monk out of his cloystre.
This is to say, a monk out of his cloister.
182 But thilke text heeld he nat worth an oystre;
But he considered that same text not worth an oyster;
183 And I seyde his opinion was good.
And I said his opinion was good.
184 What sholde he studie and make hymselven wood,
Why should he study and make himself crazy,
185 Upon a book in cloystre alwey to poure,
Always to pore upon a book in the cloister,
186 Or swynken with his handes, and laboure,
Or work with his hands, and labour,
187 As Austyn bit? How shal the world be served?
As Augustine commands? How shall the world be served?
188 Lat Austyn have his swynk to hym reserved!
Let Augustine have his work reserved to him!
189 Therfore he was a prikasour aright:
Therefore he was indeed a vigourous horseman:
190 Grehoundes he hadde as swift as fowel in flight;

He had greyhounds as swift as fowl in flight;
191 Of prikyng and of huntyng for the hare
Of tracking and of hunting for the hare
192 Was al his lust, for no cost wolde he spare.
Was all his pleasure, by no means would he refrain from it.
193 I seigh his sleves purfiled at the hond
I saw his sleeves lined at the hand
194 With grys, and that the fyneste of a lond;
With squirrel fur, and that the finest in the land;
195 And for to festne his hood under his chyn,
And to fasten his hood under his chin,
196 He hadde of gold ywroght a ful curious pyn;
He had a very skillfully made pin of gold;
197 A love-knotte in the gretter ende ther was.
There was an elabourate knot in the larger end.
198 His heed was balled, that shoon as any glas,
His head was bald, which shone like any glass,
199 And eek his face, as he hadde been enoynt.
And his face did too, as if he had been rubbed with oil.
200 He was a lord ful fat and in good poynt;
He was a very plump lord and in good condition;
201 His eyen stepe, and rollynge in his heed,
His eyes were prominent, and rolling in his head,
202 That stemed as a forneys of a leed;
Which gleamed like a furnace under a cauldron;
203 His bootes souple, his hors in greet estaat.
His boots supple, his horse in excellent condition.
204 Now certeinly he was a fair prelaat;
Now certainly he was a handsome ecclesiastical dignitary;
205 He was nat pale as a forpyned goost.
He was not pale as a tormented spirit.
206 A fat swan loved he best of any roost.
A fat swan loved he best of any roast.
207 His palfrey was as broun as is a berye.

His saddle horse was as brown as is a berry.
208 A FRERE ther was, a wantowne and a merye,
There was a FRIAR, a pleasure-loving and merry one,
209 A lymytour, a ful solempne man.
A limiter (with an assigned territory), a very solemn man.
210 In alle the ordres foure is noon that kan
In all the four orders of friars is no one that knows
211 So muchel of daliaunce and fair langage.
So much of sociability and elegant speech.
212 He hadde maad ful many a mariage
He had made very many a marriage
213 Of yonge wommen at his owene cost.
Of young women at his own cost.
214 Unto his ordre he was a noble post.
He was a noble supporter of his order.
215 Ful wel biloved and famulier was he
Very well beloved and familiar was he
216 With frankeleyns over al in his contree,
With landowners every where in his country,
217 And eek with worthy wommen of the toun;
And also with worthy women of the town;
218 For he hadde power of confessioun,
For he had power of confession,
219 As seyde hymself, moore than a curat,
As he said himself, more than a parish priest,
220 For of his ordre he was licenciat.
For he was licensed by his order.
221 Ful swetely herde he confessioun,
He heard confession very sweetly,
222 And plesaunt was his absolucioun:
And his absolution was pleasant:
223 He was an esy man to yeve penaunce,
He was a lenient man in giving penance,
224 Ther as he wiste to have a good pitaunce.
Where he knew he would have a good gift.
225 For unto a povre ordre for to yive

For to give to a poor order (of friars)
226 Is signe that a man is wel yshryve;
Is a sign that a man is well confessed;
227 For if he yaf, he dorste make avaunt,
For if he gave, he (the friar) dared to assert,
228 He wiste that a man was repentaunt;
He knew that a man was repentant;
229 For many a man so hard is of his herte,
For many a man is so hard in his heart,
230 He may nat wepe, althogh hym soore smerte.
He can not weep, although he painfully suffers.
231 Therfore in stede of wepynge and preyeres
Therefore instead of weeping and prayers
232 Men moote yeve silver to the povre freres.
One may give silver to the poor friars.
233 His typet was ay farsed ful of knyves
His hood was always stuffed full of knives
234 And pynnes, for to yeven faire wyves.
And pins, to give to fair wives.
235 And certeinly he hadde a murye note:
And certainly he had a merry voice:
236 Wel koude he synge and pleyen on a rote;
He well knew how to sing and play on a rote (string instrument);
237 Of yeddynges he baar outrely the pris.
He absolutely took the prize for reciting ballads.
238 His nekke whit was as the flour-de-lys;
His neck was white as a lily flower;
239 Therto he strong was as a champioun.
Furthermore he was strong as a champion fighter.
240 He knew the tavernes wel in every toun
He knew the taverns well in every town
241 And everich hostiler and tappestere
And every innkeeper and barmaid
242 Bet than a lazar or a beggestere,
Better than a leper or a beggar-woman,
243 For unto swich a worthy man as he

For unto such a worthy man as he
244 Acorded nat, as by his facultee,
It was not suitable, in view of his official position,
245 To have with sike lazars aqueyntaunce.
To have acquaintance with sick lepers.
246 It is nat honest; it may nat avaunce,
It is not respectable; it can not be profitable,
247 For to deelen with no swich poraille,
To deal with any such poor people,
248 But al with riche and selleres of vitaille.
But all with rich people and sellers of victuals.
249 And over al, ther as profit sholde arise,
And every where, where profit should arise,
250 Curteis he was and lowely of servyse;
He was courteous and graciously humble;
251 Ther nas no man nowher so vertuous.
There was no man anywhere so capable (of such work).
252 He was the beste beggere in his hous;
He was the best beggar in his house;
252a [And yaf a certeyn ferme for the graunt;
[And he gave a certain fee for his grant (of begging rights);
252a Noon of his bretheren cam ther in his haunt;]
None of his brethren came there in his territory;]
253 For thogh a wydwe hadde noght a sho,
For though a widow had not a shoe,
254 So plesaunt was his "In principio,"
So pleasant was his "In the beginning,"
255 Yet wolde he have a ferthyng, er he wente.
Yet he would have a farthing, before he went away.
256 His purchas was wel bettre than his rente.
His total profit was much more than his proper income.
257 And rage he koude, as it were right a whelp.
And he knew how to frolic, as if he were indeed a pup.

258 In love-dayes ther koude he muchel help,
He knew how to be much help on days for resolving disputes,
259 For ther he was nat lyk a cloysterer
For there he was not like a cloistered monk
260 With a thredbare cope, as is a povre scoler,
With a threadbare cope, like a poor scholar,
261 But he was lyk a maister or a pope.
But he was like a master of arts or a pope.
262 Of double worstede was his semycope,
Of wide (expensive) cloth was his short cloak,
263 That rounded as a belle out of the presse.
Which was round as a bell fresh from the clothespress.
264 Somwhat he lipsed, for his wantownesse,
Somewhat he lisped, for his affectation,
265 To make his Englissh sweete upon his tonge;
To make his English sweet upon his tongue;
266 And in his harpyng, whan that he hadde songe,
And in his harping, when he had sung,
267 His eyen twynkled in his heed aryght
His eyes twinkled in his head exactly
268 As doon the sterres in the frosty nyght.
As do the stars in the frosty night.
269 This worthy lymytour was cleped Huberd.
This worthy friar was called Huberd.
270 A MARCHANT was ther with a forked berd,
There was a MERCHANT with a forked beard,
271 In mottelee, and hye on horse he sat;
Wearing parti-coloured cloth, and proudly he sat on his horse;
272 Upon his heed a Flaundryssh bever hat,
Upon his head (he wore a) Flemish beaver hat,
273 His bootes clasped faire and fetisly.
His boots were buckled handsomely and elegantly.
274 His resons he spak ful solempnely,
His opinions he spoke very solemnly,

275 Sownynge alwey th' encrees of his wynnyng.
Concerning always the increase of his profits.
276 He wolde the see were kept for any thyng
He wanted the sea to be guarded at all costs
277 Bitwixe Middelburgh and Orewelle.
Between Middelburgh (Holland) and Orwell (England).
278 Wel koude he in eschaunge sheeldes selle.
He well knew how to deal in foreign currencies.
279 This worthy man ful wel his wit bisette:
This worthy man employed his wit very well:
280 Ther wiste no wight that he was in dette,
There was no one who knew that he was in debt,
281 So estatly was he of his governaunce
He was so dignified in managing his affairs
282 With his bargaynes and with his chevyssaunce.
With his buying and selling and with his financial deals.
283 For sothe he was a worthy man with alle,
Truly, he was a worthy man indeed,
284 But, sooth to seyn, I noot how men hym calle.
But, to say the truth, I do not know what men call him.
285 A CLERK ther was of Oxenford also,
There was also a CLERK (scholar) from Oxford,
286 That unto logyk hadde longe ygo.
Who long before had begun the study of logic.
287 As leene was his hors as is a rake,
His horse was as lean as is a rake,
288 And he nas nat right fat, I undertake,
And he was not very fat, I affirm,
289 But looked holwe, and therto sobrely.
But looked emaciated, and moreover abstemious.
290 Ful thredbare was his overeste courtepy,
His short overcoat was very threadbare,
291 For he hadde geten hym yet no benefice,
For he had not yet obtained an ecclesiastical living,

292 Ne was so worldly for to have office.
Nor was he worldly enough to take secular employment.

293 For hym was levere have at his beddes heed
For he would rather have at the head of his bed

294 Twenty bookes, clad in blak or reed,
Twenty books, bound in black or red,

295 Of Aristotle and his philosophie
Of Aristotle and his philosophy

296 Than robes riche, or fithele, or gay sautrie.
Than rich robes, or a fiddle, or an elegant psaltery.

297 But al be that he was a philosophre,
But even though he was a philosopher,

298 Yet hadde he but litel gold in cofre;
Nevertheless he had but little gold in his strongbox;

299 But al that he myghte of his freendes hente,
But all that he could get from his friends,

300 On bookes and on lernynge he it spente,
He spent on books and on learning,

301 And bisily gan for the soules preye
And diligently did pray for the souls

302 Of hem that yaf hym wherwith to scoleye.
Of those who gave him the wherewithal to attend the schools.

303 Of studie took he moost cure and moost heede.
He took most care and paid most heed to study.

304 Noght o word spak he moore than was neede,
He spoke not one word more than was needed,

305 And that was seyd in forme and reverence,
And that was said with due formality and respect,

306 And short and quyk and ful of hy sentence;
And short and lively and full of elevated content;

307 Sownynge in moral vertu was his speche,
His speech was consonant with moral virtue,

308 And gladly wolde he lerne and gladly teche.
And gladly would he learn and gladly teach.

309 A SERGEANT OF THE LAWE, war and wys,

A SERGEANT OF THE LAW (high-ranking attorney), prudent and wise,
310 That often hadde been at the Parvys,
Who often had been at the Porch of St. Paul's (where lawyers gather)
311 Ther was also, ful riche of excellence.
Was also there, very rich in superior qualities.
312 Discreet he was and of greet reverence —
He was judicious and of great dignity —
313 He semed swich, his wordes weren so wise.
He seemed such, his words were so wise.
314 Justice he was ful often in assise,
He was very often a judge in the court of assizes,
315 By patente and by pleyn commissioun.
By royal appointment and with full jurisdiction.
316 For his science and for his heigh renoun,
For his knowledge and for his excellent reputation,
317 Of fees and robes hadde he many oon.
He had many grants of yearly income.
318 So greet a purchasour was nowher noon:
There was nowhere so great a land-buyer:
319 Al was fee symple to hym in effect;
In fact, all was unrestricted possession to him;
320 His purchasyng myghte nat been infect.
His purchasing could not be invalidated.
321 Nowher so bisy a man as he ther nas,
There was nowhere so busy a man as he,
322 And yet he semed bisier than he was.
And yet he seemed busier than he was.
323 In termes hadde he caas and doomes alle
He had in Year Books all the cases and decisions
324 That from the tyme of kyng William were falle.
That from the time of king William have occurred.
325 Therto he koude endite and make a thyng,
Furthermore, he knew how to compose and draw up a legal document,
326 Ther koude no wight pynche at his writyng;

So that no one could find a flaw in his writing;

327 And every statut koude he pleyn by rote.
And he knew every statute completely by heart.

328 He rood but hoomly in a medlee cote,
He rode but simply in a parti-coloured coat,

329 Girt with a ceint of silk, with barres smale;
Girded with a belt of silk, with small stripes;

330 Of his array telle I no lenger tale.
I tell no longer tale of his clothing.

331 A FRANKELEYN was in his compaignye.
A FRANKLIN was in his company.

332 Whit was his berd as is the dayesye;
His beard was white as a daisy;

333 Of his complexioun he was sangwyn.
As to his temperament, he was dominated by the humour blood.

334 Wel loved he by the morwe a sop in wyn;
He well loved a bit of bread dipped in wine in the morning;

335 To lyven in delit was evere his wone,
His custom was always to live in delight,

336 For he was Epicurus owene sone,
For he was Epicurus' own son,

337 That heeld opinioun that pleyn delit
Who held the opinion that pure pleasure

338 Was verray felicitee parfit.
Was truly perfect happiness.

339 An housholdere, and that a greet, was he;
He was a householder, and a great one at that;

340 Seint Julian he was in his contree.
He was Saint Julian (patron of hospitality) in his country.

341 His breed, his ale, was alweys after oon;
His bread, his ale, was always of the same (good) quality;

342 A bettre envyned man was nowher noon.
Nowhere was there any man better stocked with

wine.
343 Withoute bake mete was nevere his hous,
His house was never without baked pies
344 Of fissh and flessh, and that so plentevous
Of fish and meat, and that so plentiful
345 It snewed in his hous of mete and drynke;
That in his house it snowed with food and drink;
346 Of alle deyntees that men koude thynke,
Of all the dainties that men could imagine,
347 After the sondry sesons of the yeer,
In accord with the various seasons of the year,
348 So chaunged he his mete and his soper.
So he varied his midday meal and his supper.
349 Ful many a fat partrich hadde he in muwe,
He had very many fat partridges in pens,
350 And many a breem and many a luce in stuwe.
And many a bream and many a pike in his fish pond.
351 Wo was his cook but if his sauce were
Woe was his cook unless his sauce was
352 Poynaunt and sharp, and redy al his geere.
Hotly spiced and sharp, and ready all his cooking equipment.
353 His table dormant in his halle alway
In his hall his dining table always
354 Stood redy covered al the longe day. Stood covered (with table cloth) and ready all the long day.
355 At sessiouns ther was he lord and sire;
He presided as lord and sire at court sessions;
356 Ful ofte tyme he was knyght of the shire.
He was a member of parliament many times.
357 An anlaas and a gipser al of silk
A dagger and a purse all of silk
358 Heeng at his girdel, whit as morne milk.
Hung at his belt, white as morning milk.
359 A shirreve hadde he been, and a contour.
He had been a sheriff, and an auditor of taxes.
360 Was nowher swich a worthy vavasour.

There was nowhere such a worthy landowner.
361 AN HABERDASSHERE and a CARPENTER,
A HABERDASHER and a CARPENTER,
362 A WEBBE, a DYERE, and a TAPYCER —
A WEAVER, a DYER, and a TAPESTRY-MAKER —
363 And they were clothed alle in o lyveree
And they were all clothed in one livery
364 Of a solempne and a greet fraternitee.
Of a solemn and a great parish guild.
365 Ful fressh and newe hir geere apiked was;
Their equipment was adorned all freshly and new;
366 Hir knyves were chaped noght with bras
Their knives were not mounted with brass
367 But al with silver, wroght ful clene and weel, But
entirely with silver, wrought very neatly and well,
368 Hire girdles and hir pouches everydeel.
Their belts and their purses every bit.
369 Wel semed ech of hem a fair burgeys
Each of them well seemed a solid citizen
370 To sitten in a yeldehalle on a deys.
To sit on a dais in a city hall.
371 Everich, for the wisdom that he kan,
Every one of them, for the wisdom that he knows,
372 Was shaply for to been an alderman.
Was suitable to be an alderman.
373 For catel hadde they ynogh and rente,
For they had enough possessions and income,
374 And eek hir wyves wolde it wel assente;
And also their wives would well assent to it;
375 And elles certeyn were they to blame.
And otherwise certainly they would be to blame.
376 It is ful fair to been ycleped "madame,"
It is very fine to be called "my lady,"
377 And goon to vigilies al bifore,
And go to feasts on holiday eves heading the procession,
378 And have a mantel roialliche ybore.

And have a gown with a train royally carried.
379 A COOK they hadde with hem for the nones
A COOK they had with them for the occasion
380 To boille the chiknes with the marybones,
To boil the chickens with the marrow bones,
381 And poudre-marchant tart and galyngale.
And tart poudre-marchant and galingale (spices).
382 Wel koude he knowe a draughte of Londoun ale.
He well knew how to judge a draft of London ale.
383 He koude rooste, and sethe, and broille, and frye,
He knew how to roast, and boil, and broil, and fry,
384 Maken mortreux, and wel bake a pye.
Make stews, and well bake a pie.
385 But greet harm was it, as it thoughte me,
But it was a great harm, as it seemed to me,
386 That on his shyne a mormal hadde he.
That he had an open sore on his shin.
387 For blankmanger, that made he with the beste. As for white pudding, he made that of the best quality.
388 A SHIPMAN was ther, wonynge fer by weste;
A SHIPMAN was there, dwelling far in the west;
389 For aught I woot, he was of Dertemouthe.
For all I know, he was from Dartmouth.
390 He rood upon a rouncy, as he kouthe,
He rode upon a cart horse, insofar as he knew how,
391 In a gowne of faldyng to the knee.
In a gown of woolen cloth (that reached) to the knee.
392 A daggere hangynge on a laas hadde he
He had a dagger hanging on a cord
393 Aboute his nekke, under his arm adoun.
About his neck, down under his arm.
394 The hoote somer hadde maad his hewe al broun;
The hot summer had made his hue all brown;
395 And certeinly he was a good felawe.
And certainly he was a boon companion.
396 Ful many a draughte of wyn had he ydrawe
He had drawn very many a draft of wine

397 Fro Burdeux-ward, whil that the chapman sleep.
While coming from Bordeaux, while the merchant slept.

398 Of nyce conscience took he no keep.
He had no concern for a scrupulous conscience.

399 If that he faught and hadde the hyer hond,
If he fought and had the upper hand,

400 By water he sente hem hoom to every lond.
He sent them home by water to every land (they walked the plank).

401 But of his craft to rekene wel his tydes,
But of his skill to reckon well his tides,

402 His stremes, and his daungers hym bisides,
His currents, and his perils near at hand,

403 His herberwe, and his moone, his lodemenage,
His harbors, and positions of his moon, his navigation,

404 Ther nas noon swich from Hulle to Cartage.
There was none other such from Hull to Cartagena (Spain).

405 Hardy he was and wys to undertake;
He was bold and prudent in his undertakings;

406 With many a tempest hadde his berd been shake.
His beard had been shaken by many a tempest.

407 He knew alle the havenes, as they were,
He knew all the harbors, how they were,

408 Fro Gootlond to the cape of Fynystere,
From Gotland to the Cape of Finisterre,

409 And every cryke in Britaigne and in Spayne.
And every inlet in Brittany and in Spain.

410 His barge ycleped was the Maudelayne.
His ship was called the Maudelayne.

411 With us ther was a DOCTOUR OF PHISIK;
With us there was a DOCTOR OF MEDICINE

412 In al this world ne was ther noon hym lik,
In all this world there was no one like him,

413 To speke of phisik and of surgerye,

To speak of medicine and of surgery,
414 For he was grounded in astronomye.
For he was instructed in astronomy.
415 He kepte his pacient a ful greet deel
He took care of his patient very many times
416 In houres by his magyk natureel.
In (astronomically suitable) hours by (use of) his natural science.
417 Wel koude he fortunen the ascendent
He well knew how to calculate the planetary position
418 Of his ymages for his pacient.
Of his astronomical talismans for his patient.
419 He knew the cause of everich maladye,
He knew the cause of every malady,
420 Were it of hoot, or coold, or moyste, or drye,
Were it of hot, or cold, or moist, or dry elements,
421 And where they engendred, and of what humour.
And where they were engendered, and by what bodily fluid.
422 He was a verray, parfit praktisour:
He was a truly, perfect practitioner:
423 The cause yknowe, and of his harm the roote,
The cause known, and the source of his (patient's) harm,
424 Anon he yaf the sike man his boote.
Straightway he gave the sick man his remedy.
425 Ful redy hadde he his apothecaries
He had his apothecaries all ready
426 To sende hym drogges and his letuaries,
To send him drugs and his electuaries,
427 For ech of hem made oother for to wynne —
For each of them made the other to profit —
428 Hir frendshipe nas nat newe to bigynne.
Their friendship was not recently begun.
429 Wel knew he the olde Esculapius,
He well knew the old Aesculapius,

430 And Deyscorides, and eek Rufus,
And Dioscorides, and also Rufus,
431 Olde Ypocras, Haly, and Galyen,
Old Hippocrates, Haly, and Galen,
432 Serapion, Razis, and Avycen,
Serapion, Rhazes, and Avicenna,
433 Averrois, Damascien, and Constantyn,
Averroes, John the Damascan, and Constantine,
434 Bernard, and Gatesden, and Gilbertyn.
Bernard, and Gaddesden, and Gilbertus.
435 Of his diete mesurable was he,
He was moderate in his diet,
436 For it was of no superfluitee,
For it was of no excess,
437 But of greet norissyng and digestible.
But greatly nourishing and digestible.
438 His studie was but litel on the Bible.
His study was but little on the Bible.
439 In sangwyn and in pers he clad was al,
He was clad all in red and in blue,
440 Lyned with taffata and with sendal.
Lined with taffeta and with silk.
441 And yet he was but esy of dispence;
And yet he was moderate in spending;
442 He kepte that he wan in pestilence.
He kept what he earned in (times of) plague.
443 For gold in phisik is a cordial,
Since in medicine gold is a restorative for the heart,
444 Therefore he lovede gold in special.
Therefore he loved gold in particular.
445 A good WIF was ther OF biside BATHE,
There was a good WIFE OF beside BATH,
446 But she was somdel deef, and that was scathe.
But she was somewhat deaf, and that was a pity.
447 Of clooth-makyng she hadde swich an haunt
She had such a skill in cloth-making
448 She passed hem of Ypres and of Gaunt.

She surpassed them of Ypres and of Ghent.
449 In al the parisshe wif ne was ther noon
In all the parish there was no wife
450 That to the offrynge bifore hire sholde goon;
Who should go to the Offering before her;
451 And if ther dide, certeyn so wrooth was she
And if there did, certainly she was so angry
452 That she was out of alle charitee.
That she was out of all charity (love for her neighbour).
453 Hir coverchiefs ful fyne weren of ground;
Her kerchiefs were very fine in texture;
454 I dorste swere they weyeden ten pound
I dare swear they weighed ten pound
455 That on a Sonday weren upon hir heed.
That on a Sunday were upon her head.
456 Hir hosen weren of fyn scarlet reed,
Her stockings were of fine scarlet red,
457 Ful streite yteyd, and shoes ful moyste and newe.
Very closely laced, and shoes very supple and new.
458 Boold was hir face, and fair, and reed of hewe.
Bold was her face, and fair, and red of hue.
459 She was a worthy womman al hir lyve:
She was a worthy woman all her life:
460 Housbondes at chirche dore she hadde fyve,
She had (married) five husbands at the church door,
461 Withouten oother compaignye in youthe —
Not counting other company in youth —
462 But thereof nedeth nat to speke as nowthe.
But there is no need to speak of that right now.
463 And thries hadde she been at Jerusalem;
And she had been three times at Jerusalem;
464 She hadde passed many a straunge strem;
She had passed many a foreign sea;
465 At Rome she hadde been, and at Boloigne,
She had been at Rome, and at Boulogne,
466 In Galice at Seint-Jame, and at Coloigne.

In Galicia at Saint-James (of Compostella), and at Cologne.
467 She koude muchel of wandrynge by the weye.
She knew much about wandering by the way.
468 Gat-tothed was she, soothly for to seye.
She had teeth widely set apart, truly to say.
469 Upon an amblere esily she sat,
She sat easily upon a pacing horse,
470 Ywympled wel, and on hir heed an hat
Wearing a large wimple, and on her head a hat
471 As brood as is a bokeler or a targe;
As broad as a buckler or a shield;
472 A foot-mantel aboute hir hipes large,
An overskirt about her large hips,
473 And on hir feet a paire of spores sharpe.
And on her feet a pair of sharp spurs.
474 In felaweshipe wel koude she laughe and carpe.
In fellowship she well knew how to laugh and chatter.
475 Of remedies of love she knew per chaunce,
She knew, as it happened, about remedies for love
476 For she koude of that art the olde daunce.
For she knew the old dance (tricks of the trade) of that art.
477 A good man was ther of religioun,
A good man was there of religion,
478 And was a povre PERSOUN OF A TOUN,
And (he) was a poor PARSON OF A TOWN,
479 But riche he was of hooly thoght and werk.
But he was rich in holy thought and work.
480 He was also a lerned man, a clerk,
He was also a learned man, a scholar,
481 That Cristes gospel trewely wolde preche;
Who would preach Christ's gospel truly;
482 His parisshens devoutly wolde he teche.
He would devoutly teach his parishioners.
483 Benygne he was, and wonder diligent,

He was gracious, and wonderfully diligent,
484 And in adversitee ful pacient,
And very patient in adversity,
485 And swich he was ypreved ofte sithes.
And such he was proven many times.
486 Ful looth were hym to cursen for his tithes,
He was very reluctant to excommunicate for (nonpayment of) his tithes,
487 But rather wolde he yeven, out of doute,
But rather would he give, there is no doubt,
488 Unto his povre parisshens aboute
Unto his poor parishioners about
489 Of his offryng and eek of his substaunce.
Some of his offering (received at mass) and also some of his income.
490 He koude in litel thyng have suffisaunce.
He knew how to have sufficiency in few possessions.
491 Wyd was his parisshe, and houses fer asonder,
His parish was wide, and houses far apart,
492 But he ne lefte nat, for reyn ne thonder,
But he did not omit, for rain nor thunder,
493 In siknesse nor in meschief to visite
In sickness or in trouble to visit
494 The ferreste in his parisshe, muche and lite,
Those living farthest away in his parish, high-ranking and low,
495 Upon his feet, and in his hand a staf.
Going by foot, and in his hand a staff.
496 This noble ensample to his sheep he yaf,
He gave this noble example to his sheep,
497 That first he wroghte, and afterward he taughte.
That first he wrought, and afterward he taught.
498 Out of the gospel he tho wordes caughte,
He took those words out of the gospel,
499 And this figure he added eek therto,
And this metaphor he added also to that,
500 That if gold ruste, what shal iren do?

That if gold rust, what must iron do?
501 For if a preest be foul, on whom we truste,
For if a priest, on whom we trust, should be foul
502 No wonder is a lewed man to ruste;
It is no wonder for a layman to go bad;
503 And shame it is, if a prest take keep,
And it is a shame, if a priest is concerned:
504 A shiten shepherde and a clene sheep.
A shit-stained shepherd and a clean sheep.
505 Wel oghte a preest ensample for to yive,
Well ought a priest to give an example,
506 By his clennesse, how that his sheep sholde lyve.
By his purity, how his sheep should live.
507 He sette nat his benefice to hyre
He did not rent out his benefice (ecclesiastical living)
508 And leet his sheep encombred in the myre
And leave his sheep encumbered in the mire
509 And ran to Londoun unto Seinte Poules
And run to London unto Saint Paul's
510 To seken hym a chaunterie for soules,
To seek an appointment as a chantry priest (praying for a patron)
511 Or with a bretherhed to been withholde;
Or to be hired (as a chaplain) by a guild;
512 But dwelte at hoom, and kepte wel his folde,
But dwelt at home, and kept well his sheep fold (parish),
513 So that the wolf ne made it nat myscarie;
So that the wolf did not make it go wrong;
514 He was a shepherde and noght a mercenarie.
He was a shepherd and not a hireling.
515 And though he hooly were and vertuous,
And though he was holy and virtuous,
516 He was to synful men nat despitous,
He was not scornful to sinful men,
517 Ne of his speche daungerous ne digne,
Nor domineering nor haughty in his speech,
518 But in his techyng discreet and benygne.

But in his teaching courteous and kind.
519 To drawen folk to hevene by fairnesse,
To draw folk to heaven by gentleness,
520 By good ensample, this was his bisynesse.
By good example, this was his business.
521 But it were any persone obstinat,
Unless it were an obstinate person,
522 What so he were, of heigh or lough estat,
Whoever he was, of high or low rank,
523 Hym wolde he snybben sharply for the nonys.
He would rebuke him sharply at that time.
524 A bettre preest I trowe that nowher noon ys.
I believe that nowhere is there a better priest.
525 He waited after no pompe and reverence,
He expected no pomp and ceremony,
526 Ne maked him a spiced conscience,
Nor made himself an overly fastidious conscience,
527 But Cristes loore and his apostles twelve
But Christ's teaching and His twelve apostles
528 He taughte; but first he folwed it hymselve.
He taught; but first he followed it himself.
529 With hym ther was a PLOWMAN, was his brother,
With him there was a PLOWMAN, who was his brother,
530 That hadde ylad of dong ful many a fother;
Who had hauled very many a cartload of dung;
531 A trewe swynkere and a good was he,
He was a true and good worker,
532 Lyvynge in pees and parfit charitee.
Living in peace and perfect love.
533 God loved he best with al his hoole herte
He loved God best with all his whole heart
534 At alle tymes, thogh him gamed or smerte,
At all times, whether it pleased or pained him,
535 And thanne his neighebor right as hymselve.
And then (he loved) his neighbour exactly as himself.
536 He wolde thresshe, and therto dyke and delve,

He would thresh, and moreover make ditches and dig,
537 For Cristes sake, for every povre wight,
For Christ's sake, for every poor person,
538 Withouten hire, if it lay in his myght.
Without payment, if it lay in his power.
539 His tithes payde he ful faire and wel,
He paid his tithes completely and well,
540 Bothe of his propre swynk and his catel.
Both of his own labour and of his possessions.
541 In a tabard he rood upon a mere.
He rode in a tabard (sleeveless jacket) upon a mare.
542 Ther was also a REVE, and a MILLERE,
There was also a REEVE, and a MILLER,
543 A SOMNOUR, and a PARDONER also,
A SUMMONER, and a PARDONER also,
544 A MAUNCIPLE, and myself — ther were namo.
A MANCIPLE, and myself — there were no more.
545 The MILLERE was a stout carl for the nones;
The MILLER was a stout fellow indeed;
546 Ful byg he was of brawn, and eek of bones.
He was very strong of muscle, and also of bones.
547 That proved wel, for over al ther he cam,
That was well proven, for wherever he came,
548 At wrastlynge he wolde have alwey the ram.
At wrestling he would always take the the prize.
549 He was short-sholdred, brood, a thikke knarre;
He was stoutly built, broad, a large-framed fellow;
550 Ther was no dore that he nolde heve of harre,
There was no door that he would not heave off its hinges,
551 Or breke it at a rennyng with his heed.
Or break it by running at it with his head.
552 His berd as any sowe or fox was reed,
His beard was red as any sow or fox,
553 And therto brood, as though it were a spade.
And moreover broad, as though it were a spade.
554 Upon the cop right of his nose he hade

Upon the exact top of his nose he had
555 A werte, and theron stood a toft of herys,
A wart, and thereon stood a tuft of hairs,
556 Reed as the brustles of a sowes erys;
Red as the bristles of a sow's ears;
557 His nosethirles blake were and wyde.
His nostrils were black and wide.
558 A swerd and a bokeler bar he by his syde.
He wore a sword and a buckler by his side.
559 His mouth as greet was as a greet forneys.
His mouth was as large as a large furnace.
560 He was a janglere and a goliardeys,
He was a loudmouth and a buffoon,
561 And that was moost of synne and harlotries.
And that was mostly of sin and deeds of harlotry.
562 Wel koude he stelen corn and tollen thries;
He well knew how to steal corn and take payment three times;
563 And yet he hadde a thombe of gold, pardee.
And yet he had a thumb of gold, indeed.
564 A whit cote and a blew hood wered he.
He wore a white coat and a blue hood.
565 A baggepipe wel koude he blowe and sowne,
He well knew how to blow and play a bag-pipe,
566 And therwithal he broghte us out of towne.
And with that he brought us out of town.
567 A gentil MAUNCIPLE was ther of a temple,
There was a fine MANCIPLE of a temple (law school),
568 Of which achatours myghte take exemple
Of whom buyers of provisions might take example
569 For to be wise in byynge of vitaille;
For how to be wise in buying of victuals;
570 For wheither that he payde or took by taille,
For whether he paid (cash) or took (goods) on credit,
571 Algate he wayted so in his achaat
Always he watched so (carefully for his opportunity)

in his purchases
572 That he was ay biforn and in good staat.
That he was always ahead and in good state.
573 Now is nat that of God a ful fair grace
Now is not that a very fair grace of God
574 That swich a lewed mannes wit shal pace
That such an unlearned man's wit shall surpass
575 The wisdom of an heep of lerned men?
The wisdom of a heap of learned men?
576 Of maistres hadde he mo than thries ten,
He had more than three times ten masters,
577 That weren of lawe expert and curious,
Who were expert and skillful in law,
578 Of which ther were a duszeyne in that hous
Of whom there were a dozen in that house
579 Worthy to been stywardes of rente and lond
Worthy to be stewards of rent and land
580 Of any lord that is in Engelond,
Of any lord that is in England,
581 To make hym lyve by his propre good
To make him live by his own wealth
582 In honour dettelees (but if he were wood),
In honour and debtless (unless he were crazy),
583 Or lyve as scarsly as hym list desire;
Or live as economically as it pleased him to desire;
584 And able for to helpen al a shire
And (they would be) able to help all a shire
585 In any caas that myghte falle or happe.
In any emergency that might occur or happen.
586 And yet this Manciple sette hir aller cappe.
And yet this Manciple fooled them all.
587 The REVE was a sclendre colerik man.
The REEVE was a slender choleric man.
588 His berd was shave as ny as ever he kan;
His beard was shaved as close as ever he can;
589 His heer was by his erys ful round yshorn;
His hair was closely cropped by his ears;

590 His top was dokked lyk a preest biforn.
The top of his head in front was cut short like a priest's.
591 Ful longe were his legges and ful lene,
His legs were very long and very lean,
592 Ylyk a staf; ther was no calf ysene.
Like a stick; there was no calf to be seen.
593 Wel koude he kepe a gerner and a bynne;
He well knew how to keep a granary and a storage bin;
594 Ther was noon auditour koude on him wynne.
There was no auditor who could earn anything (by catching him).
595 Wel wiste he by the droghte and by the reyn
He well knew by the drought and by the rain
596 The yeldynge of his seed and of his greyn.
(What would be) the yield of his seed and of his grain.
597 His lordes sheep, his neet, his dayerye,
His lord's sheep, his cattle, his herd of dairy cows,
598 His swyn, his hors, his stoor, and his pultrye
His swine, his horses, his livestock, and his poultry
599 Was hoolly in this Reves governynge,
Was wholly in this Reeve's control,
600 And by his covenant yaf the rekenynge,
And in accord with his contract he gave the reckoning,
601 Syn that his lord was twenty yeer of age.
Since his lord was twenty years of age.
602 Ther koude no man brynge hym in arrerage.
There was no man who could find him in arrears.
603 Ther nas baillif, ne hierde, nor oother hyne,
There was no farm manager, nor herdsman, nor other servant,
604 That he ne knew his sleighte and his covyne;
Whose trickery and treachery he did not know;
605 They were adrad of hym as of the deeth.

They were afraid of him as of the plague.
606 His wonyng was ful faire upon an heeth;
His dwelling was very nicely situated upon an heath;
607 With grene trees yshadwed was his place.
His place was shaded by green trees.
608 He koude bettre than his lord purchace.
He could buy property better than his lord could.
609 Ful riche he was astored pryvely.
He was secretly very richly provided.
610 His lord wel koude he plesen subtilly,
He well knew how to please his lord subtly,
611 To yeve and lene hym of his owene good, By giving
and lending him some of his lord's own possessions,
612 And have a thank, and yet a cote and hood.
And have thanks, and also a coat and hood (as a reward).
613 In youthe he hadde lerned a good myster:
In youth he had learned a good craft:
614 He was a wel good wrighte, a carpenter.
He was a very good craftsman, a carpenter.
615 This Reve sat upon a ful good stot
This Reeve sat upon a very good horse
616 That was al pomely grey and highte Scot.
That was all dapple gray and was called Scot.
617 A long surcote of pers upon he hade,
He had on a long outer coat of dark blue,
618 And by his syde he baar a rusty blade.
And by his side he wore a rusty sword.
619 Of Northfolk was this Reve of which I telle,
Of Northfolk was this Reeve of whom I tell,
620 Biside a toun men clepen Baldeswelle.
Near to a town men call Bawdeswelle.
621 Tukked he was as is a frere aboute,
He had his coat hitched up and belted, like a friar,
622 And evere he rood the hyndreste of oure route.
And ever he rode as the last of our company.

623 A SOMONOUR was ther with us in that place,
There was a SUMMONER with us in that place,
624 That hadde a fyr-reed cherubynnes face,
Who had a fire-red cherubim's face,
625 For saucefleem he was, with eyen narwe.
For it was pimpled and discoloured, with swollen eyelids.
626 As hoot he was and lecherous as a sparwe,
He was as hot and lecherous as a sparrow,
627 With scalled browes blake and piled berd. With black, scabby brows and a beard with hair fallen out.
628 Of his visage children were aferd.
Children were afraid of his face.
629 Ther nas quyk-silver, lytarge, ne brymstoon,
There was no mercury, lead monoxide, nor sulphur,
630 Boras, ceruce, ne oille of tartre noon,
Borax, white lead, nor any oil of tarter,
631 Ne oynement that wolde clense and byte,
Nor ointment that would cleanse and burn,
632 That hym myghte helpen of his whelkes white,
That could cure him of his white pustules,
633 Nor of the knobbes sittynge on his chekes.
Nor of the knobs sitting on his cheeks.
634 Wel loved he garleek, oynons, and eek lekes,
He well loved garlic, onions, and also leeks,
635 And for to drynken strong wyn, reed as blood;
And to drink strong wine, red as blood;
636 Thanne wolde he speke and crie as he were wood.
Then he would speak and cry out as if he were crazy.
637 And whan that he wel dronken hadde the wyn,
And when he had drunk deeply of the wine,
638 Thanne wolde he speke no word but Latyn.
Then he would speak no word but Latin.
639 A fewe termes hadde he, two or thre,
He had a few legal terms, two or three,
640 That he had lerned out of som decree —
That he had learned out of some text of ecclesiastic

al law—
641 No wonder is, he herde it al the day;
That is no wonder, he heard it all the day;
642 And eek ye knowen wel how that a jay
And also you know well how a jay
643 Kan clepen "Watte" as wel as kan the pope.
Can call out "Walter" as well as the pope can.
644 But whoso koude in oother thyng hym grope,
But whoever knew how to examine him in other matters,
645 Thanne hadde he spent al his philosophie;
(Would find that) he had used up all his learning;
646 Ay "Questio quid iuris" wolde he crie.
Always "The question is, what point of the law applies?" he would cry.
647 He was a gentil harlot and a kynde;
He was a fine rascal and a kind one;
648 A bettre felawe sholde men noght fynde.
One could not find a better fellow.
649 He wolde suffre for a quart of wyn
For a quart of wine he would allow
650 A good felawe to have his concubyn
A good fellow to have his concubine
651 A twelf month, and excuse hym atte fulle;
For twelve months, and excuse him completely;
652 Ful prively a fynch eek koude he pulle.
Secretly he also knew how to pull off a clever trick.
653 And if he foond owher a good felawe,
And if he found anywhere a good fellow,
654 He wolde techen him to have noon awe
He would teach him to have no awe
655 In swich caas of the ercedekenes curs,
Of the archdeacon's curse (of excommunication) in such a case,
656 But if a mannes soule were in his purs;
Unless a man's soul were in his purse;
657 For in his purs he sholde ypunysshed be.

For in his purse he would be punished.
658 "Purs is the ercedekenes helle," seyde he.
"Purse is the archdeacon's hell," he said.
659 But wel I woot he lyed right in dede;
But well I know he lied right certainly;
660 Of cursyng oghte ech gilty man him drede,
Each guilty man ought to be afraid of excommunication,
661 For curs wol slee right as assoillyng savith, For
excommunication will slay just as forgiveness saves,
662 And also war hym of a Significavit.
And let him also beware of a Significavit (order for imprisonment).
663 In daunger hadde he at his owene gise
In his control he had as he pleased
664 The yonge girles of the diocise,
The young people of the diocese,
665 And knew hir conseil, and was al hir reed.
And knew their secrets, and was the adviser of them all.
666 A gerland hadde he set upon his heed,
He had set a garland upon his heed,
667 As greet as it were for an ale-stake.
As large as if it were for the sign of a tavern
668 A bokeleer hadde he maad hym of a cake.
He had made himself a shield of a cake.
669 With hym ther rood a gentil PARDONER
With him there rode a fine PARDONER
670 Of Rouncivale, his freend and his compeer,
Of Rouncivale, his friend and his companion,
671 That streight was comen fro the court of Rome.
Who had come straight from the court of Rome.
672 Ful loude he soong "Com hider, love, to me!"
Very loud he sang "Come hither, love, to me!"
673 This Somonour bar to hym a stif burdoun;
This Summoner harmonized with him in a strong bass;

674 Was nevere trompe of half so greet a soun.
There was never a trumpet of half so great a sound.
675 This Pardoner hadde heer as yelow as wex,
This Pardoner had hair as yellow as wax,
676 But smothe it heeng as dooth a strike of flex;
But smooth it hung as does a clump of flax;
677 By ounces henge his lokkes that he hadde,
By small strands hung such locks as he had,
678 And therwith he his shuldres overspradde;
And he spread them over his shoulders;
679 But thynne it lay, by colpons oon and oon.
But thin it lay, by strands one by one.
680 But hood, for jolitee, wered he noon,
But to make an attractive appearance, he wore no hood,
681 For it was trussed up in his walet.
For it was trussed up in his knapsack.
682 Hym thoughte he rood al of the newe jet;
It seemed to him that he rode in the very latest style;
683 Dischevelee, save his cappe, he rood al bare. With hair unbound, save for his cap, he rode all bare-headed.
684 Swiche glarynge eyen hadde he as an hare.
He had glaring eyes such as has a hare.
685 A vernycle hadde he sowed upon his cappe.
He had sewn a Veronica upon his cap.
686 His walet, biforn hym in his lappe,
Before him in his lap, (he had) his knapsack,
687 Bretful of pardoun comen from Rome al hoot.
Brimful of pardons come all fresh from Rome.
688 A voys he hadde as smal as hath a goot.
He had a voice as small as a goat has.
689 No berd hadde he, ne nevere sholde have;
He had no beard, nor never would have;
690 As smothe it was as it were late shave.
It (his face) was as smooth as if it were recently shaven.

691 I trowe he were a geldyng or a mare.
I believe he was a eunuch or a homosexual.
692 But of his craft, fro Berwyk into Ware
But as to his craft, from Berwick to Ware
693 Ne was ther swich another pardoner.
There was no other pardoner like him.
694 For in his male he hadde a pilwe-beer,
For in his pouch he had a pillow-case,
695 Which that he seyde was Oure Lady veyl;
Which he said was Our Lady's veil;
696 He seyde he hadde a gobet of the seyl
He said he had a piece of the sail
697 That Seint Peter hadde, whan that he wente
That Saint Peter had, when he went
698 Upon the see, til Jhesu Crist hym hente.
Upon the sea, until Jesus Christ took him.
699 He hadde a croys of latoun ful of stones,
He had a cross of latten (brass-like alloy) covered
with stones,
700 And in a glas he hadde pigges bones.
And in a glass container he had pigs' bones.
701 But with thise relikes, whan that he fond
But with these relics, when he found
702 A povre person dwellynge upon lond,
A poor parson dwelling in the countryside,
703 Upon a day he gat hym moore moneye
In one day he got himself more money
704 Than that the person gat in monthes tweye;
Than the parson got in two months;
705 And thus, with feyned flaterye and japes,
And thus, with feigned flattery and tricks,
706 He made the person and the peple his apes.
He made fools of the parson and the people.
707 But trewely to tellen atte laste,
But truly to tell at the last,
708 He was in chirche a noble ecclesiaste.
He was in church a noble ecclesiast.

709 Wel koude he rede a lessoun or a storie,
He well knew how to read a lesson or a story,
710 But alderbest he song an offertorie;
But best of all he sang an Offertory;
711 For wel he wiste, whan that song was songe,
For he knew well, when that song was sung,
712 He moste preche and wel affile his tonge
He must preach and well smooth his speech
713 To wynne silver, as he ful wel koude;
To win silver, as he very well knew how;
714 Therefore he song the murierly and loude.
Therefore he sang the more merrily and loud.
715 Now have I toold you soothly, in a clause,
Now have I told you truly, briefly,
716 Th' estaat, th' array, the nombre, and eek the cause
The rank, the dress, the number, and also the cause
717 Why that assembled was this compaignye
Why this company was assembled
718 In Southwerk at this gentil hostelrye
In Southwark at this fine hostelry
719 That highte the Tabard, faste by the Belle.
That is called the Tabard, close by the Bell.
720 But now is tyme to yow for to telle
But now it is time to tell to you
721 How that we baren us that ilke nyght,
How we conducted ourselves that same night,
722 Whan we were in that hostelrie alyght;
When we had arrived in that hostelry;
723 And after wol I telle of our viage
And after that I will tell of our journey
724 And al the remenaunt of oure pilgrimage.
And all the rest of our pilgrimage.
725 But first I pray yow, of youre curteisye,
But first I pray yow, of your courtesy,
726 That ye n' arette it nat my vileynye,
That you do not attribute it to my rudeness,
727 Thogh that I pleynly speke in this mateere,

Though I speak plainly in this matter,
728 To telle yow hir wordes and hir cheere,
To tell you their words and their behavior,
729 Ne thogh I speke hir wordes proprely.
Nor though I speak their words accurately.
730 For this ye knowen al so wel as I:
For this you know as well as I:
731 Whoso shal telle a tale after a man,
Whoever must repeat a story after someone,
732 He moot reherce as ny as evere he kan
He must repeat as closely as ever he knows how
733 Everich a word, if it be in his charge,
Every single word, if it be in his power,
734 Al speke he never so rudeliche and large,
Although he may speak ever so rudely and freely,
735 Or ellis he moot telle his tale untrewe,
Or else he must tell his tale inaccurately,
736 Or feyne thyng, or fynde wordes newe.
Or make up things, or find new words.
737 He may nat spare, althogh he were his brother;
He may not refrain from (telling the truth), although
he were his brother;
738 He moot as wel seye o word as another.
He must as well say one word as another.
739 Crist spak hymself ful brode in hooly writ,
Christ himself spoke very plainly in holy writ,
740 And wel ye woot no vileynye is it.
And you know well it is no rudeness.
741 Eek Plato seith, whoso kan hym rede,
Also Plato says, whosoever knows how to read him,
742 The wordes moote be cosyn to the dede.
The words must be closely related to the deed.
743 Also I prey yow to foryeve it me,
Also I pray you to forgive it to me,
744 Al have I nat set folk in hir degree
Although I have not set folk in order of their rank
745 Heere in this tale, as that they sholde stonde.

Here in this tale, as they should stand.
746 My wit is short, ye may wel understonde.
My wit is short, you can well understand.
747 Greet chiere made oure Hoost us everichon,
Our Host made great hospitality to everyone of us,
748 And to the soper sette he us anon.
And to the supper he set us straightway.
749 He served us with vitaille at the beste;
He served us with victuals of the best sort;
750 Strong was the wyn, and wel to drynke us leste.
The wine was strong, and it well pleased us to drink.
751 A semely man OURE HOOSTE was withalle
OUR HOST was an impressive man indeed
752 For to been a marchal in an halle.
(Qualified) to be a master of ceremonies in a hall.
753 A large man he was with eyen stepe —
He was a large man with prominent eyes —
754 A fairer burgeys was ther noon in Chepe —
There was no better business man in Cheapside —
755 Boold of his speche, and wys, and wel ytaught,
Bold of his speech, and wise, and well mannered,
756 And of manhod hym lakkede right naught.
And he lacked nothing at all of the qualities proper
to a man.
757 Eek therto he was right a myrie man;
Also moreover he was a right merry man;
758 And after soper pleyen he bigan,
And after supper he began to be merry,
759 And spak of myrthe amonges othere thynges,
And spoke of mirth among other things,
760 Whan that we hadde maad oure rekenynges,
When we had paid our bills,
761 And seyde thus: "Now, lordynges, trewely,
And said thus: "Now, gentlemen, truly,
762 Ye been to me right welcome, hertely;
You are right heartily welcome to me;
763 For by my trouthe, if that I shal nat lye,

For by my word, if I shall not lie (I must say),
764 I saugh nat this yeer so myrie a compaignye
I saw not this year so merry a company
765 Atones in this herberwe as is now.
At one time in this lodging as is (here) now.
766 Fayn wolde I doon yow myrthe, wiste I how.
I would gladly make you happy, if I knew how.
767 And of a myrthe I am right now bythoght,
And I have just now thought of an amusement,
768 To doon yow ese, and it shal coste noght.
To give you pleasure, and it shall cost nothing.
769 "Ye goon to Caunterbury — God yow speede,
"You go to Canterbury — God give you success,
770 The blisful martir quite yow youre meede!
May the blessed martyr give you your reward!
771 And wel I woot, as ye goon by the weye,
And well I know, as you go by the way,
772 Ye shapen yow to talen and to pleye;
You intend to tell tales and to amuse yourselves;
773 For trewely, confort ne myrthe is noon
For truly, it is no comfort nor mirth
774 To ride by the weye doumb as a stoon;
To ride by the way dumb as a stone;
775 And therfore wol I maken yow disport,
And therefore I will make a game for you,
776 As I seyde erst, and doon yow som confort.
As I said before, and provide you some pleasure.
777 And if yow liketh alle by oon assent
And if pleases you all unanimously
778 For to stonden at my juggement,
To be subject to my judgment,
779 And for to werken as I shal yow seye,
And to do as I shall tell you,
780 Tomorwe, whan ye riden by the weye,
Tomorrow, when you ride by the way,
781 Now, by my fader soule that is deed,
Now, by the soul of my father who is dead,

782 But ye be myrie, I wol yeve yow myn heed!
Unless you be merry, I will give you my head!
783 Hoold up youre hondes, withouten moore speche."
Hold up your hands, without more speech."
784 Oure conseil was nat longe for to seche.
Our decision was not long to seek out.
785 Us thoughte it was noght worth to make it wys, It seemed to us it was not worthwhile to deliberate on it,
786 And graunted hym withouten moore avys,
And (we) granted his request without more discussion,
787 And bad him seye his voirdit as hym leste.
And asked him to say his decision as it pleased him.
788 "Lordynges," quod he, "now herkneth for the beste;
"Gentlemen," said he, "now listen for the best course of action;
789 But taak it nought, I prey yow, in desdeyn.
But, I pray yow, do not take it in disdain (scorn it).
790 This is the poynt, to speken short and pleyn,
This is the point, to speak briefly and clearly,
791 That ech of yow, to shorte with oure weye,
That each of yow, to make our way seem short by this means,
792 In this viage shal telle tales tweye
Must tell two tales in this journey
793 To Caunterbury-ward, I mene it so,
On the way to Canterbury, that is what I mean,
794 And homward he shal tellen othere two,
And on the homeward trip he shall tell two others,
795 Of aventures that whilom han bifalle.
About adventures that in old times have happened.
796 And which of yow that bereth hym best of alle —
And whoever of you who does best of all —
797 That is to seyn, that telleth in this caas
That is to say, who tells in this case
798 Tales of best sentence and moost solaas —
Tales of best moral meaning and most pleasure —

799 Shal have a soper at oure aller cost
Shall have a supper at the cost of us all
800 Heere in this place, sittynge by this post,
Here in this place, sitting by this post,
801 Whan that we come agayn fro Caunterbury.
When we come back from Canterbury.
802 And for to make yow the moore mury,
And to make you the more merry,
803 I wol myselven goodly with yow ryde,
I will myself gladly ride with you,
804 Right at myn owene cost, and be youre gyde;
Entirely at my own cost, and be your guide;
805 And whoso wole my juggement withseye
And whosoever will not accept my judgment
806 Shal paye al that we spenden by the weye.
Shall pay all that we spend by the way.
807 And if ye vouche sauf that it be so,
And if you grant that it be so,
808 Tel me anon, withouten wordes mo,
Tell me straightway, without more words,
809 And I wol erly shape me therfore."
And I will get ready early for this."
810 This thyng was graunted, and oure othes swore
This thing was granted, and our oaths sworn
811 With ful glad herte, and preyden hym also
With very glad hearts, and (we) prayed him also
812 That he wolde vouche sauf for to do so,
That he would consent to do so,
813 And that he wolde been oure governour,
And that he would be our governor,
814 And of oure tales juge and reportour,
And judge and score keeper of our tales,
815 And sette a soper at a certeyn pris,
And set a supper at a certain price,
816 And we wol reuled been at his devys
And we will be ruled as he wishes
817 In heigh and lough; and thus by oon assent

In every respect; and thus unanimously
818 We been acorded to his juggement.
We are accorded to his judgment.
819 And therupon the wyn was fet anon;
And thereupon the wine was fetched immediately;
820 We dronken, and to reste wente echon,
We drank, and each one went to rest,
821 Withouten any lenger taryynge.
Without any longer tarrying.
822 Amorwe, whan that day bigan to sprynge,
In the morning, when day began to spring,
823 Up roos oure Hoost, and was oure aller cok,
Our Host arose, and was the rooster of us all (awakened us).
824 And gadrede us togidre alle in a flok,
And gathered us together all in a flock,
825 And forth we riden a litel moore than paas
And forth we rode at little more than a walk
826 Unto the Wateryng of Seint Thomas;
Unto the Watering of Saint Thomas;
827 And there oure Hoost bigan his hors areste
And there our Host stopped his horse
828 And seyde, "Lordynges, herkneth, if yow leste.
And said, "Gentlemen, listen, if you please.
829 Ye woot youre foreward, and I it yow recorde.
You know your agreement, and I remind you of it.
830 If even-song and morwe-song accorde, If what you said last night agrees with what you say this morning,
831 Lat se now who shal telle the firste tale.
Let's see now who shall tell the first tale.
832 As evere mote I drynke wyn or ale,
As ever I may drink wine or ale,
833 Whoso be rebel to my juggement
Whosoever may be rebel to my judgment
834 Shal paye for al that by the wey is spent.
Shall pay for all that is spent by the way.

835 Now draweth cut, er that we ferrer twynne;
Now draw straws, before we depart further (from London);
836 He which that hath the shorteste shal bigynne.
He who has the shortest shall begin.
837 Sire Knyght," quod he, "my mayster and my lord,
Sir Knight," said he, "my master and my lord,
838 Now draweth cut, for that is myn accord.
Now draw a straw, for that is my decision.
839 Cometh neer," quod he, "my lady Prioresse.
Come nearer," he said, "my lady Prioress.
840 And ye, sire Clerk, lat be youre shamefastnesse,
And you, sir Clerk, let be your modesty,
841 Ne studieth noght; ley hond to, every man!"
And study not; lay hand to (draw a straw), every man!"
842 Anon to drawen every wight bigan,
Every person began straightway to draw,
843 And shortly for to tellen as it was,
And shortly to tell as it was,
844 Were it by aventure, or sort, or cas,
Were it by chance, or destiny, or luck,
845 The sothe is this: the cut fil to the Knyght,
The truth is this: the draw fell to the Knight,
846 Of which ful blithe and glad was every wyght,
For which everyone was very happy and glad,
847 And telle he moste his tale, as was resoun,
And he must tell his tale, as was reasonable,
848 By foreward and by composicioun,
By our previous promise and by formal agreement,
849 As ye han herd; what nedeth wordes mo?
As you have heard; what more words are needed?
850 And whan this goode man saugh that it was so,
And when this good man saw that it was so,
851 As he that wys was and obedient
Like one who was wise and obedient
852 To kepe his foreward by his free assent,

To keep his agreement by his free assent,
853 He seyde, "Syn I shal bigynne the game,
He said, "Since I must begin the game,
854 What, welcome be the cut, a Goddes name!
What! Welcome be the draw, in God's name!
855 Now lat us ryde, and herkneth what I seye."
Now let us ride, and listen to what I say."
856 And with that word we ryden forth oure weye,
And with that word we rode forth on our way,
857 And he bigan with right a myrie cheere
And he began with a truly merry demeanor
858 His tale anon, and seyde as ye may heere.
To tell his tale straightway, and said as you may hear.

Chapter 13

Summary and Analysis of General Prologue

Fragment I

The General Prologue

As April comes, the narrator begins a pilgrimage to Canterbury from the Tabard Inn at Southwerk. Twenty-nine people make the pilgrimage toward Canterbury and the narrator describes them in turn. The pilgrims are listed in relative order of status, thus the first character is the Knight. Chaucer describes the knight as a worthy man who had fought in the Crusades. With him is a Squire, the son of the Knight and a 'lusty bachelor' of twenty. The Knight has a second servant, a Yeoman. There is also a Prioress, shy and polite. She is prim and proper, sympathetic and well-mannered.

The Prioress wears a broach with the inscription "All things are subject unto love." With the Prioress is her secretary (the Second Nun) and a Monk. The monk is a robust and masculine man who loves to hunt. The Friar, Hubert, is an immoral man more concerned with making profit than converting men from sin. The Merchant from Flanders is a pompous man who speaks endlessly on how profits may be increased. He seems grave, yet there is no better man, according to the narrator. The Clerk follows the Merchant. As an Oxford student without employment, he is impoverished and wears threadbare clothes. The Man of Law is a man who deserves to be held in awe. He knows the law to the letter and gives the impression that he is far busier than he actually is. A Franklin travels with him. He is a man who lives in comfort and is interested simply in pleasure, particularly culinary delight. There are also five guildsmen: a Weaver, a Dyer, a Carpenter, a Tapestry-maker and a Haberdasher. With them they bring a Cook. A Shipman is the next traveller, who comes from the port of Dartmouth, and with him a Physician. The Wife of Bath is next; she is a weaver who wears bright red clothing. She has been married five times (and had several companions as a youth).

The Parson is an honourable, decent man who cares for his congregation and adheres to the teachings of Christ. With him is his brother, a Plowman, who is equally kind. The final travellers are a Miller, a Manciple, a Reeve, a Summoner and a Pardoner. The Miller is a large man with an imposing physique. The Manciple is from a lawyers' college and knows every legal maneuver. The Reeve is a slender man with a fiery temper. The Summoner is quite unfair in his job (he is responsible for serving summons to court for church crimes). If he likes a scoundrel, he can ignore the man's sins. The Pardoner is an effeminate man. Each of these travellers finds themselves in the Tabard Inn, where the Host, a bold and merry man, suggests that on their way to Canterbury each traveller tell two tales, and on the way back each traveller tell two more. They draw lots to decide who will tell the first tale, and it is the Knight who has the honour.

Analysis

In the General Prologue, Chaucer sets up the general structure of the tales and introduces each of the characters who will tell the tales. The characters who tell each of the tales are as important as the characters in the tales that they tell; a significant portion of the action of the Canterbury Tales takes place within the prologues to each of the tales. The General Prologue in essence serves as a guide for the tales, giving some explanation for the motivation behind each of the tales each character tells.

The introductory imagery of the General Prologue mixes the spiritual with the secular and moves between each form with relative ease. The Canterbury Tales begins with the famous lines "Whanne that Aprill with his shoures soote / The droghte of March hath perced to the roote," setting up imagery of spring and regeneration. Yet he does not continue with the logical outcome of this springtime imagery. Instead of conforming to the cliché "in springtime a young man's fancy turns to love," Chaucer veers into more spiritual territory. In springtime these travellers make a religious pilgrimage to Canterbury. Yet Chaucer is equally uninterested in the religious details of this journey, and keeps the beginning passages of the General Prologue focused on nature and not on the human society with which the travellers will deal.

Chaucer gives relatively straightforward descriptions of the characters and has some inclination to show their best qualities. Chaucer describes virtually each pilgrimage as an exemplar - a number of these pilgrims are described as 'perfect' in some way or another, most often in their craft. Furthermore, these pilgrims exist almost entirely in terms of their profession. Chaucer gives only a few of them character names, and these emerge only in terms of conversation between the characters during each tale's prologue, and not in Chaucer's description in the General Prologue.

Yet even within these descriptions he allows for subtle criticism and sly wit. The description of the Prioress in particular, is overtly flattering yet masquerades a sharp criticism of her foolish sentimentality and oppressive attention to manners. Although she strives to be polite and refined, she spoke French "after the school of Stratford-at-Bow," the vulgar rural pronunciation compared to elite Parisian French. Furthermore, she weeps at the mere sight of a dead mouse, a gross overreaction to a small tragedy.

The descriptions of the upper members of the clergy

deserve special note in context of the tales. Each of the clergymen defy traditional expectations; the Monk is a rough labourer, while the Friar is resolutely immoral. Chaucer lists the various sins of the Friar: he sells pardon from sin for a price, seduces women who ask for pardons, and spends more time in bars than he does aiding the poor. His concern for profit is a stark contrast with that of the Merchant. While the Merchant merely dispenses advice on how to attain profit, it is the Friar who applies his entire existence to its pursuit. The Friar further contrasts with the later description of the Parson, a man who performs his duties honourably and cares for his congregation. In his description of the Parson, Chaucer lists the various admirable qualities, none of which are held by the Friar.

The description of the Merchant is also notable, for it shows the disparity between how the narrator overtly appraises a character and what he describes. After listing a number of unflattering qualities in the Merchant, the narrator still judges him to be a fine man; in these descriptions, the details and anecdotes are far more important in defining character than the final stated opinion of the narrator.

Chaucer indulges in comic criticism in his portrait of the Clerk. This Oxford student, however educated, is not worldly enough for any normal employment. He has studied only impractical knowledge, and even carries among his few possessions several volumes of Aristotle.

Most of the travellers engaged in a profession receive little description; as the travellers move down the social scale Chaucer gives them less and less detailed descriptions. The Wife of Bath is the most significant of the travellers low on the social scale. Chaucer describes her as lewd and boisterous. Her clothing, all variations of bright red, is ostentatious, meant to attract attention from others. Chaucer even indicates that she is quite promiscuous - she has been married five times and had an undetermined number of lovers. The other traveller who merits a lengthy description is the Pardoner. He has a very effeminate manner, with a high voice and soft features.

Chaucer even compares him to a gelding (a castrated horse) or a mare, which may be a subtle comment on his sexuality.

The prologue sets up the general design of the Canterbury Tales. Each character will tell four tales during the journey, leading to a grand total of 116 tales. Chaucer never completed all of the tales, starting only about one fourth of the possible stories, not all of which remain in their entirety. Some of the stories that remain are only fragments which have either been lost or were never completed by the author.

When the travellers draw lots to decide who will tell the first story, it is the Knight who has the first choice. Although the order is supposedly random, the Knight draws the first lot and thus randomly receives the rank appropriate to his status, which indicates that the Host may have fixed the lots in order to curry favor with the Knight.

Chapter 14

Study Questions

Q. Crtically Analyse Chaucer's General Prologue. ?

Or

Q. Discuss Chaucer's General Prologue as an Epic Poem.?

Or

Q. Discuss the Genral Prologue placing it in its Historical Context. ?

Or

Q. Discuss Chaucer's use of Irony and Satire in General Prologue. ?

Introduction

In addressing "The General Prologue to The Canterbury Tales" we are dealing with what has long been recognized as one of the greatest masterpieces of English literature, certainly the finest and most influential work of fiction to emerge in England from that period we call the Middle Ages. For most literary historians, English literature begins well before Chaucer's greatest poem, but this particular work marks the start of the tradition which is still readily accessible in the original language to the diligent reader, even though Chaucer's Middle English requires the constant help of a glossary.

A Note on the Term Middle Ages

One might well begin by asking "Why the Middle Ages?" Clearly people at the time did not think of themselves as living between two different time periods (they thought of themselves, as every age does, as the most recent arrivals), so where does the term come from? Well, the term Middle Ages was applied by later Renaissance writers and historians to refer to the period falling very roughly between the fall of the Roman Empire in 410 AD (when Alaric sacked Rome) and the Renaissance. The arrival of the latter has no clear date and tends to be dated earlier in southern Europe than in the north.

A convenient (but somewhat misleadingly precise) date for the arrival of the Renaissance in England might be 1485, the date of the Battle of Bosworth Field, when Richard III, the last of the Plantaganet kings, was defeated and killed by Henry Tudor, thus initiating the reign of the Tudors, which lasted in England until the death of Queen Elizabeth I in 1603.

The term Middle Ages, like so many historical terms applied to an earlier period, was deliberately pejorative. There had been the great Classical Period of Greece and Rome, and now there was the wonderful revival of classical learning, the Renaissance. In between was a period viewed by many Renaissance thinkers as a time of relatively little achievement (with some exceptions here and there), a time of ignorance, an absence of the invaluable classical inheritance, feudal oppression, and the widespread power of the church. With deliberate contempt, some writers applied the term The Dark Ages to the earlier part of this period (up to about the eleventh century).

In fact, the Middle Ages was a time of extraordinary vitality. In the first five hundred years of this period, Christianity established itself throughout Europe, developed a complex institutionalized religion capable of governing society at all levels, ministering to the sick, and dealing with judicial disputes; the Church hammered out compromises with secular rulers, an aristocracy derived from the Germanic tribal customs, and placed Europe's economy on a firm agricultural foundation (the work of the monasteries in clearing the land is one of the greatest successes of western labour, an astonishing achievement of the most effective work force our culture has every produced). During this period there were many fierce (and often bloody) disputes about Christian doctrine, about the relative distribution of power between Church and State, and about the relationship between the Church's immense economic power and its ministry to the poor. Nevertheless, for much of the Middle Ages, life was calm, orderly, stable, and relatively prosperous. If we tend to remember the excesses, like the Black Death and the persecution of heretics and witches (which is more a Renaissance phenomenon, anyway), we should not therefore forget that this period established the basis from which were to develop the institutions, customs, and power which fuelled the amazing expansion of Europe in the Renaissance and afterwards.

Medieval Christianity

It is particularly important for modern readers of medieval works not to make the common but fatal error of thinking about the Middle Ages, and especially about the Christian Church in the Middle Ages, as something monolithic, homogenous, and backward. There is a common tendency for inexperienced readers of Chaucer to offer criticisms like "Well, in the Middle Ages, everyone believed this or that." Such statements make no more sense than similar generalizations about today or, indeed, about any other time. Within the Church, as within the ranks of modern liberal capitalism, there were all sorts of tensions between traditional authoritarian conservatives, radical free thinkers, communitarians insisting on limiting individual freedom, individualists insisting on more individual freedom, reformers wanting a better deal for the poor and less money for the top bureaucrats, and so on.

The major work of the Church was to maintain, in the midst of all these tensions, a workable social community in the thousands of very small agricultural communities throughout Europe, and in this attempt it was for a long time astonishingly successful. If many of the popes and bishops, like the imperial Caesars, left behind scandalous records of personal misconduct, nevertheless many were efficient and caring administrators, and the bureaucracy of the Church could often work extremely well with corruption at the top, because it was staffed by educated and diligent human beings at lower levels.

Thus, it is very, very misleading to make any sweeping generalizations about the Middle Ages (as it is about any complex period), and you should at once check any impulse in yourself to bring to bear on Chaucer's work any preconceived general notions you have that, because the Middle Ages happened long ago and is always associated with Roman Catholic Christian hierarchy, it therefore can be easily characterized and summed up with a single pithy insight or slogan.

A much better idea (and this applies to all literature from the past or from cultures different from our own) is to set all such preconceptions aside and to enter the work as if it is describing a culture that you have suddenly come across on your travels through the forest. If you find such a culture at all intriguing, the first thing to do is not to judge it but to make some attempt to understand it. And that means, above all else, keeping your own immediate evaluative judgments at bay until such time as you have learned something more about what is going on in such a culture. If the people there are doing things which are distinctly odd or even abhorrent by our standards, then find out why they are doing them. Explore the belief system that prompts such behaviour. Find out what they value, what rules and visions guide their understanding of the world, the different varieties of conduct which go on, before determining too casually just what the entire culture is worth. And if one wants to be fair to that culture, one needs to be very precise about one's observations and scrupulous about the judgments which arise out of them.

The Renaissance

The term Renaissance is applied to the period of intellectual and cultural history which succeeded the Middle Ages. Literally the term refers to the rebirth of classical learning which swept across Italy in the late fourteenth and early fifteenth century, as old classical manuscripts were rediscovered, edited, translated, and distributed throughout southern Europe, moving slowly northward throughout the fifteenth century. The immediate impetus which launched this revival was the serious threat posed to Eastern Europe by the Turkish Muslim forces moving up towards Constantinople and Vienna throughout the early part of this period (Constantinople was captured by the Turks in 1453). The flight of Greek scholars with the manuscripts toward the West brought into the West, and especially into Italy, what had been lost long ago, Greek language and literature. The diffusion of such learning accelerated rapidly after the invention of printing in the 1450's.

But there was more to the Renaissance than just this scholarly revival. There was a renewed emphasis on classical humanism, on the view that the good life did not have to be lived under the constant supervision of the Church within the often limited restrictions of the small community. The increasing interest in exploration, the growing wealth of the towns, and the rising interest in speculating about the nature of the earth and the heavens (often supported by ambitious central monarchs growing in power) all put pressure on the static, traditional, communal model which had been the social reality of Europe for eight centuries.

Chaucer's poem was written late in the fourteenth century, in the late Middle Ages or early Renaissance, depending on how one wishes to consider the time. And a few things about the social conditions of the period are clear from the picture of society he gives us there. Let me list a few of them:

First, the Church is still clearly a major part of society. About one third of the pilgrims going to Canterbury are church officials, and the entire group is celebrating spring by taking part in a traditional Christian ritual, the pilgrimage to an important holy shrine. In doing so they are giving public testimony to things that are valued in their society and their lives, just as we would reveal a great deal about our social and personal values, if we were to write this poem today by picturing our pilgrim band as containing many people working for the government, all on their way to Disneyland in a charter jet.

Secondly, while none of the pilgrims comes from the top classes of society, the aristocracy, many of them are quite rich and sophisticated. In examining them, we are, for the most part, looking at members of the middle-class (although the concept of class did not exist at the time). Some of them have money, a few have traveled extensively. They know about good clothes and books and food. Some ordinary folk have horses. What we would call the trading and service industries are well represented by people who would not be out of place in a Nanaimo mall. And yet we are reminded, too, that the traditional roles of the Middle Ages have not yet disappeared.

Finally, there is a sense of rising individualism among them. While the ideals of the dedication to a traditional Christian communal society are still clearly there, it is equally evident that for many of these pilgrims, including the Church officials, the sense of a communal duty is being eroded by a personal desire for money and the fine things money can buy. In fact, there is a strong sense throughout The Canterbury Tales that this money is somehow a threat to something older and more valuable.

All of these details suggest a society in transition. We are not here dealing with the vision of the Middle Ages of a few hundred years before, a time when books were very scarce, traveling much more difficult, and money (and the good things it purchases) in much shorter supply. I'm going to be going into some of these points in more detail later. Here I simply want to call attention to the obvious fact that we don't have to read much of the General Prologue to sense that we are not dealing with simple agricultural folk, piously obedient to their church, and without any knowledge of the world beyond the next village or of some of the finer consumer items which make life more comfortable and fun.

Chaucer, incidentally, lived before the invention of printing and the widespread diffusion of classical literature into Northern Europe. Thus, although he was well read in French and Italian literature and drew heavily upon certain Continental works and traditions, he did not have access to Greek literature. When he wrote about Troilus and Cressida and the Trojan War, he was drawing on medieval traditions of this famous story, without direct knowledge about Greek versions in Homer or the tragedians.

The Canterbury Tales: Some Initial General Observations

I have no intention here of reviewing details of Geoffrey Chaucer's life (which are irrelevant to an understanding of the poem and which are more than adequately covered by the Norton introduction). But before looking in detail at the poem, I would like to comment on the overall plan of his masterpiece, The Canterbury Tales.

The General Prologue makes clear that the overall plan for the work called for four stories from each character, two on the way there and two on the way back. That intention was clearly not met. The manuscripts contain work on twenty-four tales, with two of these unfinished. Putting these tales together into what seems to be the most coherent form is a major editorial challenge.

The basic structure of the work, as established in the General Prologue, is simple enough and relatively conventional. A group of travellers are thrown together and, to pass the time, they determine to tell each other stories (in a manner common to all sorts of narratives like the Thousand and One Nights, The Decameron of Boccaccio, and so on). Chaucer chooses one of the oldest narrative devices, a journey, in this case a pilgrimage which includes a wide variety of social types. On this familiar narrative framework, he then hangs a series of tales in which he can display a number of different literary forms (fairy stories, prose sermons, romance narratives, bawdy tales, animal fables, and so on). In this way, he has a ready-made recipe for a wide variety of personalities and stories. And one of the greatest achievements of The Canterbury Tales is the richness of it characters and its literary styles.

The Narrator

Linking the episodic nature of the gallery of characters and their stories is the engaging presence of the narrator, who is a major presence in the poem. Chaucer presents the narrator as one of the pilgrims, a fellow Christian traveling to Canterbury and meeting the various characters and hearing their stories. This gives his descriptions the immediacy of a personal narration based upon intimate conversations and direct witnessing of the dramatic events which take place upon the way (like the different quarrels among some of the pilgrims).

At the same time, however, it is quite clear that many of the details we learn (especially in the General Prologue) are obviously based upon a perspective that cannot be simply derived from a personal encounter. The details we learn about all the Knight's achievements, for example, or the details of the Wife of Bath's behaviour back home in her own church, these are not things that a pilgrim narrator could learn in such vivid detail.

Hence, we are dealing with, in effect, two narrators. The shifts between them are unannounced, and I doubt if many readers enjoying the poem are at all disturbed by questions about how a pilgrim-narrator could possibly know so much about people he has just met. This, in itself, is a good reminder that what matters in reading a poem (as in viewing a film) is not the total absence of logical difficulties of this sort but rather the skill with which the writer (or film maker) avoids drawing attention to any such inconsistencies. The dual point of view has the great advantage, of course, of giving the poem the immediacy of a personal narrative and the wealth of background detail of the sort available only to an omniscient narrator where this is a useful supplement to a portrait or a narrative.

The General Prologue: Some Thematic Considerations

When we first start reading the General Prologue we are

likely to be drawn first to the richness and variety of the gallery of characters. That is, indeed, one of the wonderful things about this poem; as Dryden observed, "Here is God's plenty." And we can spend a lot of time, as we have seen in our seminars, discussing particular characters in detail. I want to come back to this business of literary criticism as character analysis (which may be unfashionable in some scholarly quarters but which is still the most vital contact with narrative fictions for most readers). Before that, however, I'd like to introduce the notion of a thematic approach to the General Prologue.

To approach a work thematically is to consider what ideas or leitmotivs co-ordinate its details, how these ideas are presented, modified, challenged, and (perhaps) resolved by the end of the work. Thematic criticism will tend to see characterization as primarily important for what it contributes to the complication or presentation of such co-ordinating ideas.

It's important to stress for all those interested in thematic criticism that works of fiction are not philosophical works. They do not present rational arguments (although such arguments may exist in them at times). Thus, thematic criticism is not simply a matter of reducing a work to some simple "moral" or prose summary. What matters in thematic criticism is following the way in which a particular idea or theme is qualified, complicated, challenged, deepened, resolved, reinforced as one proceeds through the fiction. In some fictions, the thematic dimension will be very clear indeed (e.g., in allegories); in others, it may not exist at all (the point of the fiction may well be to disqualify any thematic approach to experience—which, when one thinks about it, is a theme in its own right).

To separate themes from characterization is, of course, suspect, since the two of them work together inextricably. So what we're talking about here is a matter of emphasis. Thematic critics tend to get irritated when all people want to talk about are the minute particulars of character (see L. C.

Knights' famous essay "How Many Children Had Lady Macbeth?" for a classic statement of this objection); and interpreters who like to emphasize character criticism tend to get irritated when other interpreters want to turn a narrative totally into a debate about ideas (William Empson's celebrated study of Paradise Lost in Milton's God contains a sturdy defence of character analysis as a sound basis for criticism in his spirited attacks on those who want to turn Milton's poem into a matter of doctrinaire ideas).

The Opening Sentence

So a thematic approach to the General Prologue might begin by focusing attention on the famous opening sentence. I want to call attention to some of the details of the opening lines, in order to illustrate some potentially important thematic considerations and to show how a detailed attention to what's going on in the language can alert us to what is going to emerge as an important part in the characterization of the pilgrims.

The first point to notice about that opening sentence is that it falls into two equal parts, the first focusing on the spring and the second on the holy duty of the pilgrimage. The first half really stresses the erotic energies of spring, with words like "engendred", "Inspired," "priketh," "Ram," and so on. These words often denote penetration and fertilization, and the movement of the lines and the short vowels in some of the words help to create a sense of erotic energy of a time when nature is so charged with sexual vitality that even the birds sleep with one eye open.

The second half of the sentence focuses on something entirely different, the desire of people to give thanks to God for having survived another winter, having with the help of God and his special saint overcome illnesses and threats of death. The sounds and movements of this part of the sentence is much softer and gentler.

Now this sentence holds in perfect balance the two primary motives of life—the erotic drives which come to us from spring and which push us forward into newly renewed life, and the desire for a common religious experience to thank God for our life together, something which pulls us to worship. On the basis of these two motions, the irrational push of Eros and the spiritual pull of Thanatos (to use Freudian terms) we can approach the study of society which Chaucer then depicts for us.

What I would like to suggest is that the opening sentence announces a powerful theme which runs throughout the General Prologue: that there are two essential forces of life and that what matters is that they be held in a balance (as they are grammatically in the opening sentence). This theme, you might think, is not nearly so explicit as I am suggesting in the opening sentence. But it becomes explicit as soon as we think about this opening sentence in relation to the first pair of portraits (of the Knight and Squire, father and son), a pairing which unites the highest virtues of active Christianity displayed in the lifetime of service of the Knight with the exuberant vitality of the son, an erotic love of life which yet remains in check, so that he knows his duties towards his father (as the last detail of the portrait makes clear).

If we look closely at the first pair of portraits in the light of the theme suggested by the opening sentence, then we encounter a standard of human conduct against which we will inevitably compare the later portraits. What is clear about the Knight is that he has led a active life fighting on behalf of Christianity, especially against the threat of Turkish invasion. He has displayed fortitude, courage, truth, honour, courtesy, and earned a high reputation. Yet he remains humble and does not flaunt his rank in an expensive exterior or display any sense of superiority. He has just arrived back in England and immediately joins the procession to give thanks.

His son, the Squire, shows all the virtues of youth, full of erotic energy, song, a love of the fine things of spring and a commitment to the ideals of chivalry; he is a creative spirit, able to sing, write lyric poetry, dance, and, in general, celebrate the joy of life. But, as already mentioned, this has not led him to forget the respect he owes his father.

Later in the poem, near the end, we meet another pair, the Parson and the Ploughman. They display virtues remarkably similar to those of the Knight and the Squire. They are, above all, charitable and hard working. They have dedicated their lives to the service of their fellow creatures and do not shrink from self-sacrifice or danger to stand up to injustice. What seems clear is that the energies which drive them through life (and into this pilgrimage) are in harmony with the highest ideals by which the narrator measures human conduct.

There's an important thematic point to starting the catalogue of pilgrims with an ideal standard and to reintroducing it near the end. What this achieves is to enable us to make moral judgments more easily about the other portraits. It is clear what the narrator in this poem most admires; he conveys that in these ideal portraits. In this way, we could claim that a central theme of the General Prologue is an exploration of the full range of the moral qualities of late Medieval Christianity as they manifest themselves in the daily life of the people.

The General Prologue as an Epic Poem

If we wish to address the vision of life developed in the General Prologue, we can pay tribute to its epic quality. This literary term is usually reserved for certain narrative fictions which hold up for our exploration something more than just a story. They have a social breadth and a narrative scope which provide a much wider and all-inclusive canvas than an ordinary fiction. In reading them, we are exploring, not simply particular characters in a particular setting, but an entire cultural moment. Epic narratives, from Homer onwards, celebrate civilization in a particular manifestation, and part of their power and interest comes from our sense that an entire way of life is under scrutiny. Parenthetically, what is curious about epic poems is that they tend to appear when the way of life they celebrate is the process of disappearing forever (Homer, for example, is writing about a heroic society a couple of centuries older than him, Paradise Lost appears when the great Protestant experiment under Cromwell is clearly over, many of the novels celebrating the American South come after the Civil War and the defeat of the Confederate cause).

In that sense, the General Prologue invites us to evaluate a particular society. Like all societies this culture is under tension. It has a clear sense of values, what we might call the traditional values of active Christianity, best summed up in the well known Biblical celebration of faith, hope, and charity (and the greatest of these is charity). The ideal portraits make it clear to us that the narrator of this poem admires such qualities more than any others. And the remaining portraits acquaint us with the various ways in which these qualities are under threat. Hence, reading the General Prologue is a voyage through the evaluation of an entire society.

Before moving onto other matters, I'd like to make two comments about the moral vision we encounter. First, by the end of the General Prologue we have become well acquainted with the seven cardinal virtues (prudence, fortitude, temperance, justice, faith, hope, and charity) and the seven cardinal sins (pride, envy, covetousness, sloth, anger, lust, and gluttony). And it seems clear that the narrator of the poem is developing the portraits in accordance with the thematic importance of this traditional value scheme.

Second, and related to the above point, is the emphasis on the social basis for virtue. What makes people good or bad Christians, in the world of this poem, is how they treat each other. Virtue is not an abstract matter of doctrine, a purification ritual carried out in contemplative isolation, or a challenge to the individual will. It is thoroughly social, a matter of one's obligations to help others and to refrain from mistreating them. That list of virtues and vices I recited above are primarily social and cannot be understood outside of a rich social context. This is, as we shall see, in very marked contrast to the other great Christian pilgrimage we shall be reading about in Pilgrim's Progress.

Comparative Critical Details

In this respect, you should notice how certain words and details appear from one portrait to the next. For example, we are often told about a character's attitude to or use of money. And it's worth paying attention to what each character values enough to spend money on. The Knight's price is his reputation, and he has paid for a good horse. The Parson's gold is his sense of Christian duty ("if gold rust, what shal iren do?"), the Clerk (student) spends money on books. The Ploughman dutifully gives money to the Church. Other pilgrims spend money on a wide variety of consumer goods: clothes, food, fine living. How do these people get their money? How do they use their money?

In following just this one point, we can see how that necessary balance between one's erotic and one's religious feelings can be upset, perhaps in some places corrupted. Here it is important to notice how many of the portraits are of Church officials, for whom this question is of particular importance. By looking closely at what the Monk purchases with his money or the tactics used by the Friar and the Pardoner to get money we see immediately where their particular sense of priorities drive them.

Similarly, we should pay attention to clothes. Sometimes these are quite appropriate to the social function a character occupies (e.g., the Knight and perhaps the Prioress). At other times, we might wonder. The narrator clearly likes a fine appearance and has a keen eye for good clothes, just as he values books and the ability to read and write, as well good manners (courtesy). But his highest praise is reserved, as I have mentioned, for those details which enable us to see someone as charitable, that is, as loving his neighbours more than himself. So when the words charity or charitable appear we need to be particularly alert to assessing just what the words mean in this context.

This business of love is essential. What does each

character love? Is this love a corruption of the spirit? In the Prioress we are not sure. The brooch might very well refer to love of God (for the slogan is a common religious statement). In the Monk, his love of God has become a lust for hunting and eating; the Friar's love directs him to all the common pleasures. The finest thing about the Parson is the perfect balance between his love for God and for this world. In the Pardoner, by contrast, the love of God's justice (of which he is the agent) and for humanity has become hopelessly corrupted.

We have to be careful about assessing the importance of each detail. The task asks us to evaluate, not what we think of the character in question, but what the narrator thinks. How do the details he presents about each character shape our understanding of how he feels about them? What emotional pressures is the language putting on us to understand a particular character in one way rather than another? The narrator rarely, if ever, offers an explicit judgment that is not tinged with some irony. But the list of specific details develops a latent judgment in a very delicate manner that the reader needs to attend to and respect.

Chaucer's Irony

This sort of assessment is particularly challenging in the General Prologue because of the ironic tone which pervades so many of the portraits. In fact, there could hardly be a better introduction to the importance of evaluating irony than this famous poem. So it is appropriate here to say a few words about this all-important critical term.

Irony, considered very generally, refers to the quality of language to have different levels of meaning, to be ambiguous, so that we are not entire certain how to interpret a particular phrase or descriptive detail or action. The presence of irony complicates our response because it reveals that what is being described is not a simple literal fact for all to see. It is more complex and layered than that. Irony in language is, as one might expect, not welcome in certain forms of writing, especially in scientific and legal writing, where the unambiguous clarity of clearly defined words is the essence of the prose. In poetry and fiction generally, irony is a writer's stock in trade because it is the surest way to remind the reader that the subject matter of this text is not something simple and literal, but inherently ambiguous.

How does irony work? That's a large subject. But we don't have to read very far in the General Prologue to see Chaucer's standard technique. He is always setting morally loaded language against actions which do not live up to that high praise, thus inviting us to see a discrepancy, an ambiguity between the moral language and the action. Here is a famous example from the portrait of the Wife of Bath:

She was a worthy womman al hir live
Husbondes at chirche dore she hadd five.

The word worthy in the first line sets up a very approving moral value judgment; the detail in the second line undercuts it. Note that that detail doesn't necessarily cancel the approval, but it redirects our attention. We have to wonder about just what the precise nature of the Wife's worthiness consists of. The narrator is not telling us directly; he is inviting us to explore the ambiguity in our own reaction. The irony does not directly clarify the nature of the Wife, but it complicates it, inviting us to see her in a more complex way. Yes, she is a worthy woman (a fine person), but in some ways she might not be as morally worthy as an unambiguous use of the term might suggest.

Similarly, the narrator tells us that the Prioress is charitable (very high praise indeed, given the importance of this term established in the earlier portrait of the Knight) and then, to establish that point, tells us that she weeps if she sees an animal in pain. The details add a distinct note of irony to the work charitable. We know the literal meaning of the word, but the style is asking us to qualify our literal understanding with something more ambiguous. Similarly the Friar is the best beggar in his order. What does that mean? Obviously he is a good beggar in the sense that he obtains a great deal of money, but the details of how he gets his money really qualify the moral content of the potential moral approval in that word best.

Some of the portraits are clearly not ironic; we are invited to take them as literal portraits of an ideal. I would argue, as I have mentioned, that the Knight and the Squire and the Parson and the Ploughman are such ideals. Perhaps the Clerk is as well. But almost all the rest are ironic portraits of human characters whose qualities are inherently ambiguous.

Interpreting Irony

For the literary interpreter the presence of irony is an important challenge, largely because an interpretation must explore that irony and seek to assess its effects, without being too ham fisted, that is, without resolving the irony too simplistically. If the effect of an ironic portrait is often thoroughly ambiguous, then one must acknowledge that and not close off the ironies too quickly.

For example, the portrait of the Prioress has invited some people either to claim that there is no irony in the portrait whatsoever (and thus she is as fine and elegant a person as one might wish for), while others have dismissed her as a thoroughgoing hypocrite. Both of these reactions, in my view, deal with the portrait by destroying its most obvious and interesting quality, its elusiveness. Yes, there are contradictory tendencies in the details, but (and this is a crucial point) human characters often consist of contradictory qualities bound up in a single personality, and one of the functions of poetry is to explore and illuminate such emotional contradictions, not to destroy them.

Hence, in reading the General Prologue, one has to take care to shape one's response to each character carefully, seeking to define as precisely as possible our sense of how the ironical details finally add up, what sort of critical weight we might give to the presence of irony. One of the obvious ways to do this (something the poem invites us to do) is to compare the characters with each other. We might sense, for example, that the Prioress is clearly not up to the standard of the Knight, but she does seem less corrupt than the Friar, who, in turn, is obviously not as scandalously hypocritical as the Pardoner.

Once we start comparing the characters with the theme of corruption of an ideal in mind, we will learn a great deal about the importance of making our responses to irony as precise as possible.

In this connection, it might be useful to remember and apply the concepts of sins of omission and sins of commission. The former stem from a failure to do what one's duty requires one to do; the latter stem from active deeds injuring others directly. And we might want to differentiate between sins of commission which are more serious than others. For example, the Friar commits many sins of commission, but he brings a certain amount of pleasure and fun with him, and his sexual conquests of women, although a disgrace to his order, are, we are led to believe, often well received. The Summoner and the Pardoner, by contrast, actively extort money through systematic lies, threats, and a corruption of church doctrine in their sermons.

One final comment about irony in a style. Often, the most important debates between interpreters of a particular work hinge on whether or not they both see irony in the style or, if they do, just what weight to give it. Since irony inevitably undercuts the literal meaning of particular words and phrases, its presence or absence can make a huge difference. My favourite example of this is Machiavelli's The Prince. My sense is that this was intended as a thoroughly ironic, even satiric work, but so many people failed to see the irony, that the book has been hailed or condemned as a celebration of the political life totally divorced from morality. Debates over the ending of the Odyssey, or Shakespeare's Twelfth Night or Henry V, or Paradise Lost, some of the most interesting and vital critical debates, hinge precisely on this question of detecting the presence of irony and evaluating it.

Satire

When does irony become satire? What is the difference between a thoroughly ironic portrait and a satirically ironic style? One way to sort out the difference is to remember that the purpose of satire is to hold someone up to ridicule as an example to others. Satire always has something aggressive about it, a desire to point a finger and say, in effect, "Look how ridiculous this person is." Making readers laugh at the foolishness of others is the essence of all satire. And irony is the key stylistic technique used to achieve it. All satire emerges from the ironic discrepancy between what people think they are or would like to be and what they, in fact, are. The challenge to the satirist is to make this discrepancy "witty," so that people laugh at the hypocrisy.

But there is an enormous range to satire, and we are not really saying much about a style just by labeling it satiric. We need to evaluate as best we can, on the basis of the language, the precise nature of the satire. There's a huge difference, after all, between a very good natured, even affectionate joke at someone's expense and a savagely harsh indictment of the sinful duplicity of a total hypocrite.

To make fun of people's foolishness and to hold them up as satiric targets requires the satirist to put a certain amount of distance between the target and the reader and to simplify the potential complexity of the personality under attack. This is clear enough in one powerful form of satire still common in society, the political cartoon. This depends upon distortion, simplification, and a black and white presentation of the target as an object worthy of ridicule. The current range of satiric jokes about Bill Clinton (by, for example, Jay Leno) uses the same technique. We are not invited to think about how much pain the target might be in or what psychological pressures might have prompted the error. The more complex the psychological presentation of character, the less powerful the satire becomes.

There's a old French saying, "Tout comprendre, c'est tout pardonner," to understand everything is to forgive everything. But satire is not asking the reader to forgive foolishness but to mock it. And for that to happen, a certain distance and simplification are essential.

Now, it's clear that the narrator in the Canterbury Tales

is inviting us to laugh at the foolishness of some of the portraits. In that sense, we can usefully talk about a satiric presence throughout the General Prologue. But as soon as we have acknowledged that, we would have to concede that much of this satire is extremely gentle. The narrator seems genuinely to like these people on the journey. He brings us quite close to them and indicates that he, for the most part, enjoys their company. So the potential of the satire is enormously muted, to the point where sometimes one can concede that the satiric possibility disappears completely.

For example, the portrait of the Prioress is clearly ironic. We are invited to sense ambiguities in her character, to wonder about what earthly passions might exist beneath the proper attire and the religious icons. But the narrator is clearly much taken with her fine appearance and seems to like her clothing and the way she conducts the divine service. There is an affection, even an admiration, for the woman. Hence, the irony develops little-to-no-satiric energy. We do not, I think, respond to this portrait with the sense that the narrator is inviting us to mock the woman as a hypocrite.

In other portraits where the irony is considerably stronger and more overt, the attitude of the narrator is always muting the satiric potential. The Friar is obviously a sinner, derelict in his duties, as is the Monk. But the narrator conveys a liking for these characters and an admiration for some of their qualities. This collapses the distance between the target and the readers and makes the satire, if it is there at all, much gentler than it might otherwise be. As Paul Baum has remarked, if this is satire, it is satire without indignation.

This mildly affectionate satiric tone (now you feel it, now you don't) in the General Prologue gives to the style of this poem its unique quality. There's a firm moral vision at work here, and the narrator is not afraid to let us know what he believes in. At the same time, he has such a genuine liking for people and their various silly ways that he is not going to let a censorious judgment come between them. This adds a distinct note of compassion, humour, and sociability to the narrator himself who, in some ways, emerges by the end of the General Prologue as the most interesting person on the trip.

Q. Discuss The Narrator as Writer and Pilgrim in General Prologue.

Or

Q. Discuss the role of narrator in General Prologue.

Or

Q. Does narrator in General Prologue acts as a Pilgrim? Elucidate

Introduction

The little narrator in the Canterbury Tales is an enigma. He turns his searching gaze on everyone on the pilgrimage except himself, finishing up in a rush with "Ther was also a Reve, and a Millere, A Somnour, and a Pardoner also, A Maunciple, and myself — ther were namo". Not a word about what he himself does for a living, or where he stands socially. To find out who he is and what he does, we must look for clues in the text.

We know he's not just a talker who's telling a story once, but a writer who has produced a written copy of the story, and knows it may survive to be read by others. His promise to produce a word-for-word transcript of the pilgrimage, to "reherce as ny as evere he kan Everich a word", would be a difficult promise to keep if he hadn't been taking notes the whole journey and writing up the stories to be read later. Perhaps the promise to produce a perfect copy is just hyperbole. What isn't hyperbole, however, is his caution before the Miller's Tale.

He acknowledges that his audience might "list it not yheere", not want to hear what he has to say, but then directs them in that case to "Turne over the leef and chese another tale" and to choose responsibly: "Blameth not me if that ye chese amys". His audience is not just composed of hearers but also of readers who are responsible for their own choices in a way that they could not have been if they had simply been listening while he talked.

Besides being a poet who both recites his work and writes it down, the narrator is also a pilgrim. He says it clearly: "in that seson on a day, In Southwerk at the Tabard as I lay Redy to wenden on my pilgrymage". But the fact that he is a pilgrim gives no clue to what he does in real life; beggars and kings alike could be pilgrims.

So we know the narrator not by his vocation, but by his avocations: writer and pilgrim. So what? Why not short-circuit this elabourate search for textual clues as to what the narrator does, and just equate him with Chaucer? After all, the narrator and Chaucer are both literate, so they belong to a relatively small segment of Medieval society and are likely to have had similar interests, jobs, and education. Also, to Chaucer's contemporary audience, Chaucer and the narrator could have been one; it's possible that Chaucer read his own poems aloud to the court. As Chaucer read the words of his narrator, "I was of hir felaweship anon", his listeners easily could have merged the government employee with the narrator of the poem, and Chaucer the courtier could have ridden wrapped in pilgrim's robes.

But while Chaucer's hearers may have conflated him with the narrator, we can't know exactly how. It's impossible to question an audience that's been dead for 600 years, and without knowing more about author or audience, it's dangerous to equate an author automatically with his/her characters; Shakespeare was not Hamlet, Herman Melville was not Ishmael even though Moby Dick begins "Call me Ishmael," and Mary Shelley, author of Frankenstein, was not a hodgepodge of resurrected body parts. Neither was Chaucer identical with the narrator in the Canterbury Tales. Chaucer was at various times a courtier, civil servant, ambassador, and prisoner of war, but the text doesn't indicate that the plump little narrator tagging along with the jingling, colourful group speaks as any of those. The narrator remains a writer and a pilgrim, and it is as a writer and pilgrim we must consider him.

The Writer

Calling the narrator a reciter and writer is a redundancy, because the first thing the narrator would have been prepared to do as a writer is to read out loud. Medieval writers were not only wordsmiths but also performance artists. William Woods considers the Medieval connection between silent reading and vocalization so strong that reading silently to oneself in the Middle Ages would have seemed as insufficient as reading musical notation would be to a modern music lover. Modern authors are rarely adept at communicating their works vocally, but to the Medieval author, writing a manuscript was only half the job; the other half was reciting it.

The narrator is like Chaucer in that Chaucer may have introduced the Canterbury Tales to the world by reading them out loud. While there's no absolute proof of Chaucer's performing his works aloud, there are two pieces of circumstantial evidence. The first is simply that many other authors read their own works out loud, so there's no reason to suppose Chaucer didn't. The second is more individualized. A frontispiece of Troilus and Criseyde, painted shortly after Chaucer's death, shows a man who resembles Chaucer, standing behind a lectern declaiming to an audience. Of course, though the narrator of the Canterbury Tales might have had an audience, he wouldn't necessarily have had the apparently noble one pictured in the frontispiece. Recitations appealed to the citizenry and peasants as well, and the entertainers known as jongleurs made their livings off that fact.

A significant difference between modern writers and Medieval ones is that Medieval authors made no money with their pens. Only scriveners (copyists) made money from writing. For authors, there was no market and no reading public, because the number of people able to read was relatively small. And even if a writer could have captured the imagination of every reader in England, other writers could have copied his work freely. There were no copyright laws, so every writer, including Chaucer, freely borrowed from other written works;

such borrowing benefited the public because borrowers, by retelling others' tales, made information available to a wider audience than the original authors could reach. Between the lack of readers and the lack of exclusive rights to any story, the narrator of the Canterbury Tales never could have paid his bills by selling copies of his work. Few would have bought it, and many would have copied it.

Even if literacy had been universal and copyright laws had existed, the narrator still could not have earned money by writing: there was no way to flood the market with books because there was no quick way to reproduce them. The first book printed in Europe with movable type emerged from Johann Gutenberg's press more than 50 years after Chaucer died. Until then, books had had to be written out individually by hand — a labour-intensive process that could take months per copy, and put the price of books beyond the reach of any but the most dedicated reader.

Therefore, authors had to do something besides write if they were to earn a living. Once men had become educated, they had three choices of jobs: Church, government, or, if they were free-spirited or desperate and one doesn't define "literacy" too strictly, the itinerant entertainer's life of the jongleur.

For centuries the source of literacy in England had been the Church, which not only taught its clergy to read and write, but taught them to teach others to do so. ("Clergy" here refers to male clergy. Literacy doesn't seem to have extended as uniformly through the nunneries as it did the monasteries, and nuns confined themselves to teaching their novitiates, while male clergy could instruct members of the secular world as well.) The literacy of the humbler village clerics was often barely above that of their flock, but still, until the end of the 12th century education was connected with monasteries or cathedrals so inextricably that to be a scholar was to be religious: G. G. Coulton tells of a religious official who entered religious life only to have a teaching career. "Samson, abbot of Bury St. Edmunds, told Jocelin frankly that, if he could have made bread and cheese by teaching outside, he would never have become a monk" (Medieval).

Great numbers of grade schools, universities and colleges were founded throughout England during the 14th century. Children of both sexes could receive some schooling, but higher education was reserved for males; if females continued past the grade-school level, they generally did so at home. Many grade schools and "public" (privately funded) institutions were supported by individual philanthropists, churches, and workmen's guilds. The institutions of higher learning were for the most part at least nominally under religious control, but at least the Oxford students were such dedicated drinkers and brothel-visitors that in 1355 they clashed in open warfare with the citizens of the town. Still, even in Chaucer's time, secular teachers owed their abilities to the religious masters who had taught them, or to the religious masters who had taught those masters before. One didn't have to intend to enter the Church to receive an education, but the education available was strongly flavoured by that Church.

Writers in the Church not only taught in grammar schools, cathedral schools, and universities; they also preserved old manuscripts and produced new ones. For hundreds of years the high ranking church and monastic officials (who were generally the most educated of the churchmen) acted as the wardens of books, and kept Greek and Latin alive so that ancient documents could be read. The churchman had a double intellectual duty: to protect this storehouse of wisdom, and to add to it by writing new texts on history, theology, and philosophy.

But, because of the technical demands of producing books, not every writer in the Church was a writer as we think of writers now. Rather than creating new books or even cataloguing old ones, many writers were copyists. With no copy machines, no typewriters, and no printing presses, the only way to multiply manuscripts was to copy each one out by hand. Many monks spent their lives doing just that.

They glorified God, and relieved what must have been unutterable tedium, by "illuminating," or illustrating, appropriate places in their manuscripts with ornate lettering, Biblical figures, animals, angels, and demons.

If the narrator of the Canterbury Tales were a cleric at all, the life of a copyist/monk, or of a frugal parson like the "Poor Parson" on the pilgrimage, would be his most likely niche. He would be of fairly low rank because it's unlikely that a bishop, say, would have joined such a ragtag crew, or that he would have been treated as informally by the innkeeper if he had. He's certainly placed no higher than the Priest because the innkeeper addresses even the Priest casually, reserving nominal deference for the Knight, and teases the narrator unmercifully; the only way it's conceivable for the narrator to be a high-ranking churchman is if he has first deliberately disguised himself and then left that fact out of the Canterbury Tales altogether.

Even though the Church educated writers, it did not retain every one it taught. If the narrator wasn't a cleric, he could have been one of many Englishmen of letters who clustered in the courts to become either courtiers or government officials.

A courtier's duties in the royal household were wide-ranging; for instance, a Yeoman of the King's Chamber (as Chaucer once was) was a live-in high-class servant/attendant who carried messages, went on errands, made beds, and did whatever else the chamberlain told him to. Squires (the rank Chaucer eventually achieved) might execute these same housekeeping duties, taste the King's food to test for poison, or entertain royalty, nobility and visitors by singing, harping, and telling stories.

A government official's job sometimes overlapped with that of the courtier, and also depended upon literacy — either an instant familiarity with Italian and French literature (to which he could refer in elabourate ambassadorial speeches) or an ability to write (which he would have needed in a job such as customs-official or comptroller, both of which Chaucer held).

But whether a writer became a civil servant or a courtier, he wasn't limited to legal writing. Courtiers, of course, might have needed to be expert creators of tales and poems for entertainment on long evenings. But civil servants, too, produced not only import/export documents and bills of lading, but also translations, romances, and poems for the amusement of their peers. And "for the amusement of their peers" is an important qualifier; poetry might have won a writer favor or prestige in the English court, but it's not certain that such poets were paid any money.

In fact, even Chaucer may not have earned anything for writing. Though some authorities believe that Chaucer received grants and pensions for his poems, others point out that there's no inevitable cause and effect between Chaucer's writing for the court and his receiving money from it. V. J. Scattergood deduces from the value of Chaucer's pensions (about what any competent government man would get) that Chaucer wasn't a paid writer but rather a paid public official, and that he wrote as a sideline. Again, D. W. Robertson, Jr., asserts that Chaucer "was always a member of the court first — whether as squire, customs official, or Clerk of the Works" (London,). 0

The narrator could have been, like Chaucer, a non-nobly-born citizen who became a courtier or civil servant, with the pensions and grants attached to such a position. But no matter what court connections or pensions the narrator had, he probably was not a writer with a patron. Patrons were the rich and influential who paid money — sometimes irregularly, sometimes like any other wage — and even offered room and board in their households to writers.

In return for financial support, a writer saturated his works with compliments to his patron. But although the custom of patronage was established in the French court by Chaucer's time, the English court didn't embrace the practice until well afterward, when John Lydgate was financed for his praises of Henry V. Chaucer's The Book of the Duchess did commemorate the death of John of Gaunt's wife, but even if John of Gaunt rewarded Chaucer for that particular poem, patronage probably would not have been a steady source of income for either Chaucer or the narrator.

Besides the writers in government and religion, another kind of writer/reciter existed. The jongleur, "half-minstrel, half-buffoon" (Coulton, Medieval), was a travelling entertainer for occasions such as funerals and weddings. Whether or not he could actually write, he had to be familiar with the classical, romantic, and popular sources that informed Medieval literature, and able to rapidly adapt and recite stories from them at will. He had to be good at gauging his audience, too; he subsisted by passing the hat after his performances, and a performance that didn't please didn't pay.

Jongleurs drifted from house to house and village to village, pursued by the imprecations of clergymen, who regarded them as ministers of Satan. It's unlikely that the narrator is this impoverished kind of entertainer. He has enough money to stay at inns during his pilgrimage (no easy task on the usual income of a jongleur). And though Bailey teases the narrator remarkably freely, he does not describe the narrator as a jongleur. Bailey does not say the that the narrator is ragged or a crowd-pleaser, or that he pesters people for handouts. Rather, Bailey sketches the narrator as a small, silent, doll-like man who stares at the ground as if to search for rabbits, and who probably shrinks from the very kind of hearty cheer Bailey thrusts upon him.

> And thanne at erst he looked upon me,
> And seyde thus: "What man artow?" quod he;
> "Thou lookest as thou woldest fynde an hare,
> For evere upon the ground I se thee stare.
> "Approche neer; and look up murily.
> Now war yow, sires, and lat this man have place!
> He in the waast is shape as wel as I;
> This were a popet in an arm t'embrace
> For any womman, smal and fair of face.
> He semeth elvyssh by his contenaunce,

For unto no wight dooth he daliaunce."

The narrator could indeed have been a courtier or a cleric (albeit not very high-ranking in either profession), but here on the road he is quiet, teasable, merely one of a crowd of pilgrims. And that's the second part of what the narrator does. Not only is the narrator a writer; he's also "Redy to wenden". He's a pilgrim.

The Pilgrim

Like saying prayers or giving alms, a pilgrimage was a devotion to God. It was a road trip to one of various holy places, planned for one or more reasons. The pilgrim omight have been ordered by a religious leader to make a pilgrimage as a penance for sin; omight have vowed, in the midst of sickness or trouble, to go on a pilgrimage as a kind of bargain with God to "buy" better times; omight have survived sickness or trouble and wanted to thank God more tangibly than with prayers; or omight simply have wanted to go on a journey.

In theory, the purpose of a pilgrimage was religious. In practice, especially by Chaucer's time, pilgrimages could be excursions with a sense of religious duty scarcely more, and a noise level scarcely less, than a vanload of students setting out for spring break.

Despite a handful of devout companions, the narrator has joined a rowdy bunch: the Summoner drapes himself in flowers and food, the Pardoner is a shyster, the Friar is a lecher, and at one point the Cook is so drunk that he falls off his horse, requiring "greet showvyng bothe to and fro To lift hym up". Even the Miller's "baggepipe," with which "be broughte us out of towne", is noisily inappropriate to play on a holy trip, or so one complaint (by a Lollard called Thorpe, discussed below) would have us believe. Bagpipes at the beginning of a journey are the Medieval version of slapping a raucous cassette into a car's tape player, turning the volume up, and roaring onto the highway.

Despite extremely secular distractions, a pilgrimage was supposed to pay a debt to, or fulfill a contract with, God.

Making a pilgrimage entailed much more than worshipping at the destination: travelling itself was usually so difficult that the journey itself was privation for the Lord's sake. The expense, danger, and time involved in a pilgrimage of course increased dramatically when the pilgrim travelled overseas to the most holy of holy places, Rome or Jerusalem, but even a local pilgrimage like the Canterbury trip had great potential for unpleasantness and danger.

The dangers of travel began with the daunting logistics of simply getting from point to point. Roads were not paved outside London; beyond the city gates, the flat, wide strip we think of as a road degenerated into the weedy ruts of cart-tracks, and those cart-tracks degenerated into mires. In 1499, bad road conditions actually killed one unfortunate glove-maker who had started out at night from Leighton Buzzard to Aylesbury on a horse laden with panniers of gloves. In the dark, neither rider nor horse saw a huge hole that had been dug in the middle of the road by a miller who had needed some clay to repair his mill. The pit that the miller left had filled with rain, and both rider and horse fell in and were drowned (Coulton, Medieval -). Though the records don't indicate that this particular kind of disaster was common, or that clay pits dotted England's roads, travel was quite dangerous enough anyway. Besides being so dark at night that it was indeed possible for travellers to blunder into danger, even during daylight travel wasn't easy. Bridges and roads were muddy, rocky, desolate, and so subject to ruinous bad weather that maintaining them was a charity and a duty to God.

Bridge and road maintenance was charitable and holy because it mitigated the terrible problems travellers had to face, and therefore relieved human suffering. Since maintenance work was charitable and holy, who better to do it than monks? Their tasks were sometimes shared by merchants, who had a financial interest in reliable transportation. But though monks and merchants worked diligently to serve God and their purses, travel could not be made entirely easy. Rain turned dirt roads into soup; the mud caked walkers' shoes and spattered riders' clothes; if streams had no bridges, sometimes the shallow spots were not obvious, so people and horses blundered into deep water; when streams did have bridges, the bridges could collapse; wolves lurked in the forests, waiting for stragglers; and, generally, the outdoors often got closer to the traveller than the traveller wanted it to.

Even if travellers could keep Nature at a safe distance, they still had to deal with fellow humans, including convicted thieves and murderers sentenced to walk the main road to the closest seaport for passage out of England. Any offender so sentenced had to dress like "a felon condemned to death — a long, loose white tunic, bare feet, and a wooden cross in his hand to mark that he was under protection of Holy Church." (Coulton, Medieval) But though these criminals were thus easily identified, nobody accompanied them to be sure they kept wearing their felon's robes, behaved well on the journey, or reached the seaport at all. A criminal might set up an anonymous life in another town, become a mercenary soldier, or live in the wilds by scavenging, hunting, and preying on travellers.

Not every dangerous person on the road was a white-robed felon. Some were employed by the most powerful people in the area. Any man or woman who could afford the wages could hire retainers to defend his/her administration, land, or person, but protectors often became a kind of goon squad or mini-Mafia that robbed, vandalized, raped, and assaulted. A traveller set upon by these brigands had no legal recourse, because the local authorities either supported the brigands or were intimidated into silence. This practice of employing quasi-hit-men was called "maintenance," and was so widespread in Chaucer's day that both Edward III and Richard II constantly issued edicts against it. The number and frequency of edicts shows how little attention anyone paid to them. Townspeople and travellers alike feared maintenance, but at least the townspeople knew when and where to be on the lookout. Travellers could be taken by surprise.

Yet despite bad weather, dangerous roads, marauders, and other perils, the pilgrims of the Canterbury Tales are so unconcerned that they tell stories. Why aren't they worried? Because these pilgrims are dangerous. Setting out from the Tabard Inn, fully half are bristling with blades, are experienced brawlers, or are accustomed to bloodletting. The group includes:

The Knight, armored, armed, and fresh from battle; oHis son, who at an early age has already fought in several cavalry expeditions; oThe efficient, silent Woodsman who is a walking armoury: arrows, bow, sword, and dagger;

The Monk, who, even if not a fighter, is a huntsman; oThe Friar, whose neck "strong was as a champioun" and who has a collection of knives to hand out to pretty matrons; oThe Frankeleyn, who carries an "anlaas" (a broad, double-edged dagger that tapers to a sharp point); oThe Haberdasshere, Carpenter, Webbe, Dyere, and Tapycer, who own "knyves... chaped... al with silver"; oThe Shipman, who carries a dagger under his arm and dispatches losers quickly, sending them "hoom to every lond"; oThe Miller, who carries a sword, is a champion wrestler, and can rip a door off its hinges or smash through it with his head; oThe Reve, armed with "a rusty blade"; oAnd the innkeeper Harry Bailey, who boasts, "I am perilous with knyf in honde".

Even the Wife of Bath reminisces about her free-for-alls. "I with my fest so took him on the cheke That in our fyr he fil backward adoun. And he up stirte as dooth a wood leoun, And with his fest he smoot me on the heed That in the floor I lay as I were deed.... And neer he cam, and kneled faire adoun,... I hitte hym on the cheke". She's a strong, dirty fighter: she punches hard enough to knock a man into fire, and when he returns the blow, she plays possum until she can get a good shot at him.

Nor are the other pilgrims pushovers. The Summoner "quook for ire" at the Friar, the Friar insults the Summoner as "a rennere up and doun With mandementz for fornicacioun", the Cook "wax wrooth and wraw" at the

Manciple... this group is a 14th-century Magnificent Seven.

The narrator wasn't an original member of this group; he joins them after they arrive at the Tabard. He had started on his journey alone. But he doesn't fit the picture of the stereotypical solitary pilgrim, who travelled on foot, wearing a traditional gown or hair shirt and carrying a staff topped with a shepherd's hook or a cross. Such pilgrims were protected without weaponry; the robe and staff stated clearly that God's eye was on them. Human predators must have respected the robe and staff at least occasionally, because some professional pilgrims spent their lives on the road travelling alone from shrine to shrine, and couldn't have spent much time in solitary humility if doing so always meant being beaten, robbed, and left to die.

It would have been suicidally foolish to start out alone on a journey with neither a weapon nor an obvious sign of God's patronage, and the narrator doesn't seem to possess either. He doesn't say he carries a weapon himself, and we can be sure that he's not dressed in the attention-getting garb of the professional pilgrim because Harry Bailey teases him unmercifully about his appearance but doesn't mention the narrator's clothes. So with no spiritual or physical weaponry, the narrator wasn't intending to travel alone the whole way to Canterbury. He certainly ingratiates himself with the group quickly enough — between its arrival "at nyght" and the time that "the sonne was to reste", he is "of their felawshipe anon". And since the group includes people as ill-assorted as a Prioress, a Miller, and a group of tradesmen rich enough to bring their own cook, this pilgrimage (despite warnings issued in Medieval travel books against making friends with travelling strangers) seems to have made a practice of picking up stragglers.

So the fierce, armed pilgrims, fortified with weapons, noise, jokes, and religious purpose, start out from the Tabard. It's unclear how long they spend travelling, but a four-day trip would mean they could keep a reasonable pace and still have time to argue, jostle for position on the road, and retrieve the Cook when he falls off his horse. Four travel days from Southwark (just outside London) to Canterbury could have been apportioned like this: o1st day: Southwark to Dartford (15 miles) o2nd day: Dartford to Rochester (14 miles) o3rd day: Rochester to Ospringe (18 miles) o4th day: Ospringe to Canterbury (9 miles)

(Timetable from Coulton, Chaucer 154-168; distances are my approximations from Jennett's map of the Pilgrim's Way, facing 296.)

This well-used route was dotted with inns and places to hire horses. One could ride a horse from Southwark to Rochester for twelvepence, and another horse from Rochester to Canterbury for the same price. But even if travellers owned their horses, travellers (and horses) needed food and places to sleep, and therein lay the next travail of travel: night-time lodging.

Inns were usually set up with the sleeping quarters on the second floor, directly above the dining room, and smells and noise could filter up through the floorboards. A fifteenth-century manuscript (Coulton, Chaucer,) illustrates the casual way strangers slept naked side by side on featherbeds or straw mattresses, or on straw pallets on the floor. The straw in the bedchamber and the food in the kitchen so often attracted bedbugs, fleas, lice, and rodents that travellers addressed the issue as matter-of-factly as modern road manuals warn of speed traps. J. J. Jusserand mentions a 14th-century manual of French conversation that includes a sample exchange between an innkeeper and a potential customer.

The servant sent forward to engage the room utters the fond hope "that there are no fleas, nor bugs, nor other vermin." "No, sir, please God," replies the host, "for I make bold that you shall be well and comfortably lodged here — save that there is a great peck of rats and mice."

Lodging was not only uncomfortable but also expensive, especially when combined with meals. The 1331 expense account of six travellers from Oxford to Durham is instructive. One night's food, horse fodder, beds, fuel to heat the bedroom, and candles to light it, cost each traveller "about four times a ploughman's daily wage" (Woods -). However, every pilgrim in the Canterbury Tales seems to have brought money to spare. They agree to Harry Bailey's suggestion that they all chip in after their return to buy the best storyteller a supper at the Tabard. This is a shrewd move on Bailey's part, for he isn't giving the supper away, just spreading the cost among himself and the 30 paying members of the party in such a way that they will be tempted to buy supper from him for themselves as well. After that, who knows? Some pilgrims may then eat and drink until it's too late to start back home, and must spend yet another night at the Tabard at still more profit to Bailey. No matter who gets the free meal, there are two winners in this bargain: the storytelling champion, and Bailey himself.

Pilgrims could spend hefty sums for food and lodging on the way through town, but local residents weren't always happy to see the pilgrims coming. In 1410, a Lollard called Thorpe complained of how disruptive pilgrimages could be. His complaint should not be taken as the last word on the subject, because Lollards disagreed with the religion that sent pilgrims through town in the first place. Still, Thorpe's vivid description could have come straight out of the pages of Chaucer, from the Miller's pipes to the Monk's bells to the Pardoner and Summoner as they sing "Com hider, love, to me!": I know well that when divers men and women will goe thus after their own willes, and finding out one pilgrimage, they will ordaine with them before, to have with them both men and women that can well sing wanton songes, and some other pilgrimes will have with them bagge pipes; so that everie towne that they come through, what with the noise of their singing, and with the sound of their piping, and with the jangling of their Canterburie bels, and with the barking out of dogges after them, that they make more noise, then if the king came there away, with all his clarions, and many other minstrels.

(Coulton, Chaucer -.)

Religious or irreligious, holy journey or pleasure trip,

the pilgrimage eventually ended at the shrine: a church, monastery, abbey, or convent that purportedly could heal body or soul. The shrine's curative powers derived either from its location — usually where a miracle had occurred — or from something it possessed. This possession could be a piece of religious artwork or, more importantly, a relic, which was a tangible scrap of anything connected with a holy person or event. The list of relics at various shrines reads like a combination junk shop and natural disaster: it's a jumble of the property, bodies, and severed limbs of the devout. Canterbury possessed the following:

Thomas Becket's coffined body ohis severed head, which the privileged could kiss ohis haircloth underclothes oa jewelled statue of the Virgin, which was said to have spoken to Becket when he prayed to it othe whole arms (not weaponry, but body parts) of eleven saints including St. George ofragments of the arms of two other saints oAaron's rod (Rome also claimed to own the original) ofragments of the Holy Sepulchre, the manger, and the rock on which the Cross stood; othe column to which Christ was tied to be whipped othe stone on which Christ stood before the Ascension othe bed of the Virgin owool woven by the Virgin oa piece of the clày from which Adam was made

Of all the English shrines, Canterbury was the most enduringly popular. Others went in and out of favor as they acquired different attractions, but Canterbury was a constant draw. Its resident saint, Thomas Becket, was murdered in Canterbury Cathedral on December 29, 1170, by four of Henry II's knights. In penance for this murder, Henry II journeyed to the shrine, thus initiating the tradition of other British kings' doing the same; this royal luster and Becket's dramatic martyrdom attracted thousands of pilgrims annually.

Canterbury Cathedral lived up to the pilgrims' expectations with an extremely theatrical presentation of the blessed relics. The Cathedral itself was good theater, because upon entering it, the first thing the pilgrim saw was an awe-inspiring series of steps with Becket's coffin looming distantly and magnificently at the top. After recovering from this sight, the pilgrim would be shown various relics. Which relics were shown depended on the rank of the pilgrim, with rarer relics exhibited as the rank increased, but everyone saw the bejeweled statue of the Virgin. Then the pilgrim would ascend the steps to the altar, perhaps crawling on his or her knees. At the altar, the coffin supported on arches held the remains of Thomas Becket. Derek Brewer describes the dramatic ritual that attended the viewing of the shrine: sick and lame pilgrims were allowed to place themselves between these [arches], rubbing their afflicted limbs against the marble which held the body. The shrine proper was at first invisible, concealed by a wooden canopy; at a sign this was raised, and the shrine appeared blazing with gold and innumerable jewels. While the pilgrims knelt, an officer of the monastery came forward and pointed out the various jewels with a white wand, naming them in English and, for the benefit of foreigners, in French, telling their values and the marvellous magical properties which were normally attributed to jewels in the Middle Ages.

After the official finished the lecture, the wooden canopy was again lowered over the shrine. The pilgrims were then free to pray and exit past an offering-box strategically located at the foot of the stairs. Religious demands on the pilgrim's purse continued long after the offering: outside the Cathedral, souvenirs were available for purchase. Each shrine sold a distinctive style of medallion or amulet, made of lead, silver, or pewter, and meant to be sewn onto clothing or worn as a necklace. To anyone familiar with the symbols of the various shrines, it would have been immediately obvious where any pilgrim had journeyed.

Canterbury: St. Thomas, miniature jar oSt. James's Compostella: shell oAmiens: head of St. John the Baptist oRocamadour: Holy Virgin oRome: a "vernicle," or reproduction of the cloth with which St. Veronica wiped Christ's face when he was on his way to Calvary. The cloth miraculously received the imprint of Christ's features. (A vernicle was sewn to the cap of Chaucer's Pardoner.)

Canterbury sold two styles of amulet. The little lead or silver jar sometimes held holy water. The St. Thomas was a sketch in lead of a full-face view of the mitered head of Becket, in a circular frame or against a background of decorated arches that provided plenty of open spaces through which to pass needle and thread when sewing it to cloth.

If the pilgrim wanted something besides religious souvenirs, the town of Canterbury could provide it. If a pilgrim needed to eat but didn't want to stop at an inn, a long row of street stalls sold food and drink. And if the sight of the relics within the Cathedral hadn't been enough, the pilgrim could see more relics outside. Local residents, or itinerants like Chaucer's Pardoner, sometimes passed off common objects as relics, selling glimpses of the objects — or sometimes the objects themselves. Chaucer's Pardoner is an effective salesman with a good stock in trade:

For in his male he hadde a pilwe-beer,
Which that he seyde was Oure Lady veyl;
He seyde he hadde a gobet of the seyl
That Seint Peter hadde, whan that he wente
Upon the see, til Jhesu Crist him hente.
He hadde a croys of latoun ful of stones,
And in a glas he hadde pigges bones.
But with thise relikes, whan that he fond
A povre person dwellynge upon lond,
Upon a day he gat hym moore moneye
Than that the person gat in monthes tweye;
And thus, with feyned flaterye and japes,
He made the person and the peple his apes.

Suitably purified, decorated, gorged, and entertained, the pilgrims would retrace the path homeward, still travelling together. Harry Bailey assumes that nobody will depart from the group until after they reach the Tabard.

ech of yow,
In this viage shal telle tales tweye
To Caunterbury-ward,...
And homward he shal tellen othere two...

And which of yow that bereth him best of alle —...
Shal have a soper at oure aller cost
Heere in this place...
Whan that we come agayn fro Caunterbury.

Bailey's game depends on everyone's returning to the Tabard together. Company would lessen the dangers and increase the potential pleasures on the second half of the journey as well as on the first; it would have been common sense to travel both ways in a group.

So the little narrator is a writer and a pilgrim, but that still doesn't tell us what his actual job was. He's not indubitably Chaucer, or a civil servant, or a courtier, or a cleric, or in any obvious career path; he's not even labelled by his marital status as is the Wife of Bath. The only thing that the narrator indubitably is, is the man who went on an ordinary pilgrimage and then preserved the memory of it in an extraordinary way. But perhaps that, after all, is his job. The job of entertainer existed before the job of Reeve or of Summoner, and has outlived them as well.

As an entertainer, the narrator isn't necessarily a member of the ragtag class of jongleurs, just as he isn't necessarily a courtier passing the long winter evenings away, or a cleric stealing time from recopying the Book of Matthew to scribble his own words. He is son to the Old English scop, the honourable minstrel-poet who entertained the Anglo-Saxons; he's brother to Scheherazade, to Sherlock Holmes's Doctor Watson, even to Uncle Remus — any fictional retailer of others' stories.

Ultimately this narrator's spare-time amusement is his full-time profession. All the other characters tell stories only if there's a supper to be won, but the narrator tells and tells even if there's nothing to tempt him. His entire narration of the Canterbury Tales is not an entry in the pilgrimage's storytelling contest, because he couches not only the stories but the pilgrimage itself in the past tense. Presumably the pilgrimage is over, along with the contest, by the time he starts telling about it. But even though the journey and the free supper are both a memory, he still revels in stories. For him, and for us, that is enough.

Q. Discuss the presence of Carnival Imagery in General Prologue.

Or

Q. How does Chaucer implements imagery in Genral Prologue.

Chaucer introduced in the General Prologue and in some of the tales a side of medieval culture now unfamiliar, the carnival world of medieval popular life, which the Soviet scholar Mikhail Bakhtin discerned as the true context of Rabelais. The tradition is still known to us in certain survivals of celebrations and images—carnivals and circuses, clown faces and such. Carnival imagery is first placed before us in the General Prologue to prepare us for what follows in the tales. How different this is from the Decameron: Boccaccio in his prologue and frame made his ten young ladies and gentlemen examples of perfect decorum, and permitted the carnival world of buffoonery and grotesquerie to appear only in the stories, where we get wild images of an abbess throwing her lover's trousers over her head thinking they're her wimple, or of a lecherous monk led into the public square on a chain disguised as a wild man and there recognized and apprehended, images of popular medieval folk comedy, mocking and overblown. In Chaucer such images, though they appear in the stories too, are associated with the pilgrims themselves, whose behavior on the pilgrimage is itself carnivalesque.

This medieval idiom belonged to fold culture; it was not "theater." In the modern world clowns and fools and jesters are played by actors, but in medieval life they were real crackbrains. "(They) remained," writes Bakhtin, "fools and clowns always and wherever they made their appearance"; by the same token madmen, dwarfs, and blind men were objects of fascination and mirth. There was a whole world of carnival with its own activities and tastes, its own sensibility and imagery, that survived in some places many centuries after the Middle Ages. In 1788 the poet Goethe described in his Italienishe Reise the carnival in Rome, preceding Ash Wednesday, no doubt an actual survival of medieval traditions though changed in many ways. The last vestiges survive still, fragmented in grotesque art, circuses with their "freaks" and spectacles, "amusement parks," and in such festivals as Halloween or, closer to the medieval tradition, Mardi Gras. In medieval times carnival was, according to Bakhtin's analysis, "the people's second like, "festive, parodic, egalitarian. The carnival spirit, in such medieval traditions as the Feast of Fools, mocked and degraded official life: it put laughter temporarily in place of official seriousness. To medieval people official life meant fear, humiliation, submission to the whims of those in power; the carnival spirit, in reaction, cultivated the misshapen and incongruous, combining images of birth and life with images of death, disfigurement or dismemberment.

It is not accurate to think of carnival only as a temporary and permitted reaction of the underprivileged/ Bakhtin, as a Marxist, over-emphasizes this side, but he recognizes the positive side that celebrated human life per se. The best description of carnival from this view point was made by a Christian writer, W.H. Auden, who was it in juxtaposition against the transcendent and eschatological aspects of Christianity:

Carnival celebrates the unity of our human race as mortal creatures, who come into this world and depart from it without our consent, who must eat, drink, defecate, belch and break with in order to live, and procreate if our species is to survive. Our feelings about this are ambiguous. To us as individuals, it is a cause for rejoicing to know that we are not alone, that all of us, irrespective of age or sex or rank or talent, are in the same boat. As unique persons, on the other hand, all of us are resentful that an exception cannot be made in our own case. We oscillate between wishing we were unreflective animals and wishing we were disembodied spirits, for in either case we should not be problematic to ourselves.

The Carnival solution of this ambiguity is to laugh, for laughter is simultaneously a protest and an acceptance. During

Carnival, all social distinctions are suspended, even that of sex. Young men dress up as girls, young girls as boys. The escape from social personality is symbolized by the wearing of masks. The oddity of the human animal expresses itself through the grotesque—false noses, huge bellies and buttocks, farcical imitations of childbirth and copulation. The protest element in laughter takes the form of mock aggression....In medieval carnivals, parodies of the rituals of the Church were common, but what Lewis Carroll said of literary parody—"One can only parody a poem one admires" —is true of all parody. One can only blaspheme if one believes. The world of Laughter is much more closely related to world of Worship and Prayer than either is to the everyday, secular world of Work, for both are worlds in which we all are equal....

This explains what is, after all, the preponderant aspect of The Canterbury Tales until its end. The General Prologue from the start gives attention to almost microscopic details of physical life and the body. Springtime is represented with the microscopic image of sap flowing in twigs and leaves. We are drawn up close to people's faces; the Prioress, though in a nun's habit, displays a graceful nose, gray eves, a small mouth soft and red, a broad forehead. Noses and mouth, Bakhtin tells us, dominated the medieval popular image of the body, whereas in modern times expressive features like the eyes dominate; even with the Lady Prioress the nose is mentioned first.

We are drawn up to their skin and facial hair—the white skin of the Friar's neck, the Merchant's forked beard, the Franklin's white beard and red complexion, the Shipman's browned skin. The Cook's physical appearance is represented with a single grotesque detail, and open sore on his knee. Some physical details, as we move down the social scale, have significance in the light of medieval science: the Wife's being "gat-toothed," it is said, signifies a lascivious character, the Miller's physical traits show him to be of sanguine complexion, the Reeve's of a choleric one. The dominant detail about the Monk as we encounter him is the jingling bells on his horses, for the image of bells always appears among what are termed "popular festive" images.

The Miller, the first of the "churls" introduced at the end of the General Prologue, is a generic image of carnival man, with gaping mouth and prominent nose. The Miller has on the tip or bridge of his nose a wart or mole, on which is a tuft of hairs, "Red as the bristles of a sowe's eares" (line 556), and his nose has black, wide nostrils. "his mouth," we learn, "as great was a great furnais" —the conventional carnival image of a hell-mouth. Of the last pilgrims described, the Summoner with his "fire-red" inflamed face has a form of acne possibly associated in the popular mind (as in medical authorities) with leprosy—"whelkes white" (great white pustules), and "knobbes" (boils or running sores) on his cheeks. Reeking of garlic, onions, and leeks, he incongruously wears a large garland of flowers on his head. And with him rides the Pardoner, not so much loathsome as sexually anomalous, spooky: his hair, "yellow as wax," hangs over his shoulders, thin and in strips, and he has glaring eyes like a hare's, conjectures that he is "a gelding or a mare," a castrated male or a hermaphrodite.

This grotesque element in the imagery of the General Prologue prepares us for the carnival spirit of the pilgrimage itself. The pilgrimage setsËm the tavern in Southwark, a festive banquet setting, and proceeds to Saint Thomas 'a Watering, a place of execution. Against this menacing background, the Knight is chosen by lot to tell the first tale; the Host then calls on the Monk as the person next highest in rank, but the Miller drunkenly cries out "in Pilate's voice," swearing "By armes and by blood and bones!": As carnival man the Miller behaves in the carnival idiom: his drunkenness, his boisterousness, his oaths by the parts of Christ's body are all characteristics. He swears he will tell his tale or go his way, and the Host in resignation says, "Tell on, a devil way! / Thou art a fool." Chaucer even takes occasion to make a brief, ironic apology (line 3167): he will, he regrets to say, have to tell the churl's tale or else falsify his "mattere." Addressing us directly, he assures us he does not speak with evil intent. If we don't care to hear it, "Turn over the leaf and chese another tale" — and don't blame me, he adds, if you choose amiss.

Some dozen of the tales are an extension of the carnival spirit introduced through particular pilgrims. There is parody of official culture in Sir Thopas, the Nun's Priest's Tale, and elsewhere. The carnival imagery in the tales goes beyond that of the General Prologue—we get gross images of excrement, fornication, and farting (in the Reeve's and Miller's tales and others), of great oaths especially by the parts of God's body (as in the Host's speeches or the Pardoner's sermon), of a comic devil (in the Friar's Tale), of dismemberment (in relics, the true ones of Saint Thomas 'a Becket or the Pardoner's false ones), of lechery (in the Merchant's Tale and elsewhere), drunkenness (in the Cook's fall from his horse in the Manciple's Prologue. And gluttony: the banquet image of popular-festive forms, where gluttony triumphs, notable in Rabelais, hovers over the whole of The Canterbury Tales: the prize supper at the Tabard Inn, planned at the beginning, is the pilgrims' ostensible goal. When the work actually ends just outside Canterbury, the last image in the last tale, the Manciple's, is the key carnival image of the gaping mouth—this one, very appropriate to the end of a tale-tell game, with a wagging tongue.

Such imagery stands out more in Chaucer's work than in the Decameron. While Boccaccio did of course include tales of official culture, of pathos and heroism and patient suffering, Chaucer included a broader spectrum: from him we have a romance of aristocratic idealism, a tale of allegory, even a prose "meditation" on penance—he shows more of official life. And while Boccaccio altogether excluded the carnivalesque from the refined company of his prologue, Chaucer lets it emerge by stages or degrees among the pilgrims until it becomes preponderant.

But in the end Chaucer turned the carnival tradition on its head. There was a whole side of it that he pointedly mitigated, what Bakhtin calls the "material bodily lower stratum." Such imagery descended from head to bowels or genitals, from earth to hell; it involved fights and beatings, swabbings of the body, debasement. "Carnival celebrates the destruction of the old and the birth of the new world—the new year, the new spring, the new kingdom," Bakhtin observed. The material world was always the focus: the future lay in the next generation, not the other world, and death was viewed as the other side of birth. Carnival showed the defeat of fear by laughter: its images of hell—as in Bosch and the elder Breughel—were grotesque, absurd, and extreme. The idiom produced gross contradictions—mixtures of praise and abuse, the praise of folly, images of things upside down, inside out, bottoms up. In The Canterbury Tales the material world is the focus and the lower stratum is by no means ignored.

We have the "mooning" or "bum-baring" in the Miller's Tale, elsewhere the upside-down abuse of official life and religious custom, a comic devil and comic hell in the Friar's Tale, excremental imagery in the Summoner's Prologue (the friars' place in hell is in the devil's ass), possibly a scatological satire of Pentecost at its close, where a fart is to be divided in twelve, and the Host's praise of Bacchus at the end of the Manciple's Tale. The last tales before the Parson's meditation may present images of this kind: The Canon's Yeoman's Tale, about false and swindling alchemy and the impossibility of turning base metals into gold is and upside-down image of transcendental and eschatological ideas, and the Manciple's Tale is about the debasement of language, the very stuff of which the work is made.

But The Canterbury Tales ends with the image of the cathedral on the horizon, symbol of the Heavenly Jerusalem. It is the reverse of the banquet image of carnival tradition, the prize supper at the Tabard that has until now been the presumed destination. Carnival mocks official culture on certain licensed occasions; but pilgrimage reverses forever the pilgrim's sense of his true destination and ultimate home.

The material world is the focus and the lower stratum is by no means ignored. We have the "mooning" or "bum-baring" in the Miller's Tale, elsewhere the upside-down abuse of official life and religious custom, a comic devil and comic hell in the Friar's Tale, excremental imagery in the Summoner's Prologue (the friars' place in hell is in the devil's ass), possibly a scatological satire of Pentecost at its close, where a fart is to be divided in twelve, and the Host's praise of Bacchus at the end of the Manciple's Tale. The last tales before the Parson's meditation may present images of this kind: The Canon's Yeoman's Tale, about false and swindling alchemy and the impossibility of turning base metals into gold is and upside-down image of transcendental and eschatological ideas, and the Manciple's Tale is about the debasement of language, the very stuff of which the work is made.

But The Canterbury Tales ends with the image of the cathedral on the horizon, symbol of the Heavenly Jerusalem. It is the reverse of the banquet image of carnival tradition, the prize supper at the Tabard that has until now been the presumed destination. Carnival mocks official culture on certain licensed occasions; but pilgrimage reverses forever the pilgrim's sense of his true destination and ultimate home.

Q. Comment on The Nun Prioress of the General Prologue.

Or

Q. Chaucer describes the nun in the opposite way. Does he do it intentionally? Discuss

In the reading "The Canterbury Tales" by Geoffrey Chaucer, there is a detailed description about the nun Prioress in the "General Prologue". Chaucer uses physical and spiritual relationships to show the characteristics of a person. When we see the nun in relationship to other characters, for example the Knight, Chaucer makes the reader see two types of people. On one hand, the nun who gives much importance to minor things. On the other hand, the Knight who gives much importance to things that really matter. To describe how the nun was Chaucer writes with irony the description of the nun Prioress, everything that Chaucer says about her means the opposite.

Chaucer describes a nun Prioress called Madame Eglantine. A nun should be modest, had to have poverty, and pity. Chaucer describes the nun in the opposite way to show us, how the nun Prioress had all the characteristics that a nun should not have. She was a nun modest, well educated and with good manners. She also had tender feelings, and a strong love for God and his creations. The author connects the relationship between how she sang and with her nose. He is sarcastic when relating her physical and spiritual beauty. "She sang the divine service well, entuning it in her nose in a most seemly way." She was a well educated person, who reflects her manners in her language and with her actions. "She spoke French well and properly" in this quote properly means with good manners, not with slang words or with the popular language used in France. "For the French of Paris was unknown to her." All of these characteristics show how the nun Prioress was focused on things that should not be important for a nun.

Among her minor things, the nun in the tale actions was cautious and splendid. Her manners were unique, and practiced with perfection. "Her table manners were admirable: she never let a morsel fall from her lips, nor wet her fingers too deeply in the sauce; daintily she carried a morsel to her lips, taking care that no drop should fall on her breast: she took much pleasure in proper etiquette." The author makes us understand that her behavior with such perfection was not because she was obligated to act in this way. It was because having manners and being educated gave her joy, something that is wrong for a nun. Having manners for her was like giving a candy to a little boy. Also the author describes with a lot of details her manners to show us how important her behavior was for herself, an a nun's behavior should be reflected on other people not on herself.

All of Chaucer's nun actions as behaving and acting as nun were superb, in an ironic way. Her physical description was described with perfection nun showing the irony in these minor details. "Her nose well-shaped; her eyes bright as glass; her mouth very small, and soft and read; an indeed she had a fine forehead." The description of her beauty reflects how she was from her inside. The author gives great importance to small things to makes us see how the nun Prioress was. One example is when he wrote about her fine forehead. To most people the forehead is not an important aspect of the physical characteristics of a person, only in some cases where the forehead is tremendously big or very small. However, the author talks about her fine forehead with sarcasm because he is telling us how this small characteristic, were reflected so well in the nun Prioress. Every small detail is what made her perfection as a whole, perfection meaning the opposite.

One thing the nun had that showed irony in her behavior, was her tender feelings. The author is sarcastic when he uses the example of her feelings for a mouse and that she was so charitable and full of pity. "She was so charitable and so full of pity that she would weep if she saw a mouse caught in a trap and dead or bleeding." Another example that illustrates the irony and how the author was sarcastic is by showing her big actions on animals rather than to human beings. "She had a few small dogs that she fed with roast meat, or milk and fine bread; but she wept indeed if one of them died, or if someone hit it smartly with a stick-she was feeling tender heart."

This example illustrates how soft she was, and also that she gave great importance to little things rather than great importance to big ones. The Knight is one example of a person in the general prologue, who gave importance to great things, which fought for big reasons. In contrast the author illustrates the nun Prioress, as a person with the opposite view of the world. The knight would never give better food to some dogs rather that to the people who needed it. On the other hand the nun gave great importance and attention to her dog, or a mouse that was bleeding, rather than to people. That is why the author does not give examples of the nun helping people, or doing well.

Q. Draft a Character Sketch of Chaucer's Knight in General Prologue.

Or

Q. Why is Knight an important character in Chaucer's General Prologue?

Geoffrey Chaucer's Canterbury Tales, written in approximately 1385, is a collection of twenty-four stories ostensibly told by various people who are going on a religious pilgrimage to Canterbury Cathedral from London, England. Prior to the actual tales, however, Chaucer offers the reader a glimpse of fourteenth century life by way of what he refers to as a General Prologue. In this prologue, Chaucer introduces all of the characters who are involved in this imaginary journey and who will tell the tales. Among the characters included in this introductory section is a knight. Chaucer initially refers to the knight as "a most distinguished man" (l. 43) and, indeed, his sketch of the knight is highly complimentary.

The knight, Chaucer tells us, "possessed/Fine horses, but he was not gaily dressed" (ll. 69-70). Indeed, the knight is dressed in a common shirt which is stained "where his armor had left mark" (l. 72). That is, the knight is "just home from service" (l. 73) and is in such a hurry to go on his pilgrimage that he has not even paused before beginning it to change his clothes.

The knight has had a very busy life as his fighting career has taken him to a great many places. He has seen military service in Egypt, Lithuania, Prussia, Russia, Spain, North Africa, and Asia Minor where he "was of [great] value in all eyes (l. 63). Even though he has had a very successful and busy career, he is extremely humble: Chaucer maintains that he is "modest as a maid" (l. 65). Moreover, he has never said a rude thing to anyone in his entire life (cf., ll. 66-7).

Clearly, the knight possesses an outstanding character. Chaucer gives to the knight one of the more flattering descriptions in the General Prologue. The knight can do no wrong: he is an outstanding warrior who has fought for the true faith—according to Chaucer—on three continents. In the midst of all this contenton, however, the knight remains modest and polite. The knight is the embodiment of the chivalric code: he is devout and courteous off the battlefield and is bold and fearless on it.

In America, we would like to think that we have many people in our society who are like Chaucer's knight. During this nation's altercation with Iraq in 2003, the concept of the modest but effective soldier captured the imagination of the country. Indeed, the nation's journalists in many ways attempted to make General in command of our forces a latter day knight. The general was made to appear as a fearless leader who really was a regular guy under the uniform.

It would be nice to think that a person such as the knight could exist in America today. The fact of the matter is that it is unlikely that people such as the knight existed even in the fourteenth century. As he does with all of his characters, Chaucer is producing a stereotype in creating the knight. As noted above, Chaucer, in describing the knight, is describing a chivalric ideal. The history of the Middle Ages demonstrates that this ideal rarely was manifested in actual conduct. Nevertheless, in his description of the knight, Chaucer shows the reader the possibility of the chivalric way of life.

Q. Discuss The Canterbury Tales as Framed Narratives.

Or

Q. Explanations of the function of the Prologue and frame of the Canterbury Tales which fall back on the Gothic nature of the late medieval period may to some extent are right. Do you agree? Discuss

Or

Q. We can, if we wish, look upon two narrative levels—the level of the world of fact and the level of imaginative creation—as an imitation of life itself as it is lived. Elucidate.

Robert Jordan in his interesting book has made the point that "the Canterbury Tales... invites piecemeal criticism; it also invites the total view. In the equality of these two claims on our attention lies much of the critical problem." Jordan tends to see the historical explanation of this paradox in the Gothic nature of Chaucer's art, the dominant aesthetic mood of the period, wherein "the total form is determined by the accumulation of individually complete elements." The whole can be regarded as a collection of complete parts which involve varying perspectives and unusual juxtapositions, the very opposite of modern "organic" art wherein the parts are at least theoretically subordinate to the whole.

Although I think that the notion of modern art as organic must be qualified and questioned, there is a certain force and validity to Jordan's distinction between medieval and modern art. Modern art expects the parts to be somewhat subordinate to the whole. The dominant stress of New Criticism was on the organic nature of art. This principle applies mainly to certain poets and novelists of the Renaissance and later periods but certainly not to all. The Victorian novelists did not write organically. Many of the eighteenth-century poets did not. On the other hand, some medieval literature is organic— Gawain and the Green Knight, for instance, and some of Chaucer.

We do not, therefore, have to relate the individual Canterbury tales to the frame in any psychological, symbolic, or dramatic manner, but we can treat them as separate units. We can look at the frame separately as at another part of the poem, as well as a unifying device. We need not be concerned with the dramatic unity of the Canterbury Tales. I do not, however, deny that some relation even if not an organic one, exists between the frame and the tales. The former is at least causative and authenticating. As we shall see, it provides the narrative cause for the other narratives, and it attempts to authenticate the stories, that is, to help make the reader or audience suspend their disbelief. This is the usual procedure in most collections of tales. We shall here examine the rather complex background of the frame and its numerous aesthetic functions to see what light this knowledge may throw on Chaucer's general intention. It may help us to learn how

Chaucer himself regarded his great masterpiece.

There is a sense, it must, however, be acknowledged, in which the tales—or most of them—are also reflections of their tellers, and this relationship adds another dimension to their complexity of perspective and meaning. This aspect has, however, been much overstressed by early twentieth-century criticism, an emphasizing which has blurred the structure of the units in their own right. Chaucer is a great psychologist, but he was not the exclusive psychologist-realist and prober of the human heart that modern critics and scholars prodded by early twentieth-century interests have made him out to be. Modern criticism, with its strong mimetic bias, has tended to emphasize character and dramatic incident at the expense of structure and sequence, and it is time to redress somewhat the balance. Chaucer was influenced by the literary and rhetorical tradition as much as by life.

There were many possible precedents for a collection of tales more or less unified in some way, and before we proceed further we should glance briefly at some of these collections. As Nevill Coghill has pointed out, Chaucer's idea of a collection was novel and original, but he could also have been indebted to predecessors. He certainly would have relied in some way, no matter how original his idea was, on the tradition of a collection of tales to interest readers. We must then look at several possible exemplars.

Before we go into some detail, it is important to note the religious and moral suggestions which a collection of tales would connote to readers in fourteenth-century England. Not all of Chaucer's models are religious, but the really popular collections of tales had a didactic purpose. Collections of saints' lives, of fables, of miracles of the virgin, and of exempla for sermons certainly provided the fundamental exemplars for Chaucer and even Boccaccio.These collections had a practical purpose and came into existence for the convenience of religious teachers.

I do not wish to deny that early secular collections like The Seven Sages and other Oriental collections may have influenced Chaucer in some way. I think, however, the English audience, even a court audience, would have normally expected a didactic and religious purpose in any collection of tales presented to them inasmuch as these didactic assemblages were the most common type of narrative collections in the period.

The twelfth century for the first time in the West saw the development of collections of tales, tales primarily for the convenience of preaching and devotional purposes. The earlier collections such as the Vitae patrum and some hagiographic collections were essentially for monks, making provision for communal and spiritual readings in the monastery. The Moslem world, though these were mainly secular and entertaining, did have collected and framed tales dating from before the twelfth century—notably the Arabian Nights (in some of its forms) and The Seven Sages. Among Oriental fable collections the Arabic Kalilah and Dimnah or Fables ofBidpai are also of early date. Nevertheless The Seven Sages and Kalilah were not translated into Western languages before the twelfth century.Aesopic collections made in classical times and Ovid's Metamorphoses were, however, known. The latter at the beginning of book 4 even has three daughters of King Minyas carry on discussions between their tales.

The great upsurge in collections dating from the twelfth and thirteenth centuries is due, as might be expected, to a demand for moralizing stories as literate and religious audiences increased in size. Collections of tales were useful for preaching friars who turned increasingly to sermons to win over urban audiences. Stories and anecdotes have always been used in teaching but the notion of an organized collection of such, if not new in the West, at least received a new attention. The later Middle Ages is a great period of collected stories—the legends of the Virgin began to appear in the twelfth century, and proliferated until the Reformation; exempla books are very numerous indeed in the same period; great legendaries, especially Jacob of Voragine's Golden Legend, flourish; even works on other subjects, like Peraldus 's Summa virtutum et vitiorum, are infiltrated by exempla; older collections like those of Valerius Maximus and the Vitae patrum take on, as their MSS show, a new life in this period. We also find collections of a De casibus type wherein tragedies or strictly speaking falls are told, or of a De illustribus type wherein brief biographical lists of great people are provided.

It is possible that the Gothic spirit was responsible in part for the efflorescence of an older genre, but there is probably a more prosaic reason at the bottom—sheer convenience. These collections were useful for preachers. The authorities on preaching emphasize the importance of illustrating homiletic points by concrete stories. There is perhaps no "clear-cut treatment of the exemplum" in the Artes predicandi, those rhetoric books for preachers, but that its use was strongly urged there can be no doubt.

This passion for collecting also extended to anthologies of poetry and dictionaries of various sorts. Traditionally, in the medieval period, we find classical poetry introduced by the accessus ad auctores in which the circumstances of the composition of the work presented are often given, sometimes in terms of four Aristotelian causes. St. Jerome applied what the Rhetorica ad Herennium and Cicero's De inventione has recommended, an introduction to the beginning of each of his commentaries on the books of the Bible he translated. His example was very influential.

We sometimes find brief biographies embedded in accessus. Medieval literary history was conceived of as introductions to particular literary works. This passion extended to the Provencal razos, discussions of the external circumstances of composition of poems preceding them in a number of Provencal manuscripts. These are also accessus of a sort. Biographies of these poets, usually separate from the razos, abound. The Prologue to Canterbury Tales, if not all parts of the frame, can be regarded in part as an accessus. It exists in part to describe the fictitious authors and the "causes" of the tales themselves.

A distinction should be made between collections of tales

with a prologue from the author as a real person and framed tales with a prologue which is also a fiction and which may have, as the Decameron and Canterbury Tales do, framing interludes. The accessus is from the author as a real person. The Prologue to the Canterbury Tales is an artistic, made-up accessus, not a real one.

A frame, besides justifying the tales or collected stories, also exists for authenticating purposes. Most stories pretend to be real, to be "historical" in some sense. Part of the pleasure of a story for a reader or hearer lies in the suspension of disbelief engendered by the claim, open or implied, that the story is true. If the magic of art is to work, it must be true. This feeling that what is told really happened is a very old tradition, almost certainly going back to early oral societies. The host when he describes the Canterbury scheme says that each pilgrim will tell four tales "of aventures that whilom han bifalle" (1. 795; F. N. Robinson, 2d ed.), each tale to be about things and matters which really happened.

One of the major purposes of the frame, then, is to authenticate the tales—to play the game that the stories are real. Here, as I have elsewhere written, "Chaucer has moved from dream and past history [in his earlier poetry] to a report on the contemporary world and present history.... We are given a social world in the frame, not an individual's problems or attitudes." The "realism" of the Canterbury Tales which lies in great measure in the frame rather than the tales themselves, however, does not arise out of a desire to give us a "true" picture of fourteenth-century life as a medieval Zola might wish to do but to an important degree out of a well-known literary purpose—authentication. The attempt to show the truth of a tale; "it really happened," is its indirect theme. Besides this aim, the genre of collected tales—not only the Gothic spirit—demanded a prologue and sometimes a total frame.

Then, further, the frame is in the form of a supposititious pilgrimage to St. Thomas's shrine in Canterbury.This imagery suggests, on a literary level, the pilgrim's report, which is told in the first person, presumably of a personal experience. The pilgrimage notion, besides its obvious religious symbolism, serves as a literary authenticating device for the Chaucer persona. We are all pilgrims on the way to our different Canterburys.Life is a journey to our final homes; and besides, this governing image helps us to suspend our disbelief and listen to a pilgrim's tale, of one who has just made a voyage. A good more or less contemporary report in English is that of Margery Kempe who, in her Autobiography, tells inter alia of her journey to Palestine in Chaucer's period. Most pilgrim's tales are in Latin, but by Chaucer's time, vernacular reports were beginning to appear.

It is also significant for the understanding of the framed tales of the period that the single-centreed narrative of early Arthurian romance began to give way in the thirteenth century and even more in the fourteenth to the Arthurian prose cycle type of narrative which is formed by rambling disgressions having a common Arthurian background but introducing a vast number of what seem to and may actually be irrelevant stories. The story within the story goes wild and multiplies in a bewildering way. The collections as well as the Canterbury Tales are held together by a recognizable purpose or plan, the prose cycles are not. Yet the urge to proliferate tales is there and may also be explained by this later medieval drive to create collections. It is so urgent that Chaucer makes one of his tales, the Monk's Tale, a smaller collection of tales—"little tragedies"—within a larger collection.

All this may be seen in some great late medieval collections. In the fourteenth century, three remarkable men, Juan Ruiz in Spain, Boccaccio in Italy, and Chaucer in England, took the religious or moralizing genre of collected tales and infused it with new life and vitality in a way that few early secular collections were able to be animated. This is not the place to go into a detailed comparison, but each author had a complex artistic vision, and however different in aims and form produced masterpieces. They diversified their narratives by "retrospection and anticipation," and by subtle shifts in perspective they gave us several worlds held together in a most subtle articulation.

None of Chaucer's predecessors, however, use exactly his device. Nor does any combine the religious and secular attitudes and subjects to the degree he does. Chaucer gives us a spiritual vision both directly and indirectly.

The Decameron has no interludes except at the beginning of the whole work and between days. As Robert Pratt and Karl Young point out, "it is clear that the frame of the Decameron could not be regarded as Chaucer's model in any precise or thorough-going sense." (See Sources and Analogues of Chaucer's Canterbury Tales, ed. W. F. Bryan and Germaine Dempster.) The Ameto and Filocolo, both by Boccaccio, especially the Ameto, are somewhat closer to the Canterbury Tales but even they differ from the latter in significant ways. Sercambi, whose collection of tales used to be considered the closest Italian source of or analogue to the Canterbury Tales, now seems out of the running because of a correction in his assumed dates. The Libro del buen amor is even less like the Canterbury Tales than the Italian examples I have named. We must not forget, of course, Ovid's great collection of tales, especially because Ovid was so popular in the later Middle Ages, but the Metamorphoses is fundamentally different in structure from the Canterbury Tales.

Art traditionally teaches and amuses. These three masterpieces, the Libro del buen amor, the Decameron, and the Canterbury Tales, stress these two aims differently. Chaucer teaches most of all. They all make some use of circumstantial realism for literary ends, but they are all pictures of life only in the most profound sense. They are also partly true to life because the religious tradition out of which they come is true of life. The sermons and penitential books of the Christian tradition are realistic.

Chaucer's notions of dialogue and the elabouration of the role of the persona are too varied in origin to trace here, but they no doubt are part of the complex sense of the world which Chaucer delighted in. Wyclif, Chaucer's great contemporary, said that "pulcra alternacio delectat animam" and that "multi delectantur in loquela dialogi." Chaucer knew too that debate and dialogue delighted and soul. Many of the religious collections of tales had prefaces, but they were written by the author as author, commenting on his collection, praising God and possibly offering reasons and uses for the tales that follow. What Ruiz, Boccaccio, and Chaucer did was to make the prologues and frames linking the tales part of the artistic creation (a very rare device indeed in religious collections, and usually confined to titles). The tales themselves were pushed to a secondary level so to speak. The prologue and framing links became the setting out of which the tales came. Neither Ruiz nor Boccaccio used the links in as complete a way as nor to the same extent that Chaucer did. An imitation of reality, not an opinion of the author or presumed author speaking in his own person, provided, however, the rationale of the collection for all three.

Chaucer and his Mediterranean colleagues used circumstantial detail of time, place and description in their prologues and frames, and following an old tradition, descriptions of characters and lively dialogue. The circumstantial detail of the frame we have already discussed elsewhere. It is especially presented for its purpose in authenticating. The portrait goes back to the classical world as a literary genre and was recommended by medieval writers on rhetoric and poetics. Dialogue was considered, as we have seen, a proper form for medieval writers to use to increase the delectation of their audiences.

In making something of this genre, these writers then used dialogue, debate, and circumstantial realism to make a complex perspectivism and a rich, ironical, self-aware sense of life. Each was a maker of a world or worlds. Each "thickened the mixture" and made their audience see the bitter-sweetness of existence.

The frame of the Canterbury Tales serves many functions and is not there, as some think, only to serve as an introduction to some attractive tales. It sets the tone for the richness and complexity of human experience presented to us. It authenticates, prepares us for morality and entertainment in various subtle ways. It offers another level of experience, another world out of which the ideal, that is the unreal, world of the tales come. It introduces us to characters of extraordinary range; it universalizes, in a religious sense, the stories; it satisfies the Gothic urge for wholes within wholes; it gives a sense of completeness and plenitude such as suggests on a very small scale God's activity within the world. The practical purposes of an introduction to stories are there, of course, but above all a real act of creation is suggested in which a new world appears made out of the stuff of the old.

The spring setting of the Prologue continues the notion of creation, for God was supposed to have created the world in this season. Chaucer, following the medieval rhetoricians, is less concerned with describing spring than with emphasizing its powers (vires). The beginning of the poem then suggests creation just as the end suggests the ultimate end of man the pilgrim, and finally of the world. The world of Canterbury Tales moves from its own genesis to its final revelation in the Parson's Tale and Chaucer's palinode.

The great character of the frame is the host. He is both the speaker for Chaucer and Chaucer's great critic. He is the supposed creator of the scheme of the tales and is the sole judge of it. He is therefore a Chaucer surrogate and at a great remove a surrogate for God. Yet he lacks complete freedom to impose his will as he quickly learns. God also in a mysterious way is limitied by his creation, but it is a voluntary limitation for man's good.

When Dryden wrote of the Canterbury Tales in his Preface to the Fables, "Here is God's plenty," he no doubt had the notion of divine plenitude in the back of his mind as an enlightening metaphor, but he builded better than he knew, for the creation (both natura naturans and natura naturata) of the Canterbury Tales with its encompassing and richly variegated frame is really an artistic parallel to God's creation. Traditionally the variety of the world (its plenitude) has always been taken as evidence of God's goodness which overflows into his creation in a variety of ways and manifests itself in as many forms as possible.

Just as secondary causes operate in the world below, all ultimately dependent on God, the primary cause of all, so secondary causes in the forms of Chaucer's many characters create their own stories. But we who observe the whole scene, who read the tales and frame are aware of a mind behind it all, the controlling guide and spirit, to whose goodness we are indebted— Chaucer the man.

As Charles Owen writes, "the embracing fiction [of the pilgrimage] not only gives a value to most of the narratives more important than any they inherently possess, but it manifests itself frequently within the stories influencing their form, their ideology, their style, their language." The Prologue and frame is Chaucer's tribute to and imitation of God's creative activity. Because it is set, unlike Chaucer's other works, in the "real" world, it suggests that we too are characters in a pilgrimage and that we have our little flurries of creation, our narratives as we pass by the way. As Owen has said above, the frame penetrates the stories by creating their form and their rationale. We are both free and determined, masters and slaves, and our lives are the parameters of innumerable variables in a multidimensional continuum.

A further parallel between Chaucer and the Divine is the retrospective stance, the telling of events after they have occurred. As R. Baldwin pointed out a number of years ago, the scheme of the Canterbury Tales demands a Chaucer who has already made the journey to Canterbury and is telling it in retrospect. The pilgrim Chaucer as he tells us of the first meeting of his fellow pilgrims describes them fully, something which could only have been done after he had got to know them. The tale of Canterbury Tales is being told after the events, even if not in tranquillity. It is cast in the shape of an autobiographical reminiscence. In this, Chaucer is following a very common tradition in art which uses a retrospective teller—perhaps the best known example to him was the Divine Comedy. Dante has already completed or pretended to have completed his whole journey as he sits down to relate it to his audience. Paradise has already been reached before Dante the author sits down to write of hell. Chaucer too must have pretended to have reached Canterbury and even to have returned to London before he turned to write

> Whan that Aprill with his shoures soote
> The droghte of March hath perced to the roote.

In at least this sense then the end is the beginning and the beginning is the end in a tale in which the teller is an active character. The motto "En mon commencement est ma fin" and its converse are the truth which Christianity and life give us. This kind of reminiscence then in which the whole work is cast into retrospect is a paradigm again of God's creation and the divine attitude to existence. As in life, the end hovers over every act and all is cast in a perspective of double time. The potential pastness of the present continually being forced upon us by the conditions of this act is what gives the present its edge and its tragedy. We can forget this great truth most of the time, just as we do when we read the tales in the Canterbury Tales or as the pilgrims do as they tell their tales, but at times the warning bell clangs as the voice of the narrator, of this elvish man Chaucer, is heard above the clamour in measured tones giving us his report of this journey to Canterbury.

The Prologue and frame then of the Canterbury Tales interpenetrate the tales in many and varied ways and set the conditions for the complex worlds which are revealed. The tales are in another time than the time of the pilgrimage for the pilgrimage is given to us in the persona's retrospective time, in illo tempore. In a sense the tales then are lyric interludes or perhaps lyrico-narrative interludes, especially because we are strongly aware of most of the tellers. We are held down by the forces which control us, and yet these forces allow each one of us to tell his tale, to open up for a little while the sequence of something that has happened.

Explanations of the function of the Prologue and frame

of the Canterbury Tales which fall back on the Gothic nature of the late medieval period may to some extent be right. Obviously in some sense the spirit of the later medieval period with its preference for framed painting and framed doorway has some relation to the popularity of the framed collection of tales in the same period and with what Jordan calls "nonorganicist sensibility" so characteristic of Gothic art. Jordan himself is well aware of the difficulties in making precise such parallels. The dispute over whether we can use the term "baroque" or how to use it in discussing seventeenth-century literature is instructive in this matter. Jordan writes, "I do not press the analogy very far."

It is perhaps more helpful in our goal of understanding the function of the frame and Prologue in the Canterbury Tales to stress what Chaucer was doing in his concept of the tales; how he conceived his own masterpiece. I think the analogy of creation and God was before him deliberately and often. If we like, we may also interpret Gothic cathedrals thus—remembering though that romanesque and baroque cathedrals also aimed at creating God's house on earth and a replica of the creation and its results in salvation history. It is better to think of Chaucer as a divine surrogate in his task than only as a Gothic artist, though certainly no one can object to these analogies if they are helpful.

The poetic world created by the poet is not really ex nihilo, as Chaucer would surely not wish to put himself on a level with the real God. He is, however, analogously creating a world or several worlds, even if using already existing materials. He is creating, to use an expression of M. H. Abrams, a heterocosm, and is suggesting a parallel to the divine activity. The notion of artist as God is implicit in his greatest poems. The idea of the poet as creator only became explicit in the Renaissance. Yet the poet as vates, as prophet who is divinely inspired, is very old, older than Homer. But the notion of the prophet-poet as a god probably had to wait on Christianity and the development of Western thought, especially in the Romantic period.

The idea that the poet is a kind of god is implied in the very subject matter of The Divine Comedy. The fact that such a journey should be granted to him as it was to St Paul who visited the third heaven was a sufficient guarantee that Dante was specially favoured and was by precept and example made a special imitation of God, who in the form of Jesus made a journey similar in some respects to what his was to be.

With Chaucer the evidence is less clear but none the less impressive. His characters carry their heavens and hells about with them. They are on their way to the heavenly Jerusalem and are fortuitously joined by Chaucer just as we fortuitously join our own contemporaries at our birth. Chaucer is withdrawn and different. He is called upon by the Host twice, is poked fun at by the Man of Law, tells a dull story. All this gives us a sense of his reality and helps to guarantee his artistic truth. He gives us a world which reflects a real world and in which we find new worlds. It presents its own truth. Its epistemological guarantee is Chaucer's own retrospective report.

We can, if we wish, look upon these two narrative levels—the level of the world of fact and the level of imaginative creation—as an imitation of life itself as it is lived. We live in time punctuated by events which take us out of time, our dreams, some of our contacts with others, our hearing stories, our introspective and imaginative moments. The Canterbury Tales reflects these two basic levels of life. It lets us enjoy and lament over our scattered introspective and neighbourly moments as well as keep us aware of the pilgrimage, the via we are all bound on. We are the pilgrims, the viatores, but just as the Canterbury Pilgrims could get away from their journey carried by the wings of narrative, so we can temporarily forget the serious and fundamental passage to Canterbury we are all engaged upon. The relation between the two levels, then, need not be purely psychological, as Professor Kittredge, Lumiansky, and many others have thought, but religious and humanist.

Thus, the Canterbury Tales with its elabourate frame

and its Prologue is a prologue to a prologue—our earthly life in its plenitude, variety and multitudinousness. We recognize our world in Chaucer's world and cross in reading it another bridge in "thilke parfit glorious pilgrymage/That highte Jerusalem celestial" (. -).

We must remember that the pilgrims do not reach Canterbury.It is possible that this failure is due to the accident of Chaucer's death or it may be deliberate. I tend to the latter explanation. Chaucer may very well have decided before he reached the Parson's or Manciple's Tale not to finish his work as he had originally planned and reduced it to fewer tales, perhaps even as few as one-quarter of the number. Perhaps not. But the cessation of the work before Canterbury is reached is certainly a happy circumstance or notion in terms of the spiritual function of the Prologue and frame, and the necessity of the return to London.The heavenly Jerusalem is certainly not yet reached by the pilgrims, nor indeed us.

The heavenly Jerusalem is the ultimate goal of earthly man and until the end of time will be for all human beings still in via. Even more important, only because more immediate, is the emphasis in the Canterbury Tales on the journey of life which all who read it must still be on, with its double aspect of the travelling and the experiences within that journey which seem to take us, even if only momentarily, out of time.

Q. What is The Role of Women in The Canterbery Tales?
Or

Q. Chaucer, in his female pilgrimage thought of women as having an evil-like quality that they always tempt and take from men. Discuss

They were depicted as untrustworthy, selfish and vain and often like caricatures not like real people at all. Through the faults of both men and women, Chaucer showed what is right and wrong and how one should live, Under the surface, however, lies a jaded look of women in the form that in his writings he seems to crate them as caricatures and show how they cause the downfall of men by sometimes appealing to their desires and other times their fears. Chaucer obviously had very opinionated views of the manners and behaviours of women and expressed it strongly in The Canterbury Tales. In his collection of tales, he portrayed two extremes in his prospect of women. The Wife of Bath represented the extravagant and lusty woman where as the Prioress represented the admirable and devoted followers of church. Chaucer delineated the two characters contrastingly in their appearances, general manners, education and most evidently in their behaviour towards men. Yet, in the midst of disparities, both tales left its readers with an unsolved enigma.

The Wife of Bath represents the "liberal" extreme in regards to female stereotypes of the Middle Ages. Unlike most women being anonymous during the Middle Ages, she has a mind of her own and voices herself. Furthermore, she thinks extremely highly of herself and enjoys showing off her Sunday clothes whenever the opportunity arises. She intimidates men and women alike due to the power she possesses. Because of her obnoxious attitude Chaucer makes her toothless, fat and large. Doubtlessly, she is very ugly, almost to the point of "not-presentable. This to me shows how Chaucer depicts what men don't want. The Prioress, on the other hand, serves as a foil to the Wife of Bath.

Chaucer describes her as "tender-hearted" who cannot bear the sight of pain or physical suffering. She will cry at the thought of a dog dying. It could represent that she has a frail soul with low tolerance for pain and suffering. The latter description carries over into the modern stereotypes about women as skittish and afraid members of society who need to be cared for. Chaucer paints a very delicate and elegant picture of the Prioress. Her manners of eating are far from the brutish festivals of the time. Chaucer describes her table manners as very graceful, not a drop of anything would fall from her mouth, and she was very polite when taking thing at the table. (Lines 131-4). Chaucer's last description of Prioress - the letter "A" around her neck that stood for "Amor vincit omnia" meaning "Love conquers all." The brooch symbolizes love with which her rosaries are adorned is a common accessory for religious devotion, which carries the courtly love anthem: love conquers all. The symbol that she wears shows that she is perfect and obviously a representation of what most men of the time want but of course they can't have her. Accordingly, the Wife of Bath is daunting, ostentatious and ultimately ugly. She is nothing in comparison to the Prioress who is elegant, well mannered and above all loving.

The Prioress's superiority over the Wife of Bath is shown again in the presence of education. The Wife of Bath has travelled a great deal and seems knowledgeable about things of the world. She brings up many a valid point throughout the prologue but Chaucer voids her opinion because of her social class and looks when in truth she is actually wise. The Wife of Bath has understanding for the world and knows very well what's going on. However, during the Middle Ages, only scholarly or academic knowledge is recognized. What the Wife of Bath understands and pursues may not be commendable. On the contrary, the Prioress is considered "scholastic" and high class due to her good manners. Her ability to speak the noble language of French puts her character in a higher class as well. Thus, once again the Prioress is considered intelligent. Basically, the Wife of Bath is kind of a foil to the women during the Middle Ages. Her actions and thinking not only differ from the Prioress but almost from everyone else!!!

The Wife of Bath is radical especially when it comes to relationship with men. She is characterized as knowing much about love, which is illustrated by her physical defect-being gap-toothed symbolizing "sexual accomplishment." The Wife of Bath cannot resist telling her companions about all of her sexual experiences. She also had five husbands and countless affairs, thus breaking innocent men's hearts. Her husbands fell into two categories. The first categories of husbands were rich but also old and unable to fulfil her "sexual" demands. The other husbands were sexually vigourous, but harder to control. None of her five marriages were successful because the Wife of Bath was constantly seeking to have power and control over them, Chaucer I think characterises the Wife of Bath in this way to show men's fears. For instance, her fifth but not the last (it was said that she is on her way of marrying the sixth before she told her tale) marriage was unhappy because her husband who is half of her age beats her. To anger him, she tore three pages from his book. After this he beats her again.

She pretended to be dead and he felt so guilty that he threw his whole book in the fire. This gave her the upper hand for the rest of her life. This contrast between the Wife of Bath and the Prioress describes fully the difference between what men do and do not want in a woman. First, the violent and deceitful act of tearing books then the deceitful act of lying to her husband will never be done by the Prioress as the Prioress is well mannered, educated, "powerful" and above all, is loving. Second, is the issue of marriage and "sexual demand" which will never have its roots in the Prioress's life as she has taken the vow of chastity. This being the case appeals to both fear and desire, as all men would desire the Prioress, but fear they could not have her. The Prioress is pure in heart and thinks of men and women alike. It's interesting how the Wife of Bath was always striving to have sovereignty and the Prioress was granted sovereignty even though she didn't seek for it intentionally.

The Wife of Bath and the Prioress alike have power over men once again this characterisation would scare men. It is rare that women are given such high stature during the medieval period. The Prioress as her name suggests is "a superior being in a monastic community for women" is so important that three priests were in her company; as this shows her status as the boss, this dominance would be very fearful for men of the time. The hag, whom the Wife of Bath identifies with, initially was granted sovereignty and power over man. This is proven when the hag offers her husband the choice: he can have her old and ugly and faithful or young, beautiful, and possible unchaste. He tells her to choose; he grants her the sovereignty.

As mentioned above, the Wife of Bath desires what most women want and that is power over men, her being described as being ugly and wanting power to probably exploit that power as she did with husband number five definitely shows a representation of what men don't want. Early in the tale, there is a quotation said by the Wife of Bath supporting this idea. "I don't deny that I will have my husbands both my debtor and my slave, and as long as I am his wife he shall suffer in the flesh. I will have command over his body during all his life, not he." In other words, she is saying that she will have total control over herself, her husband, and their household and very specifically, not just the husband. However, there are also situations where she seems to submit to her husband. "Nevertheless, since I know your pleasure I will satisfy your physical pleasure." This was said by the Wife of Bath and supports the non-feministic view.

It is considered non-feministic because the woman is giving in to the man's desire, which goes against feministic beliefs. The Wife of Bath has a choice of not giving in to the man, but she decides to let the man have pleasure for his desire not hers, because from her past experience she knew how much men enjoy it when women are submissive. This quotation obviously goes against feministic beliefs, leaving an unanswered contradiction about the Wife of Bath. However, Chaucer does show through this characterisation that the Wife of Bath is desirable in one way to men because she is willing to be submissive to their desires. This raises an unseen question of desire for her as I think most men of the time would desire a woman who would grant this. The character of the Prioress in the same light, certainly keeps one guessing. Is her tale the product of the simple mind, or of one poisoned by anti-Semitism? The Prioress is, well mannered, educated, powerful, and loving. Ironically, her prologue and tale contain strong elements of anti-Semitism. This is shown through her use of the Jew as the villain of her tale.

However, there is no historical evidence of ritual murder of Christian children by Jews, but that would not have mattered to the pilgrims. Anti-Semitism, directed at a people thought to have both rejected and murdered Christ, was distressingly deep-seated. This bigotry unfortunately was rampant at the time, and both the sentiments and their being expressed in the context of a religious story would not have seemed strange to Chaucer's pilgrimage. Nevertheless, on a less depressing note, her tale can tell us something of the medieval attitude towards simple piety and miracles, which also was quite prevalent. I don't think it is about the Jews because; they were expelled from England in 1290. Yet, whether this tale is the product of the simple mind or anti-Semitism still remains an enigma. This story also reinforces her devotion to the church and this characterisation can be seen as a fear to some men as they are unable to obtain her. It is here we see the only time when the Wife of Bath and the Prioress relate to each other. In this we can see that Chaucer is telling us that the Prioress is not as perfect as she might of first seemed, and in this way we an see that both women have both got parts that men desire and men fear.

The Wife of Bath seems to be feministic yet there are also some situations in which she does as the men wish. The Prioress on the other hand keeps you wondering and seems to be a perfect lady however she is unobtainable and probably to well educated and out of reach for most men. Chaucer portrays the tale of Wife of Bath as hypocritical but between the lines there is some helpful advice for many women in the world today. In this way Chaucer is trying to educate women through her tale, and say that there are times one should be a feminist and times one should not. This characterisation of her strong head would have scared the men of the time. In his contrast with the two he shows in both women what men fear. In the Wife of Bath it's that men don't want to be controlled and in the Prioress it's the fact that she is unobtainable and maybe too clever for everyday man. These representations however when put together, create a women that seems to be perfect for what most men want and desire.

Women and Spring in The Canterbury Tales

In Geoffrey Chaucer's collection of stories; The Canterbury Tales, there is a recurring theme of love being the most important aspect of a person's life. The author enforces this theme through the usage of springtime imagery, especially an emphasis on the month of May. Not only May, but the importance of it and the flowers that bloom in it. May is when spring begins to turn into summer and flowers really bloom. This fact makes May a very pivotal month in the calendar and effects the weather and nature from there on out. If flowers bloom late then it will be different weather in June than if the flowers bloom early. In The Canterbury Tales, women are often compared to flowers and to May making them seem very powerful yet beautiful. Most of the women in this collection of tales are very beautiful, and very influential and authoritative towards men in their lives.

In the "Knight's Tale" the two prisoners see the beautiful woman in the garden and fall in love with her. When Emily is described, it is said that she was "fresher than May with its flowers." (Chaucer, pg 51) The two prisoners haven't even seen this woman yet and she is already being described like this. She is compared to flowers in May, which is a very good image to be compared to. May is known for flowers, like in the saying `April showers bring May flowers', some of the most beautiful flowers bloom then. Flowers such as daisies, poppies, lavender, baby's breath, and tulips all bloom in May, just to name a few. When a flower just blooms it is fresh, just like in spring when the snow melts and everything seems fresh and clean.

To say that Emily is like this makes a very beautiful image come to mind. The theme then comes in with this when the two prisoners fall in love with her. She is compared to spring constantly, and two men fall in love with her simultaneously, to the point where they would kill each other for her. Their lives become consumed with her, and she is identical to spring.

Emily is the springtime of these two men's lives and their love for it is the most important thing to them. She is influential on men when she begins to weep at the thought of them dying. She uses her beauty to make the Duke not sentence the two prisoners to death. He feels bad and decides to not make the order.

In "The Miller," the leading lady of the story is also very beautiful. She is well dressed, talented and good looking. "She [is] a morning glory, she [is] a daisy," (Chaucer, pg 153) both of which are May flowers. Morning glories and daisies are well known for their beauty and they both are happy flowers. They remind people of happy things, such as springtime and May. Again, comparing a woman to a flower is a very positive thing to say, and the fact that she is later on helps bring out the reoccurring theme. Many men in this woman's village are infatuated with her; including her husband, the parish clerk and Nicholas.

They all try to win her by confessing their undying love for her. The parish clerk sings to her under her window at night "like a nightingale." (Chaucer, pg 159) A bird like a nightingale is usually associated with summer or spring, in fact any bird usually is. But the making him a bird, and her a flower that he is singing to is an ultimate springtime image. May is all about flowers and birds. The men again are devoting their lives to her, and she is once again springtime. The spring makes them want to love and her beauty makes them want to love her. She has power over all of these men because she decides which one she will love.

These images occur over and over again through out the stories. Not only is love the most important thing in life, but also women are in charge when it comes to love. The women in the stories are fair and beautiful like spring, and can control when love occurs. The lusty feeling that spring causes only happens because it is spring, when women are beautiful they control men. Pretty women can with hold sexual pleasure like in the "Wife of Bath" or they can limit sex to certain men like the woman in "The Miller" does. The first sign of spring is flowers, they control when spring begins; a beautiful woman who is compared to a springtime flower can control when the lust and the love begins.

Q. Analyse the Characters of The Canterbury Tales

Or

Q. An interesting aspect of the famous literary work, "The Canterbury Tales," is the contrast of realistic and exaggerated qualities that Chaucer entitles to each of his characters. Discuss

When viewed more closely, one can determine whether each of the characters is convincing or questionable based on their personalities. This essay will analyse the characteristics and personalities of the Knight, Squire, Monk, Plowman, Miller, and Parson of Chaucer's tale.

One of Geoffrey's less believable main characters is the Knight, for reasons of chivalry. The knight displays many traits which make him seem almost too good to be true, and a true gentleman that rarely exists in reality. The narrator sums up the knights character by stating that "Though he were worthy, he was wys,/And of his port as meeke as is a mayde." (pg. 5, The Canterbury Tales) The knight holds four main admirable traits, making him the most liked traveller in "The Canterbury Tales," and also amplying the doubt of his realism.

The reader is prepared to learn of each of his noble accomplishments and importance when the narrator remarks that" A knight ther was, and that a worthy man,/That fro the tyme that he first bigan/To ryden out, he loved chivalrye,/ Trouthe and honour, fredom and curteisye." (pg. 4, The Canterbury Tales) From the characters impressive introduction, it is clear that this man is the most valued and honourable traveller among the group.

This perfect gentleman holds a love of ideals that are often not displayed by people. First and foremost, he believes in the ideals of chivalry, and always stays true to its principles. He also feels that one should be honest, truthful and faithful, which many people are not all of these ideals. The knight thinks one should only do what is right, and what will gain him honour and reputation. This character also believes in freedom and generosity towards all, and displays this ideal repeatedly throughout the novel. And lastly, the knight also strongly feels that any proper person should display courtesy and elegance at all times. Another aspect of this character's life which makes him seem too prestigious to be truthful is his impressive military career. He fought in the holy war, known as the Crusades and was involved in 15 "mortal battles."

In the prologue, the narrator informs the reader that "Ful worthy was he in his lordes werre,/And therto hadde he riden, no man ferre,/As wel in Cristendom as hethenesse,/ And ever honoured for his worthinesse." (pg. 4, The Canterbury Tales) The knight obviously held a very respectable reputation, and was treated with much honour and respect. He was a perfect gentleman, showing kindness and understanding to everyone he came in contact with.

The knight was extremely well-mannered, always being on his best behavior. His appearance was the "finishing touch," adding honour and integrity to his courageous and gentle spirit. This main character was clothed still in his armor, wearing a tunic of harsh cloth and his coat of mail is rust-stained, clearly showing remaining signs of past battles. "Of fustian he wered a gipoun/Al bismotered with his habergeoun;/ For he was late y-come from his viage." (pg. 4, The Canterbury Tales) The qualities of the knight resemble those of very few people in modern society, giving a quality of exaggeration to the perfectness found in the knight. He represents the embodiment of the ideal man as seen by Chaucer.

The knight's son however, the Squire. does not display the degree of falseness the knight does. The vivacious personality of this young man closely resembles that of a modern man. He is a "lusty bachelor" of twenty, who is ultimately concerned with his appearance. He places more importance on fighting for his lady's honour, unlike his father who fought for abstract ideals or God. He also wore stylish, but very "daring" garments. The squire was dressed in a very short gown, equal in extremity to today's modern mini-skirt, which was looked down upon by the Church.

The vain squire made every effort to ensure that he had perfectly curled hair. "With lokkes crulle as they were leyd in presse." (pg. 6, The Canterbury Tales) It seems as though it appeared that this young man purposely curled his hair, just as a woman would do. He is described as being as fresh as the month of May, showing his cleaniless and delightful appearance to which he took so much pride. "He was as fresh as is the month of May." (pg. 6, The Canterbury Tales) This young man is slowly but surely aspiring to knighthood just as his father did, therefore he's courteous, humble, and respects his father because he is an apprentice to his father.

The young man did however, hold many social talents, which were important to have when becoming a knight. He has the abilities to sing, dance, write songs and poems, and joust, which were all important social accomplishments. The vain attitude of the Squire, and his selfish outlook, relate closely to the shallow demeanor of people today. However, due to the acuteness of the squire's perfection in the sense of manlihood, he can also be viewed as a sort of a fairytale "Prince Charming." Fairytale heros relate very well to the squire, because both are willing to do whatever they can for the love of a lady.

The squire seems to possess all that a lady might dream of: agility, strength, courtesy, a nice family, manners, and good looks. Prince Charming would also possess these ideal traits and follow these lines almost exactly. Both the squire and Prince Charming are meant to be "good guys," and they both are in many aspects. They are well bred and chivalrous, fight well for honour, and have the flaw of falling in love for beauty and passion. This comparison and likeness to the fairytale prince also gives this young squire his own degree of falseness and exaggeration. In certain aspects, the Monk also displays the impression of realism through his personality and actions.

The Monk is not an ordinary holy man, but yet a worldly

man who holds dear his means of personal enjoyment. He holds a very cocky, sarcastic attitude, not normally found in men of the church, which is the biggest sign of his realistic vitality. Monks usually stay apart from the outside world, not go out for "venery," a word that carries sexual connotations, or in other words hunts for pleasure, which definately sets this Monk apart from his other church officials. The narrator states that "This ilke Monk leet olde thinges pace,/And held after the newe world the space." (pg. 10, The Canterbury Tales) This statement indicates to the reader that this Monk finds joy and happiness in modern priviladges, differing him from conventional church officials.

He is introduced as "An out-rydere, that lovede venerye;/ A manly man, to been an abbot able." (pg. 8, The Canterbury Tales) The author describes him as being a "manly man," providing the reader with the assumption that the monk took his hunting and other "manly" activites very seriously. The author also makes it a point however, to state that he was a "fat and personable priest." So in essence, this particular monk has an unusual appearance, such explained by the Host, that he appears as though he's in charge of food and drink, or like a rooster with plenty of hens. This description confirms the impression that this Monk appears quite different from other religious figures, but yet is realistic due to his actions and appreciation of worldly pleasures.

In order to explain his love of the hunt, the narrator states: "Of prikyng and of huntyng for the hare/Was al his lust, for no cost wolde he spare." (pg. 34, The Canterbury Tales, A Literary Pilgrimage) He differs greatly from other church officials in that he appears to believe its pointless to follow his monastic duties. His rejection of the life of one's mind is explicit, and the narrator agrees: "And I seyde his opinion was good./What sholde he studie and make hymselven wood." (Pg. 35, The Canterbury Tales, A Literary Pilgrimage) This Monk particularary enjoys hunting, a pastime of the nobility, which proves that the Monk cares about enjoyment rather than concerning himself with his religious duties all the time. The monk often "hunted a hare" or any other type of game that suited him. His values and attitude resemble the selfish corrupt ideals of people, who partake in actions without considering the consequences or benefit of others. This character seems to have a mix of both realistic aspects and exaggerated ones. The Monk's selfishness and desire for recreation gives him the realistic feature. However, the author's stress of his sarcassim and selfishness also applies an angle of exaggeration to his character. An emphasis of a certain trait can also be examined in the Plowman.

The Plowman is stressed as the example of an ideal middle class citizen. "A trewe swinker and a good was he,/Livinge in pees and parfit charite;" (pg. 26, The Canterbury Tales) This character is a very chivalrous workman, just as the knight was. By looking closely at this character's actions and dialogue, it can be inferred that he is the type of individual who would gladly work for a person without pay. He pays all his Church taxes on time, and is a devoted churchgoer. This citizen treats his neighbour as he would want to be treated, making him well-liked, much as the knight was. Also, he is certainly not as rowdy as the other characters. He is a decent human being, and portrays a hard-working, devoted citizen, giving him much in common with the chivalrious knight. The plowman's personality can be related to the common working class citizen of today, with the exception of a slight exaggerated flawlessness. Another character portraying an actual individual would be in the case of the Miller.

The Miller is an obnoxious character who represents the modern day bully in a sense. He is a large man with imposing figure, making him seem more powerful than the other characters. This intimidation is developed by the physical description of the miller. The workman is brawny, big-boned and muscular, and is also a good wrestler. This character is said to have a red beard and hair. He also has a rude and corrupt attitude treating his fellow travellers with contempt.

His character matches the medieval conception that millers were the most important but dishonest tenants on a manor farm. He is shameless and selfish, and has a bad temper and is easily angered. In one instance, this character stole corn and proceded to charge three times the price, thinking nothing of the person he stole from. This man shows his vulgar and rude temperment when he becomes irritated upon hearing the Knight's tale of kings and queens and knights and ladies. He drunkly shouts, "I wol now quyte the Knyghtes tale." (pg. 146, The Canterbury Tales) The Host interupts the drunken man and pleads with him to wait to tell his tale, but he refuses and the Host critisizes him for his stubborness. "Thou art a fool; thy wit is overcome." (pg. 146, The Canterbury Tales) He continues to entertain his fellow travellers by telling a tale about a devious student who plans to have an affair with the wife of a dimwitted carpenter, showing his immaturity and delight in other people's misery. He also is said to have developed a "Hell mouth," or speaks "in Pilates voys." (pg. 146, The Canterbury Tales) The miller's character can be viewed as realistic, because his personality matches that of a modern day bully, in that he is very intimidating, rude and uncaring. However, his characteristic anger is slightly overstressed.

The Parson on the other hand, was a very religious, devoted, decent man. He is described as being very principled and intelligent. The parson is very noble and sets a good example towards his fellow parishioners. It is stated by the author that he is "also a lerned man, a clerk, / That Cristes gospel trewely wolde preche" (pg. 480, The Canterbury Tales) He even hates collecting income taxes from his citizens. He is known to practice what he preaches, and his values and hard work sets a good example for the common people. He worked very hard to better the lives of others around him, and therefore worked in the absence of the comforts that tend to come along with fame and glory.

The Parson is in many ways the ideal traveller on the journey to Canterbury. He is learned, but unlike the other men, possess much virtue. He realises that if the priest that the people put their trust and faith in is machiavellian, then no one can ever expect the people to be virtuous. "For if a preest be foul, on whom we truste,/No wonder is a lewed man to ruste;/" (pg. 24, The Canterbury Tales) This Parson is favorable over many other church officials, because unline them he does not run off to bigger and better places and rent his parish to someone else. These ideal qualities make him more approved than many of the other travellers, especially spiritually. He worked hard to spread goodness, act charitably, and was never hypocritical. These commendable qualities makes him a suitable parellel to what the world might view now as a model human being. Such virtue and qualities seem too good to be true, and in a way represent what every person should be like instead of how they really are.

In essence, the plot development is also based on the development of the characters and the contrast of reality and exaggeration. Chaucer purposely chose to give his characters certain aspects of reality and exaggerated traits to help develop each of the characters' tales. It is noticeable in the novel that each character's tale matches his or her personality in one way or another. For example, the knight's heroic tale of chivalry and kings and queens obviously coinsides with his traits and lifestyle. The Miller's tale of dishonesty and cheating also matches his personality of anger and rudeness. Chaucer's use of characterization helps to establish the plot and motives of the tale. Of course, the tales told by each of Chaucer's characters reciprocates the personality traits displayed by them.

The knight spoke a tale of chivalry and virtue and of ladies in waiting, while the Squire spoke of love and intrigue in his story. The differences in their personalities leads to the conflicts and balance of reality and exaggeration. The knight for example, shows a great degree of embellishment because he is so well mannered and holds such virtuous ideals, which are not commonly displayed by normal beings, because of the selfish nature of humans. The knight seems to represent what

Chaucer believes everyone should be like, and holds the values that people seem to overlook. The Squire, on the other hand, shows a more realistic display of characteristics, and adds variety to the story line. He displays a sense of reality in that he isn't as concerned with honour and values as his father, but rather with his own enjoyment and vanity. Chaucer's novel would be incomplete without the continuing budding of his characters.

Q. Discuss The General Prologue's Development of the Dream Vision.

Or

Q. Throughout the works of Chaucer, a steady perversion of courtly/romantic tradition shows itself. Do you agree? Discuss

Or

Q. The idea of a dream vision had definite pseudoscientific significance in those times and so in Chaucer's work. Discuss

Chaucer layers in commentary satire and or even puns, ranging from Rosemounde's delightful image of love being as sweet and pervasive as a cold, jelly-fat steeped dead fishy, to the Legend of Good Women, where the moral being repeatedly reinforced is that courtly standards of virtue have nothing to do with actually being a worthwhile woman. In his longer works, the dream vision has served as a literary device to set up an objective, less hindered framework to present these layered commentaries. In The Book of the Duchess, The Parliament of Fowls, and The Legend of Good Women, a main part of the story is carried out in a dream vision.

However, at the beginning of the Canterbury Tales, this is no longer the pattern. There is no lost, frustrated Chaucer trying to probe his unconscious, no dream inspiring the narrator to wend his way to Canterbury. But on closer inspection many of the same elements and earmarks of the dream vision pattern are still present. Their presence may indicate that Chaucer's practice of toying with romantic tradition has reached the point where he no longer needs a dream vision sequence to be the spoonful of sugar around the medicine of his wry barbs. Instead he is duplicating the effect by tweaking the waking world of the story directly.

The idea of a dream vision had definite pseudoscientific significance in those times. It was a place to find answers and meaning, if the right conditions were met. Dreams also presented answers in a setting that had no obligation to be realistic. In a sense, it was a non-subjective setting through which Chaucer could subtly inject satire into his works. Instead of using it in the traditional way — as a hackneyed literary device to toss out clear-cut morals or simple conclusions — it seems Chaucer employs it more to drop a hint to the audience that there are extra layers of meaning being offered. Chaucer also includes other quirks to make it clear that these layers of meaning are more complicated than the usual simple dream vision formula, such as the narrator never waking up like he should have before composing the Good Women legends, or the narrator being improperly vague about how long after falling asleep he dreamt.

Doing so is markedly unformulaic because that information was necessary for dream science to interpret the dream "correctly". Chaucer does not want people to make simple formulaic matters out of his works, but by putting an audience in the frame of mind to look for the usual dream meanings, he is prompting them to be aware of the nonstandard extra layer he has worked into his writing. This layered structure also potentially explains why some of his work seems abrupt; the surface story is just a setup for what he really wants to cover.

But once again, why does this not occur in the Canterbury Tales? If it is assumed the dream pattern is a set-up to hint to the open-minded to look out for the true extra layer(s), the question now turns to: how does Chaucer replicate the dream sequence effect without the actual dream sequence? In the opening lines of the prologue come the words:

And smale fowles maken melodye,
That slepen al the nyght with open ye

(So pricketh Nature in hir corages),
Thanne longen folk to goon on pilgrimages,
And palmers for to seken straunge strondes,
To ferne halwes, kowthe in sundry londes;
And specially from every shires ende
Of Engelond to Caunterbury they wende,
The hooly blissful martir for to seke,
That hem hath holpen whan that they were seeke.
Befil that in that season on a day,
In Southwerk at the Tabard as I layŠ

These lines raise two issues: one is the contrast between the initial lines, which revel in the harmony of nature and the holy longings of people to go a'pilgriming, and the last two lines, which mark the beginning of a latter section characterized with happenstance phrases and slapdash language. Randomizing phrases begin appearing such as "Befil that" and "by aventure yfalle". This could potentially be a reflection of the fact that Chaucer-narrator is fully indoctrinated on how to "properly" recognize the beautiful harmony of nature and spring, but is utterly useless at reading people with the same easy polish.

However, the second point raised by those lines is that elements common to the dream vision setup are also present; the idea of spring (always present), twittering birds, (the birds were holding a Valentine's Parliament in one dream, and singing intricate harmonies in another) and furthermore on line 10 he even describes these birds being insomniacs, assumedly kept awake with love. The more obvious romantic comparison would be to describe birds composing endless love ballads to sing, but instead he summons up a picture of sleepless, love-sick birds. This image brings to mind Chaucer-poet's state which led to his dream vision in The Book of the Duchess. To further the image when the pilgrim-Chaucer finally mentions himself, the first thing he has to say is, "Befil that in that season on a day, / In Southwerk at the Tabard as I lay". Right in the same sentence where the "Befil" phrases begin to lend a sense of unpredictability, you also get your first view of Chaucer-pilgrim lying in bed, which is also strongly reminiscent of the dream sequences in previous works. Except instead of never waking up as in Legend of Good Women, in this work he never actually falls asleep. However the effect seems to be the same.

With that in mind the contrast between the tidy and properly-harmonious lines in the opening and the random language following could instead be interpreted as a literary effect to achieve the same dreamlike state he invoked more literally in those other works.

After he starts them, these little disruptions in the neatness of the story help to reinforce the feeling of unreality. Much like the find-the-meaning reflex inspired in listeners by the dream vision sequences, these disruptions keep an audience on their toes. The possibility of finding traditional meaning in numerology is dangled as a possibility when the narrator notes the number of pilgrims, but much like the vaguely worded "I fel on slepe within an houre or twoo/ Me mette how I lay in the medewe thoo" in the Legend of Good Women, Chaucer seems to intentionally frustrate people looking for easy meanings in the Canterbury Tales.

He is using the same sort of tactic previously used to make the dream visions his staging ground, only now he is expanding it to the story proper, skipping the middle step. Similarly, much in the way the Chaucer-dreamers expected their dreams to hold significance relating to their problems, Chaucer-pilgrim seems to think the mere experience of going on a pilgrimage with devout and worthy people will be a meaningful resolving experience in itself. These lines are a prime example: *"But naethelees whil I have tyme and space/ Er that further in this tale I pace/ Me thynketh it acordaunt to resoun/ To telle yow al the condicioun/ Of ech of hem"*.

Even though he has not even started on the pilgrimage he treats his experience so far like it is a meaningful story in progress. One might consider Chaucer-pilgrim could be writing about all of this after the fact, but the way he says "While I have time" makes it seem like he is writing that very evening, while he has time between talking to everyone and going to bed. Also if it was after the whole pilgrimage he was writing this, there would be no reason limited time on a given day should stop him from writing down descriptions. If he remembered how his fellow pilgrims first struck him after that long, he would be unlikely to have forgotten by the next day.

But if he is writing events down as they happen, his references to "this tale" and "accordant to reason" make it sound like the narrator expects what is happening to him to end up being some grand story governed by reason and meaning by itself. This is the same sort of assumption of significance that the dreamer in Book of the Duchess makes when he ends the poem: "This was my sweven; now hit ys doon" (1334). The dream ends and he thinks to himself, "Well that was Some Dream, I'll write it down" without even a pause to try and verify there is some worthwhile meaning in it. To Chaucer-dreamer/pilgrim, the meaning and worth are assumed.

Yet the respective Chaucer-dreamers never noticed anything worthwhile from any of their dream visions. No answers to their heartache or frustrated attempts to understand courtly love, no inspirations even. The best they got was an unfair writing assignment. The worth in the dreams was not in their expected results for the narrator, but for the freedom of expression they gave Chaucer the author. In Canterbury Tales with that device absent, the opportunity to find layered meaning through the abstraction of a dream is no longer wasted on the inept narrators. Instead the responsibility lies solely with the audience. Indeed the audience's situation of following a fictional story is an abstraction of life similar to a dream vision. Chaucer has not abandoned the objective dream pattern, he has just evolved it. The dream sequence elements are still there, just without the literal dream sequence. In the Canterbury Tales, it is now the audience's responsibility to do the dreaming, and also to do a better job than the Chaucer-dreamers did of finding the meaning in the dream they receive.

Q. Analyse the Structural Techniques and Devices in The Prologue to the Canterbury Tales.

There are several structural elements in "The Prologue to the Canterbury Tales." The first structural element is associated with nature and the physical elements. Chaucer states, "When April with his sweet showers has pierced the drought of March to the root,...(so nature pricks them in their hearts): Then people long to go on pilgrimages." April signifies a revival of spirituality in which people feel a need to take pilgrimages because they feel closer to nature and Jesus Christ. Nature is intimately connected with spiritual soul searchings. On the same line, there exists a level of correspondences in which nature and man are linked together towards a common goal.

The characters themselves are built through a concept known as the chain of being. This involves a hierarchy of character structure. The characters are introduced from their highest to their lowest status and rank. For example, the knight is described first for his bravery and honour, following the squire his son, a Yeoman, and so on.

There exists also a level of juxtaposition in which the attributing elements and characteristics are compared and contrasted. For example, one can see in the description of the knight that he possesses honour, courage, valor. In essence, he is a respectful man who wins his glory for what he stands. On the other hand, his son the squire, symbolizes youth, courtly love, romance. He is interested in nice clothes, music, nature and women.

Chaucer also employs juxtaposition involving the comparison and contrast between the knight and the squire. As seeing the knight as a bold and elegant man, the squire is described as a "lusty lover" and 'fresh flowers" in reference to the description of his dress. This is known as alliteration.

Another literary technique is the use of irony. In the description of the squire, irony is based on a gap on what is apparent and what is implied. In the lines "and in this short time he had borne himself well, in the hopes of winning his lady's favor." The reader in this respect, anticipates something bolder and intense more than just "winning his lady's favor."

Chaucer also uses similes and superlatives. When Chaucer refers to the squire's age he remarks, "he was about twenty years old, I guess;" This expresses a realistic statement of the squire's age.

Chaucer also integrates the use of superlatives in describing the squire's romantic nature. For example, "... so hotly did he love that at night he slept no more than a nightingale." Chaucer also uses exaggerated adjectives to describe the squire's body build in the line: "... and wonderly deliver, and of greet strength."

Finally, the Prologue to The Canterbury Tales is built on four distinct levels. The first level is the story itself as a whole, written by Chaucer. The second level is the narrator who participates in the pilgrimage. The third level is the host whose idea it is to create the story line of The Canterbury Tales and on the fourth level, is the character who integrates the story line as they tell their stories in a competitive group manner.

Q. Discuss Contradiction and Corruption in the Canterbury Tales.

The individual anecdotes in Geoffrey Chaucer's The Canterbury Tales make a fundamental contribution to the satire and irony of the story, but one particularly sensitive account seems to bring the chronicle full circle. The Prioress's Tale appears to intrigue readers in ways that the other tales cannot; Chaucer expresses pathos, or appeal driven by emotion, through the character of the Prioress and her tale. The Prioress appears in the General Prologue as exceptionally sophisticated and mild mannered, but Chaucer intends to prove irony through the tale she discloses in which her callow and irresponsible manners are revealed. To fully understand the tale of the Prioress, one must wholly comprehend the dynamics of her character, the character's environment, the foundation of Chaucer's depiction of her, and the sardonic parable itself.

It was likely that during her time, the Prioress was the

daughter of aristocrats who could not get her wedded; she was more concerned with acting courteous and softhearted than pious and devout to her order. In proving that her character was at odds, Chaucer dubs the Prioress "Madame Eglentyne," a name that symbolizes the Virgin Mary (Chaucer). Perhaps irony exists in her name because the Virgin Mary stood for everything amorous and gracious, and the Prioress was suffering an inner turmoil. Chaucer wildly exhibits the Prioress's attachment to animals and her paradoxical struggle for motherhood.

The Prioress is still regarded as one of the most controversial pilgrims in The Canterbury Tales; she was viewed as anti-Semitic and spiteful. She performs another stark display of irreverent behavior when she wears her veil "loosely" so that her forehead is exposed. Most pious women of her time would have worn their veils pinned tightly against their eyebrows, but the Prioress reveals hers as a symbol of excellent procreation. In addition to her tactless mannerismr, the Prioress was known for her jeweled rosary, her trendy outerwear, and her stunning brooch inscripted "Love conquers all." Poking fun at the Prioress, Chaucer proves that her rosary is an important connection between who she is and the role it plays in her tale; the Prioress "gives [the boy in her tale] the very colours of her green and coral beads to symbolize his chastity and martyrdom" (Condren).

During the middle ages when Chaucer wrote, the most tolerated and practiced religion was Roman Catholic. Chaucer was very concerned with his own personal religious views and that of the people around him. In order to satirize the church, he had to take a weak image and compare it to the behavior of the church at that time. The image Chaucer chose was a woman who was flawed, materialistic, and self-important; she was a leader of her order only because of the money and power of her family. His main objective of writing The Prioress's Tale was to demonstrate the discrepancies and imperfections within the church of his day and to bring about an awareness that would strike the people.

The Prioress's inconsistencies are further exposed when she relates her unmerciful story in the voice of a twelve-year-old to convey its innocence. The tragic story unfolds as a schoolboy learns a Latin hymn (Alma Redemptoris) about the Virgin Mary and sings it everyday as he walks through the poverty-stricken neighbourhoods of the Jewish community. The Jews think the boy is mocking them, so they slice his throat. Miraculously, his widowed mother finds him in the fertilizer trench where he is still singing his hymn. He should have been dead, but the Virgin Mary laid a pearl upon his tongue so that he may sing; the Virgin Mary said, "My little child, soon I will come for thee, / When from thy tongue the little bead they take; / Be not afraid, thee I will not forsake" (Chaucer -).

In finding connections between the character of the Prioress and her account, she most closely relates to the little boy in that she is immature. The Prioress proves to be unlike the Virgin Mary in that she is quite unmerciful, and it surfaces that she despises Jews. She herself asks for mercy at the end of her tale; she is ignorant to her plea and hypocritical to her prayer. She does not realise that by asking for mercy for Christmas and not Jews, that her hypocrisy will inescapably overcome her being. In retrospect, "the Prioress does not see that her prayer for mercy on 'us sinners' is inconsistent with this zeal for 'justice' against the Jews" (Ames). Chaucer uses the word 'mercy' three times in the last four lines to exhibit that he himself sees her as a superficial, caustic, and vile woman.

The Prioress is quite a captivating character in that her life is built on the themes of irony, hypocrisy, and ignorance. She is wedged between two appearances; the self that praises and values purity, placing emphasis on the virginity of the slain boy, which is contrasted by her own lust for blood and vengeance. Her story is a tragic one with lessons of love; "[the Prioress's] tale reads like an unhappy chapter in the history of thirteenth century England, seen through the eyes of a sentimental, pious, and bigoted woman; and that may be as

Chaucer meant us to read it" (Ames).

Her tale is full of imagery that illustrates her yearning to venture towards "[the Virgin] Mary's virtuous world of childlike spiritual perfection," yet the infantile imagery also connects the reader with the Prioress's desire for a womanhood that she cannot have (Condren). She was placed in a life that was not satisfying to her lifestyle and longing. The fact that she cannot have what she wants makes her one of the most relatable characters within The Canterbury Tales, but perhaps one of the most heartbreaking. Although I cannot share her anti-Semitic values or her undying need to use violence within her tale, I can connect to her unrelenting feeling to be close to naivety and innocence. The true story here is the struggle in the midst of who she is, who she wants to be, and who she has to be. Chaucer relates her internal strife through her spirituality, her materialism, and her ominous tale.

Chapter 15

Critical Essays

Chaucer's Theories of Textual Interpretation in the Canterbury Tales Chauntecleer, in the course of wooing his beloved Pertelote, quotes a well known 14th century proverb: "mulier est hominis confusio." He then proceeds to render the saying into English quite incorrectly:

Madame, the sentence of this Latyn is,
'Womman is mannes joye and al his blis.'

While we may appreciate Chauntecleer's talents as a lover, the quality of his translation leaves much to be desired. That Chaucer meant for Chauntecleer's misreading to be a comic moment, there is no doubt. What may give a reader pause is the motive behind the misreading. Does Chauntecleer simply not know the proper translation? Is he completely ignorant of Latin? Or is he knowingly misconstruing a popular sentiment for his own purposes? Such questions naturally lead into an examination of the character of Chauntecleer himself.

Are there textual clues that might help us understand what Chauntecleer's misreading means? Surely, his own confabulated translation works better in the context of lovemaking than the correct "woman is man's ruin." We also have ample evidence, in the form of his impressive display of authoritative citations, of this particular rooster's unexpected erudition. There is then, it seems, some evidence for a deliberate and knowing misreading. But, one might contend, if Chauntecleer is so learned, surely he could have come up with a more fitting proverb or bit of doggerel-why go to the trouble of mistranslating a less-than-apt Latin sentiment at all?

It is not my intention in this essay to delve too deeply into the Chauntecleer dilemma, but this moment in The Nun's Priest's Tale introduces, at a very straightforward and obvious level, the issue of interpretation in The Canterbury Tales. Among Chaucer's Pilgrims and the characters that inhabit their tales, there are many readers, and many characters who interpret linguistic utterances (both written and verbal). Some of these "readers" are obvious, such as the Parson and the Wife of Bath, both Biblical exegetes. Other characters, like the Summoner in "The Friar's Tale" and (neatly and conversely) the Friar in "The Summoner's Tale," while never seen engaged in literal "reading," exemplify certain theoretical aspects of 14th century interpretation. Like Chauntecleer, the majority of Chaucer's readers are far from perfect, but it is often through their various "misreadings" (be they literal misreadings or more complex methodological errors) that we are able to understand their full significance to Chaucer and his 14th century audience.

For an example even more straightforward than Chauntecleer's mangled Latin, there is John, the bumbling carpenter in "The Miller's Tale." Although we never witness John performing anything as intellectually complicated as reading the scriptures (it seems highly doubtful that he can read at all), he does enact a "misreading" of sorts when he buys into Nicholas' whopper about the coming second flood. In believing that God will flood the world a second time, John betrays his own ignorance of the actual Biblical story of Noah, wherein God promises mankind he shall never drown the world again. Ruth M. Ames convincingly argues that John here conflates the actual Biblical text with the popular mystery play of Noah's Flood, with which he was more likely to be familiar than the written scripture.

John's misinterpretation is of the most basic kind-he is simply ignorant in matters of scripture. However, the formula is rarely that simple in Chaucer. Theories of interpretation in the Middle Ages were not, like our theoretical approaches of today, simply aesthetic or epistemological paradigms. The text at the centre of every interpretive theory born in the Middle Ages is, of course, the Bible, and therefore it is impossible to completely separate artistic questions from moral and spiritual concerns. It was in the early years of the church that Christians first adopted an allegorical approach to interpretation, especially as concerns the inherited books of the Old Testament.

Early Christian fathers such as Tertullian argued that Old Testament events could be read as allegorical types for the events of th New Testament. This idea was picked up and developed by many of the most influential Christian writers of the West, including Augustine and Jerome. By the end of the first millennium, scripture was understood to hold two general levels of meaning, what Medieval theologians called the "letter," the literal meaning, and the "spirit" (the terms themselves are first used by Paul in Cor:). In the first book of the Summa Theologica, for example, Thomas Aquinas writes:

Therefore that first signification whereby words signify things belongs to the first sense, the historical or literal. That signification whereby things signified by the words have themselves also a signification is called the spiritual sense, which is based on the literal, and presupposes it.

The spiritual sense itself was further divided into three generally accepted subcategories, what Aquinas calls (though the categories predate him) the moral, the allegorical and the anagogical. These categories were learned by generations of Medieval students with the help of a well known mnemonic couplet:

Littera gesta docet; quid credas allegoria
Moralis quid agas; quo tendas anagogica.

While Robertson correctly warns that such forumulae can lead modern students to think of Medieval allegory in a reductive or simplistic way (Robertson,), this neat couplet, with its syntactic symmetry and well-balanced versification (unlike a Classical couplet, it both begins and ends with a dactyl) makes apparent a fundamental truth about Medieval exegesis. Overly literal interpretation is dangerous, especially when dealing with the non-Christian texts of the Old Testament. However, it is no more desirable to discount the letter completely, a practice which can open the door to an abuse of allegory and the manipulation of scriptural meaning to suit any purpose. The ideal interpretation was one that balanced the two, and it is by this test that we can begin to judge the characters of The Canterbury Tales as readers.

Among the Biblical exegetes in The Canterbury Tales, the most literal is The Wife of Bath. Robertson aptly describes her exegesis as "carnal," for her concern above all is the flesh and its representation on the Biblical page. As a reader, the Wife is almost exclusively concerned with the letter over the spirit. Mounting a defence of her libidinous history in "typical medieval style," The Wife comes prepared with a list of Biblical authorities and exempla (Ames,). Early on in her prologue, for instance, she cites the example of Solomon (who else?):

Lo, here the wise kyng, daun Salomon;
I trowe he hadde wyves mo than oon.
As wolde God it leveful were unto me
To be refreshed half so ofte as he!
Which yifte of God hadde hefor alle his wyvys.

Forced to defend her own sexual predispositions, she first hauls out the old Israelite king, who, she claims, surely received his 700 wives as gift from God. She also invokes the patriarchs:

I woot wel Abraham was an hooly man,
And Jacob eek, as ferforth as I kan;
And ech of hem hadde wyves mo than two,
And many another holy man also..

In citing the examples of Solomon and the Patriarchs, the Wife of Bath is attempting to use Old Testament examples as behavioral models. Her argument echoes the anxieties of the Anglo-Saxon bishop Aelfric, who was so nervous about the discrepancies between Old and New Law that he almost abandoned his own English translation of the Pentateuch.

In the preface to his translation of Genesis, he stresses the importance of making the distinction between gastlice andgit (the spiritual meaning) and eo nacede gerecednis (the naked, or literal, meaning).

The danger was obvious to Aelfric. By making the Old Testament more readily available to the unlearned (ða ungelaerdan), men not trained in the proper allegorical method of Old Testament exegesis, the possibility existed that well-meaning Christians might become confused about exactly what kind of moral code was sanctioned by scripture. Latin had provided an effective buffer, keeping the untrained at arms length from the unfiltered content of the Bible.

Aelfric was particularly squeamish about the realities of marriage in the Old Testament:

Hwilon ic wiste þæt sum mæssepreost, se þe min magister wæs on þam timan, hæfde þa boc Genesis, and he cuðe be dæle Lyden understandan: þa cwæþ he be þam heahfædere Iacobe, þæt he hæfde feower wif, twa geswustra and heora twa þinena. Ful soð he sæde, ac he nyste, ne ic þa git, hu micel todal ys betweohx þære ealdan æ and þære niwan (A while back I knew that some masspriest, he who was my teacher in those days, had the book Genesis, and he could understand in part the Latin: he said of the Patriarch Jacob that he had four wives, two sisters and their two handmaids. He spoke full truth, but he did not know, no did I yet, how great the difference is between the old law and the new). (Mitchell and Robinson,).

Just as Aelfric feared in his preface to Genesis, The Wife of Bath uses the examples of Abraham and Jacob as strict behavioral guides. While The Wife demonstrates familiarity with the Old Testament stories, she either lacks the exegetical faculties to make good Christian sense of them, or she is shrewd enough to manipulate the scripture to her advantage. She does not mention, of course, the standard "spiritual" explanation for the polygamy of Solomon and other Old Testament figures that had already been provided by, among others, St. Augustine in "On Marriage and Concupiscence":

That the holy fathers of olden times after Abraham, and before him, to whom God gave His testimony that "they pleased Him," thus used their wives (for procreation), no one who is a Christian ought to doubt, since it was permitted to certain individuals amongst them to have a plurality of wives, where the reason was for the multiplication of their offspring, not the desire of varying gratification. (Augustine,.)

Augustine explains the need for polygamy in pragmatic terms. The justification for God's allowance of multiple wives to the Old Testament fathers was that it furthered the expansion of the Israelite nation.

It would be a mistake to think of the Wife of Bath as ignorant, however. While she may be a "failure" as a Medieval exegete, she is profoundly successful as a rhetorician. Her concerns are with the flesh, not the mind or the spirit, and so it is not surprising that she ignores the "spirit" in her reading. She shrewdly takes what she needs from the scripture and ignores the arguments of the opposition, except to debunk them. We can justly call her overly literal reading of The Old Testament a "misreading," for she fails to meet the exegetical criteria laid out by Aquinas. However, hers is a misreading based not in ignorance, but in purposeful misuse. Thus it is not surprising, as Kittredge points out, that she garners the praise of that most famous Chaucerian charlatan, The Pardoner:

Up stirte the Pardoner, and that anon;
"Now dame, " quod he, "by God and by Seint John!
Ye been a noble prechour in this cas. (163-165).

Perhaps, as Kittredge writes, the Wife of Bath should not be taken too seriously, even if she is worthy of some rebuke (Kittredge,). But, it seems to me, Chaucer very much means for her "misreading" of scripture to cast light on her character. Like the Pardoner, she uses religion for her own ends, and her culpability in this regard must be acknowledged, even if we take pleasure, as Kittredge does, in her "infinite zest" (Kittredge,).

Chaucer's Theories of Textual Interpretation in the Canterbury Tales

As a literalist, The Wife of Bath has no peer among the Pilgrims. The closest match for her is the unscrupulous summoner in "The Friar's Tale." This unnamed huckster, while existing on a different ontological level than the Wife of Bath, can nonetheless be said to share some of her shortcomings as an exegete. While we never see the summoner engaged in literal Biblical analysis, we do get, in his dealings with his demonic cohort, a sense of his literalist nature. The Friar's tale is based on a very old story, one which usually starred a tax collector or lawyer or other unsavory public figure (Benson,). In this instance, the Friar has chosen to serve as the moral example of the story a summoner, one of an order of ecclesiastical bailiffs who "were quite as pervasive and unpopular in the middle ages as catchpolls were in the 18th century" (Kittredge,).

We already sense from their exchanges during the Wife of Bath's prologue that the Summoner and the Friar have no love for one another, and in his tale the Friar makes his utter disdain abundantly clear. The General Prologue tells us that the Friar is a skilled preacher, good enough to move even the most destitute woman to charity. It is not surprising that a character so skilled at using the scripture effectively for his own means should list among his protagonist's faults a certain denseness as an interpreter of language. The actual Summoner of the pilgrimage, for his part, seems to know what's coming, and tries his best to derail the tale before it gets going, only to be scolded into silence by the host: The Friar will tell his tale, and the Summoner will have to wait for his own turn to enact payback for ecclesiastical reasons, the Friar has no qualms about exposing the "harlotrye" of summoners-as a member of the religious clergy, he is not subject to the authority of the ecclesiastical courts, of which the summoners were agents (Benson,).

The Friar pulls no punches. His summoner is a lecher, always with "bawdes redy to his hond," and this charge probably hit particularly close to home for the Summoner of the company (as Janette Richardson explains, the "scall" that mars his face was very likely a form of syphilis) (Benson,). This summoner soon happens upon a devil, displaying an almost bizarre lack of concern for being in the company of such a creature. However, of greatest interest for my current purpose is the moment when the summoner and his hellish companion happen upon a man driving his horses through a patch of muddy ground:

Deep was the wey, for which the carte stood.
The cartere smoot, and cryde as he were wood,
"Hayt, Brok! Hayt, Scot! what spare ye for the stones?
The feend," quod he, "yow fecche, body and bones,
As ferforthly as evere were ye foled,
So muche wo as I have with yow tholed!
The devel have al, bothe hors and cart and hey!
This somonour seyde, "Heere shal we have a pley."

The summoner, upon hearing the oath of the driver, immediately thinks that he has forfeited himself and his property to the Devil's possession. His reading, like The Wife of Bath's reading of scripture, is excessively literal, focusing entirely on the letter while ignoring the spirit. The demon, obviously more experienced in the realm of ghostly forfeiture, quickly corrects the summoner's misreading:

"Nay," quod the devel, "God woot, never a deel!
It is nat his entente, trust me weel.
Axe hym thyself, it thou nat trowest me;
Or elles stynt a while, and thou shalt see."
This cartere thakketh his hors upon the croupe,
And they bigonne to drawen and to stoupe.
"Heyt! Now," quod he, "ther Jhesu Crist yow blesse,
And al his handwerk, bothe moore and lesse!

The devil, a better exegete than the summoner, can see what his companion cannot-the intent behind the driver's language. "Intent" in this instance seems to be roughly synonymous with exegetical term "spirit"-it is the "true" meaning behind the veil of literal utterance. As with the Wife of Bath, this summoner's excessively literal misreading accompanies more obvious moral shortcomings, such as those laid out by the Friar in the tale's opening. It probably isn't a coincidence that Chaucer's two most famous literalists are both excessively carnal in their appetites, but there is also an important distinction to be made between the Wife and the Friar's summoner. The Wife "misreads" with a rhetorical purpose, and there is something to be admired in the particularly Medieval way in which she builds her case. Wayne Shoemaker tallies the impressive count of her literary sources and references:

In the eight hundred twenty-eight lines of her prologue she refers...to Jesus, Solomon, St. Paul, Lamech, Abraham, Jacob, Mark Ptolemy, Argus, job, Metellius, Venus, Darius, Appelles, Mars, Simplicius Gallus, Ecclesiastes Valerius, Theophrastus, Jerome, Jovinian, Tertullian, Chrsippus, Trotula, Heloise, Ovide, Midas, Adam, Mercury, Eve, Sampson, Hercules, Dejanira, Socrates, Xantippe, Pasiphae, Clytemnestra, Amphiaraus, Eriphyle, Livia, Lucilia, Latumyus (whoever he is), and Arrius...an average of better than one new literary or mythological reference to every twenty lines. (quoted in Muscatine,)

Of course, it is not necessarily clear that the Wife understands all the references she makes, but at the very least her arguments are backed up by the marshaling of innumerable authorities. The Friar's summoner, meanwhile, is hardly so impressive-his misreading is merely a symptom of greed and ignorance. He lacks both the intellect and the essential vitality that makes the Wife, in the estimation of Muscatine and others, "possibly the most fully realised character in Chaucer" (Muscatine,). This shouldn't come as a surprise, for the Friar purposely paints the summoner in his tale as one completely without redeeming qualities. While in this task he is irreproachably successful, he must then receive the Summoner's counterattack in kind.

Like the Wife of Bath and the Friar's summoner, the friar of the Summoner's tale is a character who falls short in several categories of Christian morality. Also like those individuals, his methods as an exegete are part of the problem. Having been forced to endure the slanders of the Friar, the Summoner wastes no time in showing his fellow pilgrims that "freres and feendes been but lyte asonder." The tale, "an incomparable satire on begging friars" (Kittredge,), proceeds as we might expect, but perhaps the more astute reader is a bit taken aback when this friar begins espousing on exegesis to a sick man:

I have to day been at youre chirche at messe,
and seyd a sermon after my symple wit,
Nat al after the text of hooly writ;
For it is hard to yow, as I suppose,
And therfore wol I teche yow al the glose.
Glosynge is a glorious thyng, certeyn,
For lettre sleeth, so as we clerkes seyn.

The last line, of course, paraphrases the ur-text of the letter vs. spirit debate, St. Paul in the second epistle to the Corinthians: "not of the letter, but of the spirit: for the letter killeth, but the spirit giveth life." Unlike the Wife of Bath and the Friar's summoner, this unnamed Friar does appear to have some understanding of what it means to read allegorically. Indeed, he speaks with reverence about the "glorious" talent of glossing, or interpretation. A quick assumption might then be that we should consider this friar a "better" reader than either of the two literalists described above.

But that, I think, would be a rush to judgment, especially when we consider the source of this friar. The Summoner, we know, has no intention of talking about a friar who has any redeeming qualities whatsoever. His entire purpose is to cast the mendicant orders in as poor a light as possible. A first clue to the solution to this dilemma can be found with the help of the Middle English Dictionary. While "glose" in one sense simply means to interpret or provide the meaning for a written text, as in the sense of our modern word gloss, it also from before Chaucer's time through the Renaissance carried a more negative connotation: to provide a specious or false meaning, i.e., to "misinterpret." Hence Milton writes of the flattering serpent:

So glozed the Tempter, and his proem tuned:
Into the heart of Eve his words made way,

Though at the voice much marvelling...

The Summoner in these lines is not praising his friar for the ability to read allegorically, but drawing attention to his misuse of the scripture for his own means. Here, as with the Wife of Bath, we have another purposeful "misreading," where misinterpretation is a vital part of the character's rhetoric. However, the Summoner's Friar is at the opposite end of the spectrum from The Wife of Bath. While the former ignored the spirit, focusing instead on the literal sense, the latter, as Robertson points out, ignores the letter entirely, "substituting for it ideas of his own" (Robertson,). And despite their fondness for allegory, Medieval thinkers recognized that such casting aside of the of the letter was as serious an error as ignorance of the spirit. I return to the Summa:

Thus in Holy Scripture no confusion results, for all the senses are founded on one-the literal-from which alone can any argument be drawn, and not from those intended allegorically, as Augustine says (Aquinas,, emphasis mine).

Chaucer's Theories of Textual Interpretation in the Canterbury Tales

What difference is bitwixe an ydolastre and an avaricious man, but that an ydolastre, per aventure, ne hath but o mawmet or two, and the avaricious man hath manye? For certes, every floryn in his cofre is his mawmet. And certes, the synne of mawmettrie is the firste thyng that God deffended in the ten comaundementz as bereth witnesse in exodi capitulo vicesimo. Thou shalt have no false Goddes bifore me, ne thou shalt make to thee no grave thyng. Thus is an avaricious man, that loveth his tresor biforn God, an ydolastre, thurgh this cursed synne of Avarice.

As the Parson explains, the commandment exists not simply as a literal injunction against idolatry, but also as a law that looks forward in time to the New Testament and the deadly sin of avarice. In the tradition of Jerome, Augustine, and Aelfric, the New Law is used to shine light upon the Old, and vice versa. This kind of multifaceted exegesis recurs again and again in the Parson's tale. The words of the Israelite kings

Solomon and David are read as prefigurations of the Christian doctrine of Hell, while Isaiah's warnings against lying are explained in the light of Christ, who is "verray trouthe."

The Parson, so clearly the ideal cleric in many ways, is also the most versatile reader in The Canterbury Tales. He "neither reads the text carnally, abuses the spirit for his own interest, nor denies the validity of the spirit beneath the letter" (Robertson,). The example of the Parson seems to confirm the pattern in the Tales that links moral quality with exegetical talents. The Wife is purely a creature of the flesh and also a rhetorical powerhouse-thus her reading of the scripture is highly literal yet painstakingly authorized. The Friar's summoner is as carnal as the wife, yet he lacks her intellect; his reading is both literal and simplistic. The greedy Friar, meanwhile, knows just how to manipulate the gastlice andgit to garner a living wage. The Parson, who shows up at the end of the tales to denounce all the hedonism he has just been subjected to, is alone in his talents as a true exegete after the fashion of Paul and Aquinas.

The question for many readers in the end will be: which of these readers is closest to Chaucer? Accepting for the moment that Chaucer feels little regard for the friar of the Summoner's Tale or the summoner in The Friar's Tale, can it be ascertained if his sympathies lie more with The Wife of Bath or the Parson? Chaucer's esteem for the Parson seems beyond doubt: he is given the special honour of closing the tales, and by word count alone his tale is the longest of the collection.

On the other hand, countless critics, including Kittredge and Muscatine, have marveled at the Wife of Bath's "personality" and her iconoclastic stances on male domination and "received authorities." To a moralist like Robertson, however, the Wife of Bath can do no good: critics like Muscatine and Kittredge who "grow sentimental over [The Wife of Bath's] human qualities are, from a fourteenth century view, merely being misled" (Robertson, 3).

Robertson's attempts to remove the fog of alterity from

the Tales and understand these characters as a 14th century audience would is a noble effort, but in doing so he finds it necessary to paint the very concept of "personality" as a mere invention of the modern mind.

The purpose of The Wife of Bath is to amuse readers and audiences, this is true, but to claim that Chaucer or his audience would have been incapable of sympathizing with such an overwhelming personality (and I use the term with purpose) seems to me an unnecessarily reductive stance on the makeup of the medieval mind. Even the probably small minority of Chaucer's audience who recognized the Wife's ignorance of Pauline allegorical principals or Augustinian theory would not necessarily have cared. These shortcomings are part of what made the character amusing to Chaucer and still make her amusing to us, but they do not, in and of themselves, qualify as proof of Chaucer's disdain. Had Chaucer wanted to make the Wife an object of ridicule, he could have easily made her a buffoon like the Friar's summoner. The overwhelming quality of her rhetoric is proof enough for me that Robertson's claim—that the Wife's prologue serves as Chaucer's "scathing denunciation" of such carnality—is simply a case of overzealous moralism (Robertson,).

At the very least, she is not a hypocrite, a characteristic which Chaucer seems to hold in clear disdain, judging by the countless examples presented in the Tales. In this respect, it is defensible to say that Chaucer feels more sympathy with The Wife of Bath than with the more refined Prioress, whose merciless howling for Jewish blood seems at odds with the Amor vincit omnia engraved on her brooch. I thus end how I began, with a misreading of a Latin proverb. That the Prioress doesn't understand the spirit of the very words she wears upon her breast seems to me the most subtle, and perhaps the most telling, example of Chaucerian misreading.

Through "glosynge," by creating his own meaning, the friar can make the Bible say whatever he wants it to say. Robertson sums it up best: "The object of the friar's "glosynge" is not to further a love for God and for one's neighbour, but to persuade the people to be 'charitable' by giving their wealth to him" (Robertson,). The actual Friar of the pilgrimage seems to share this talent; his "in principio" doesn't save souls, it loosens purse-strings:

For thogh a wydwe hadde noght a sho,
So plesaunt was his "In principio"
Yet wolde he have a ferthyng, er he wente;

Any final summation of the rivalry between the Friar and the Summoner must acknowledge the sad fact that each pilgrim's caricature of the other turns out to be dismayingly accurate, at least if the General Prologue is to be believed.

We have looked at some examples of "misreading" in The Canterbury Tales, but to find an example of an exegete who clearly has Chaucer's admiration, one must look for a reader who can properly balance understanding of the littera and the spiritus. The most obvious character to look at is, of course, The Parson, a learned cleric trained in Augustinian hermeneutics and familiar with the writings of St. Jerome. The Parson quotes extensively from both the Old and New Testament and in his explications he displays a clear ability to comprehend meaning at more than one level. For example, he says of the second commandment:

The Question of Genre: The Canterbury Tales as Dantean Epic

The nineteenth-century notion of The Canterbury Tales as an anthology or collection of miscellaneous tales is no longer widely accepted, yet there has been little discussion in modern times about the genre to which The Canterbury Tales ought to be assigned. Not one of the notable discussions of the poem to appear in recent years, so far as I am aware, devotes any space to the question. Donald R. Howard, for example, whose book is significantly entitled The Idea of the Canterbury Tales, begins like most Chaucerians today, with the premise that despite its variety Chaucer's poem has a conceptual unity. He argues persuasively that the "inner form" of The Canterbury Tales can be understood in terms of the metaphors of speculum and labyrinth, but aside from a reference to the "interlace" of medieval romance, he does not attempt to connect the poem to any of the recognized medieval literary genres. One reason for the neglect of this topic in contemporary Chaucer studies has doubtless been a justifiable distrust of genre criticism, a distrust that could only be magnified in the case of a fragmentary text like The Canterbury Tales, which is itself already composed of a prolific variety of genres, from the fabliau to the sermon. How is one going to fit such variousness into a single generic category? For these and other reasons the reluctance to speculate about the genre of The Canterbury Tales seems understandable, and yet I believe that the attempt to establish a genre for the poem as a whole has value.

It can only help to clarify the "idea" of Chaucer's unfinished poem by suggesting its primary literary antecedents and the general shape it might have had when completed. Not that the genre I am proposing for The Canterbury Tales, that of the medieval epic as an extension of the classical, Greco-Roman epic, has a very clearly defined shape. Its narrative begins, or should begin, according to Horace's verse epistle, in "the middle of things" ("De Arte Poetica," l. 148), and it has a tendency to end there, with many loose strands and most questions unresolved. As a genre, indeed, the epic is perhaps the most perfect example of the way some recent theory views all genre: as a nonlimiting form in which heterogeneous conventions and narrative patterns compete with each other but are ultimately harmonized. At least since Virgil, the epic as a genre has been perhaps rather like a problem or project an author takes on involving history in a dual sense: political, dealing with the destiny of peoples, Horace's "res gestae regumque ducumque et tristia bella" (things done by kings and leaders and dire wars, "De Arte Poetica,".); and literary, the evocation of a past literature as providing a model to be imitated and revised.

The epic poet's self-imposed task as interpreter and mediator of this twofold past may well have prompted Virgil to begin the Aeneid with an uncharacteristic bit of literary "autobiography":

Ille ego, qui quondam gracili modulatus avena carmen, et egressus silvis vicina coegiut quamvis avido parerent arva colono, gratum opus agricolis; at nunc horrentia Martis arms virumque cano.(I am he who once tuned my song on a slender reed, then, leaving thewoodland, constrained the neighbouring fields to serve thehusbandmen, however grasping—a work welcome to farmers: butnow of Mars' bristling arms I sing and the man).

But it is scarcely surprising that the authenticity of the first four lines has often been questioned, for Virgil otherwise adheres strictly to the impersonality of classical epic. Nowhere else in the Aeneid does he draw attention to himself as a poet with a career, however symbolically idealized, of his own. In countless ways, however, the text of the Aeneid shows a poet working in full awareness of his literary predecessors, epitomized for him by Homer. The poet is literally a textor, a weaver combining strands from the Iliad and the Odyssey to tell his story of Aeneas.

This point has often been noted and has at times led to the judgment that Virgil was excessively dependent on his exemplary texts, allowing his project to be overwhelmed by them. It seems possible that Virgil's own reputed dissatisfaction with his poem sprang from similar doubts, but such a negative opinion surely ignores the extraordinary originality with which he forged his Homeric materials into a quite non- or post-Homeric vision of human destiny where men and gods are, as it were, "historicized," that is, seen to derive their being from their place in a historical continuum. This continuum is dominated by a succession of different ethe, now passionate, violent, unselfconscious, now detached, inward, cunning, and so forth. These do not, however, cancel each other out but in their mutual strife or competition constitute a kind of historical "deep structure" of which earthly events are the visible manifestation.

For all the sense of a ceaseless and mysterious process

that the Aeneid presents, its reflective style implies a kind of superior vantage point from which the bewildering scene can be viewed and analysed. It is this effect of the style, I suggest, that Dante personifies in the figure of Virgil in the Comedy, giving it the role of the Pilgrim's guide through hell and purgatory. "You are my master and my author" ("Tu se' lo mio maestro e'l mio autore," Inf. I.), the Pilgrim tells him when he first meets Virgil, and the words reverberate throughout the Comedy. Now, the extensive medieval legend of Virgil the magus and proto-Christian undoubtedly contributed to the creation of Dante's fictional Virgil, yet the primary source was surely the authorial personality Dante inferred from the poems, particularly the Aeneid. In that sense, I would say, the Virgil of the Comedy is "textual," the result of a bold act of literary interpretation in which author and text are identified.

Dante thus makes explicit from the beginning of his poem what remains implicit throughout the Aeneid: his Comedy acknowledges one master-text and will engage in a form of dialogue with it. This has the further effect of placing the Comedy in the epic tradition, a tradition Dante brings to a kind of life when the Pilgrim and Virgil join the shades of Homer, Horace, Ovid, and Lucan in Limbo. Dante-the-poet-pilgrim is invited to be the sixth in this group of classical poets (Inf. IV.–), which constitutes what admittedly looks like a rather idiosyncratic line of epic descent. The presence of Horace, the one decidedly nonepic poet in the group, might be accounted for, I suggest, by the fact that like Ovid he was a contemporary of Virgil and thus underscores the centrality, in Dante's scheme, not just of Virgil but also of the Rome of Virgil's time.

The figure of Virgil is a major crux in the Comedy, full discussion of which is well beyond the scope of this chapter. It epi[illegible]omizes the momentous transformation of the epic genre [illegible]ht by the Comedy; thereafter, the personal role of the poet [illegible] absolutely central. At the same time Dante's Virgil [illegible]ds a problem that in the classical epic remains altogether submerged: the relation between individual, personal history and collective, "universal" history. In the classical epic the individual tends to be treated as part of the great historical scheme of things (whether as victim, victor, or mere bystander).

Not so in Dante's epic. There the individual has his or her own history, and the question is how that fits into the pattern of a larger, global history. Thus Virgil, the poet who in the famous sixth book of his epic described his hero's visit to the underworld, is ideally qualified to serve as guide and model for the story of a pilgrimage through the otherworld. As a historical individual, however, born sub Iulio, "nel tempo de li dei false e bugiardi" ("in the time of the false and lying gods," Inf. I.), he suffers from a fatal flaw or disability: he is eternally barred from entrance into the heavenly city, having been in life, as he affirms, a rebel to the heavenly emperor's law (Inf. I.–). The pagan poet is thus, in the perspective of the Christian scheme of history, a problematical, even paradoxical, guide in this Christian pilgrimage.

As such, Virgil also raises a personal question for the poet of the Comedy: Is Dante's ambition to be the author of a great Christian epic perhaps a terrible mistake or an anachronism? In other words, is the very idea of Christian literature a contradiction in terms? Virgil's paganism, and that of his fellow poets in Limbo, might suggest that in the perspective of a Christian dispensation the very pursuit of literature leads only to a dead end, to a way of condemning oneself

to a life of desire without hope. Or is there a specifically Christian kind of poetry that can escape this sense of futility? Perhaps that is what the Comedy is intended to figure forth. Giuseppe Mazzotta seems to believe that such is the case when he speaks of "the radical predicament of a Christian poet [like Dante] who seeks more than an esthetic humanistic redemption and less than to perform the supreme transgression of writing an appendix to the Bible." The dilemma represented by these alternatives undoubtedly played its part in the composition of the Comedy, but my hunch is that what the Comedy is concerned with in the first place is the redemption of poetry, or literature, as such, regardless of its doctrinal or other orientation. Let us not forget that Dante is proud to count himself as one of the select company of pagan poets in Limbo.

The figure of Statius, which appears in Purgatorio XXI–XXVII, illustrates the complexity of the problem and simultaneously, I believe, hints at a resolution. Statius attributes both his becoming a poet and his becoming a Christian to Virgil's influence—"Per te poeta fui, per te cristiano," "Through you I was a poet and, through you, / a Christian" (Purg. XXII.)—but though by Dante's historical fiction Statius was a Christian before he finished his first epic, neither the Thebaid nor the unfinished Achilleid was explicitly Christian in content. There is thus a certain irony in his enthusiastic tribute to the Aeneid:

Al mio ardor fuor seme le faville, chemi scaldar, della divine flammaonde sono allumati più di mille; dell'Eneida dico, la qual mamma fummi e fummi nutrice poetando: sanz'essa no fermai peso di dramma. Purg. The sparks that warmed me, the seeds of my ardor, were from the holy fire—the same that gave more than a thousand poets light and flame. I speak of the Aeneid; when I wrote verse, it was mother to me, it was nurse: my work without it, would not weigh an ounce.)

The words recall Dante-the-pilgrim's passionate acknowledgment of his debt to Virgil (Inf. I.ff.) and remind us that Statius is yet another "mirror" for the Pilgrim. The implied judgment on Statius as a poet, however, is that he represents a weak or an inadequate link in the heroic tradition. This is not primarily a matter of his self-confessed cowardice in refusing to declare himself openly a Christian in his poems; that merely obscures, I believe, what is in reality to be seen as his imaginative failure. As his wonderfully hyperbolic language intimates—mamma / fummi e fummi nutrice poetando —he had a childlike dependence on the Aeneid, drew too much of his poetic sustenance from it, so that when it came to writing his own poems he was unable to move beyond the Virgilian model. His lukewarm Christianity, it could almost be said, results from his failure to take his poetry seriously enough, to see it as a vital and integral part of his existence. Had he taken it more seriously, he might have gained the courage to write an overtly Christian epic. As it is, not he but Dante is the next in line of succession from Homer.

Statius, or rather the myth Dante has fashioned of him in the Purgatorio, thus provides in the first instance a negative answer to the question concerning a specifically Christian poetry. For Statius, even though he was converted to Christianity by the reading of a poem—Virgil's fourth Eclogue (Purg. XXII.ff.)—Christianity and poetry exist in separate compartments; in his mind there is clearly no connection between them. This is, I believe, one of a number of reasons that Statius does not replace Virgil as the Pilgrim's guide, despite the fact that he now reveals himself as somewhat of an authority on theological matters. Poetry plus theology is not what the Pilgrim—or the poet of the Comedy —is after. Instead, he continues to be guided by the pagan poet ignorant of the mysteries of Christian revelation. The implication, as I see it, is that any poetry, if pursued seriously, so far from being antagonistic to religious truth, is integral to it. And one further conclusion I should like to draw from the foregoing considerations is that there is no specifically Christian poetry. There is only poetry written by Christian, Jew, Muslim, "pagan".

Virgil's sudden and wordless disappearance once the Pilgrim has entered the Earthly Paradise seems to accord with this conclusion. Here is no violent rupture, like the earthquake signaling that Statius has been cleansed of his sin (Purg. XX and XXI.ff.), but a natural progression. The Pilgrim was about to speak to Virgil—who by now is a fellow traveller rather than a guide or master—and he has already formed the sentences in his head, but Virgil, he discovers, is no longer by his side (Purg. XXX.ff.). The dialogue with Virgil, in other words, is not concluded, indeed, cannot be concluded, because Virgil and all that that name stands for has been fully internalized by the Pilgrim-poet, who is now ready to move on to the next stage of his pilgrimage, his encounter with Beatrice.

In the preceding paragraphs I have tried to sketch in rough outline what I believe may have been Dante's understanding of the epic tradition and of his poem's place in it, from the evidence of the Comedy itself. My emphasis has been on Dante because I start from the premise that for his epic project Chaucer chose his Italian predecessor for a guide as Dante had chosen Virgil for his. In two poems composed before The Canterbury Tales, we can observe Chaucer looking ahead to and meditating upon his project. In both he has Dante in mind and alludes to the group of poets assembled in Dante's Limbo. First, there is the envoy to Troilus and Criseyde:

Go, litel bok, go, litel myn tragedye,
Ther God thi makere yet, er that he dye,
So sende myght to make in some comedye!
But litel book, no makyng thow n'envie,
But subgit be to alle poesye;
And kis the steppes, wher as thow seest pace
Virgile, Ovide, Omer, Lucan, and Stace.

That last line does not, of course, refer to Chaucer's "sources," for which he has already created the fiction of "Lollius" (I.)—notoriously, he nowhere in his works mentions Boccaccio. Rather, like Dante's poets in Limbo, Chaucer's are mentioned to place the book of Troilus in the line of epic that they created. That the list reflects Dante's group seems clear enough. It may also allude, as it has at times been suggested, to the end of the Filocolo, where Boccaccio addresses "mio libretto" and names the same authors, except that Chaucer puts Homer where Boccaccio had Dante!

There are other hints of Dante's presence in our passage. When Chaucer describes Troilus and Criseyde as "litel myn tragedye" and expresses the hope that before he dies he will "make in some comedye" he may well be echoing Dante's references to his poem as "questa comedìa" (Inf. XVI.) and "la mia comedìa" (Inf. XXI.) over against Virgil's reference to his poem as "l'alta mia tragedìa" (XX.). In his characteristically understated, self-deprecatory way Chaucer could here be insinuating an extraordinary ambition that matches Virgil in tragedy, Dante in his comedy.

The idea of the Troilus as somehow modeled on the Aeneid is not as farfetched as it might at first appear to be. It would require, in the first place, a focus on the early books of the Aeneid dealing with the destruction of Troy and Dido's love tragedy as the real centre of the epic. That is precisely the focus we get in the dream-vision summary of the Aeneid at the beginning of the House of Fame: lines for the first four books, 33 for the rest. I mention this because I believe that the House of Fame is Chaucer's fullest meditation on the nature and meaning of epic and the second of the two poems in which he most clearly looks ahead to The Canterbury Tales with Dante in mind.

The connections between fame and the epic are clear enough: traditionally, they may be said to depend or "feed" upon each other. Fame supplies the motives and the materials that inspire the epic poet, but in this poem, which Alfred David has aptly characterized as a mock-epic, fame is also scrutinized for what it is and how it operates. In the course of the scrutiny there is a hint of a possible redefinition of the idea of fame and thus of the traditional focus of epic. All this fits very well, of course, with Dante's Comedy, but what makes the House of Fame most obviously an exploration of Dante's epic manner in the mode of parody is the fact that the poet-figure is made the dramatic centre of his narrative. The poem as a whole, we might say, serves as Chaucer's announcement or preparation for the new departure that is to be The Canterbury Tales, in which Chaucer will, in effect, manifest himself as "Dante in Inglissh," to use Lydgate's characterization of the House of Fame.

The seed of the idea developed in the House of Fame derives from Dante's Limbo (Inf. IV). There, it will be remembered, the Pilgrim and his guide encounter crowds of the unbaptized and the great poets and sages, as well as heroes and heroines of antiquity, all, in a manner of speaking, at home there. Who, the Pilgrim wants to know, are those so honoured that they are segregated from the others (–)? Virgil answers, in words pregnant with implications for the House of Fame:

L'onrata nominanzache di lor suona sù ne la tua vita, grazïa acquista in ciel che sì li avanza. (Inf. IV.–) (The honour of their name, which echoes up above within your life, gains Heaven's grace, and that advances them.)

The assumption in Virgil's speech of a correlative between earthly fame and divine grace comes in for extended mockery in the House of Fame, whose lady seems to hold the key to one of the central jokes in that work: the name that "resounds" (suona) on earth receives its reward in Fame's "heaven" by being amplified as sound, noise, moving air, wind.

The Proem of the House of Fame —whose narrator, as I said, is Dante's histrionic "I" that typically makes itself the centre of a drama of writing—begins with a discussion (anticipating the Nun's Priest's Tale) of dreams, which retrospectively we can recognize as a veiled if lighthearted inquiry into the sources, value, and authority of poetic visions like Dante's. In the Invocation this inquiry is extended to the problem of communicating the vision when the poet prays to Morpheus for help "my sweven for to telle aryght".

The same problem occupies Dante at the very opening of the Paradiso, which the Invocation may well echo with its reference to "he that mover ys of al" (;cf. "La gloria di colui che tutto move" [Par. I.]). There follows the Story of the actual dream, which takes place inside Venus's glass temple containing, as in the Knight's Tale, "portreytures." Somewhat anticlimactically, however, these merely retell in slightly garbled fashion the familiar story of the Aeneid. Why? Is this Chaucer's humourous and half-ironic comment on his lack of visionary powers? Or on the tyrannical hold the Virgilian model has on the poet's very unconscious? Whatever the answer, the "reading" of this miniature version of the Aeneid leaves the dreamer thoroughly disoriented: he knows not "where I am, ne in what contree".

Such disorientation is not uncommon in the Comedy, and Chaucer's parody seems aimed in part at the "autobiographical" cast of Dante's vision, the idea that it will serve as a way of resolving the poet-pilgrim's existential dilemma. In the House of Fame the vision inside the temple has obviously had the contrary effect, but when he leaves the temple to look for someone "that may telle me where I am", he begins, in effect, that quest for "authority" which comes to such an ambiguous conclusion in the last line of the poem. Once outside the temple, he finds himself in a deserted field reminiscent of the Libyan desert and of the "gran diserto" of Inferno I., where Virgil suddenly appears to rescue a Dante terrified by the beasts on the hillside. An eagle comes to save the Chaucerian dreamer from his terror (ff.), but it also may be said to have flown out of one of Dante's dreams, the one in Purgatorio IX, where it carried the pilgrim aloft to the sphere of fire below the moon (IX.). Like Virgil (and Beatrice) in the Comedy, the eagle was sent down, as he tells the dreamer, by Jupiter, not to give him a vision of heaven, to be sure, but to bear him to the House of Fame and so compensate him for his seemingly fruitless devotion to Cupid, Venus, and his books.

In the guise of the eagle, so I would interpret the "dark conceit" of Chaucer's parody here, Dante carries or guides the English poet away from his dependence on learned and aristocratic models toward the contemporary world buzzing with everyday speech that Dante incorporated so triumphantly into his poem. A perfect example of this speech is the dialogue between the eagle and the dreamer, which echoes so many of the dialogues that make up a major portion of the Comedy. "A ha!" says the eagle, as if he had just discovered a new form of discourse, "lo, so I can, / Lewedly to a lewed man / Speke". Indeed, there may be a hint here that Chaucer, who had demonstrated his artistry in this kind of dialogue ever since the Book of the Duchess, has nothing much to learn from his master in this area, except perhaps for the idea of an essentially theatrical poem that incorporates various kinds of speech and stylistic levels of everyday life.

Books II and III of the House of Fame parody Dante's otherworld fiction with their description of the house and the companies of people who come there for favors from its lady. The "afterlife" here is chaotic and as seemingly capricious as the life we know; despite the eagle's energetic flight we seem not to have left earth at all. Chaucer's otherworld, unlike Dante's, never really pretends to the "otherness" of visionary experience, and it contains nothing that seems designed to help our poet-dreamer to orient himself. There is, of course, the house—variously also called a castle or palace—but it is built on a rock of ice, "a feble fundament / To bilden on a place hye", and what is inside it has no apparent bearing on the dreamer's concerns. Its "hall of fame" contains statues of authors among whom there are again four of the five poets who in Limbo welcome Dante into their company (Inf. IV.), a scene that underlines the contrast between the two castles of fame, because in the Chaucerian one the dreamer is never more than an awestruck spectator and outsider among the statues. These, furthermore, include a representation of "Lollius," Chaucer's playful invention in the Troilus and a perfect exemplum of the questionableness that must attach to all of Fame's institutions. How far, after all, is the revered name of Homer from "Lollius"?

Does Dante's Limbo guarantee its distinguished residents a more substantial immortality than Fame's hall? Not necessarily. True, the elabourate structure of the Comedy suggests that in the Dantean universe, as in God's, all is purposeful, nothing and nobody is ultimately overlooked. The significance of the structure can, however, be over-emphasized, and often has been, in Dante criticism. At least as important, and certainly more mysterious, is the temporal dimension in Dante's poetic scheme, and it is this, obviously, that bears crucially on the question of poetic, or generally intellectual, posthumous fame.

It seems to me we get a clue regarding an answer to the

question very early in the Comedy when the Pilgrim first sees Virgil as one "chi per lungo silenzio parea fioco" (Inf. I.). The interpretation of this line has aroused controversy that shows no sign of flagging and which I am not competent to resolve even if such were possible. Ignoring all the difficulties, including the fact that the Italian has no explicit reference to "voice," I accept Sinclair's translation: Virgil first appeared to the Pilgrim as "one whose voice seemed weak from long silence." A possible interpretation of the line, then, seems to me that Virgil was silent until he got back his voice through Dante when he wrote the Comedy.

The obvious implication with respect to immortality is that a poet depends upon succeeding generations of poets—and commentators—to be heard, to remain alive after he has died. After death, in other words, a poet becomes identified with the texts he produced: they are his potential voice because, until brought back to life by one of the living, the poet-text is a mute shade languishing in Limbo. In light of what I said earlier about the epic poet's master project being the creative reinterpretation and renewal of the past, it follows that he is both aspirant to fame and the one peculiarly responsible for preserving the fame of others. Through him the ghosts in Limbo can hope to live again, momentarily. Through Virgil, who is the Aeneid, Homer speaks again, even for those who have never read Homer; through Dante, Virgil speaks once again, after how long a silence?

Now, the House of Fame, I have argued, shows us Chaucer aspiring to carry on the epic tradition as redefined by Dante—to make Dante speak "in Inglissh"—and at the same time, as befits a true continuator, detaching himself from some central aspects of Dantean epic. Detachment here does not mean repudiation, of course, but skepticism or at least a refusal to accept at face value. That would apply, as was already indicated, to the visionary element so central to Dante, and here also belongs the idea of poetic authority. It is, I believe, no accident that the House of Fame breaks off at the point when the dreamer sees a man who "seemed for to be / A man of great auctorite." Who this might be has been the subject of considerable scholarly speculation, but the prior point I would insist on concerns the inherent unlikelihood that a person of actual, let alone great, authority would make his appearance in this context. It is true, as I argued earlier, that the dreamer leaves Venus's temple looking for someone with sufficient authority to set him straight, that is, to tell him "where I am." This is assuredly part of the poem's parody of Dante, and it seems entirely appropriate to this parody that the poem would stop abruptly at the apparent culmination of the quest (whose point the dreamer has meanwhile characteristically forgotten). As a culmination turned into anticlimax, it is meant, I think, to be seen in relation to the moment at the beginning of the Comedy when the Pilgrim saw a man "whose voice seemed weak from long silence," and the slightly later occasion when the six poets in Limbo are in a meadow below the castle, "where there were people with grave and slow-moving eyes and looks of great authority" (S) ("Genti v'eran con occhi tardi e gravi / Di grande autorità ne' lor sembianti," Inf. IV.–).

Looking once again past or through the parody, we can say that Chaucer, too, is searching for a "Virgil figure," has in fact found it, but simultaneously hesitates or refuses to commit himself to one. Indeed, in The Canterbury Tales such a figure is notable for its absence. Where we might look for a "man of gret auctorite" to lead the pilgrimage, we find only—the Host! Paradoxically, however, the Host proves to be a not altogether inappropriate surrogate for the absent authority figure, as we shall see. The reason is that the concept of poetic—as of religious—authority is not, as we might expect, vested in an individual, an institution (like the court), or a text (like the Aeneid), but belongs instead to a group, any group, that has gathered for the purpose of telling and listening to tales. In The Canterbury Tales the fictive representatives of this group are of course the twenty-nine persons gathered in Southwark "from every shires ende," for whom the Host decides to act as master of ceremonies. This group very quickly evolves into a "felaweshipe" (General Prologue, ll.,) that spontaneously gathers to itself its own authority.

My suggestion of a poetic authority that is collective but also temporary and provisional is based on the Turners' idea of the religious, social, and political community formed by groups of people—like pilgrims—whose common pursuit has somehow placed them outside the boundaries of their customary social structure. The crucial feature of such a community is its "liminality," the fact that it is on the threshold (limen) between an established community temporarily left behind and a new one that springs from the spontaneous collabouration of people pursuing a common goal. Authority in this kind of community will itself be "liminoid," strictly provisional, and the collective expression of its individual members, like Bakhtin's "carnival spirit." In the tale-telling community the authority that I have called poetic, but that is of course also "critical," in a sense will be redefined with every tale that is told, but as a group the pilgrims and their tales also establish their collective authority.

The idea of a collective poetic authority paralleling that of the pilgrimage fellowship is based on the fiction that the Canterbury pilgrims in their dual role as tale-tellers and audience somehow mirror or stand in for the author-audience relationship that is projected in The Canterbury Tales. What I am saying is that Chaucer the narrator treats his readers as if they were an audience for whose collective benefit and approbation he is not simply reporting but also reenacting in its various roles the tale-telling game of the Canterbury pilgrimage. I shall return to this point when I come to discuss the whole idea of epic theater. Meanwhile, the distinction I suggested between Dante's and Chaucer's concepts of authority is tied in, as will be evident, with the different ways in which they treat the pilgrimage idea, the structural backbone of their respective poems.

In the Comedy, the pilgrimage is essentially metaphorical, an individual's ascent (starting with his apparent descent) to heavenly vision. In The Canterbury Tales it is literal and collective, moving horizontally over familiar ground to Canterbury and (in principle) back to its starting point. Dante's Pilgrim, furthermore, journeys through a precisely articulated tripartite setting, which simultaneously orders and mirrors the stages of moral instruction and spiritual reformation through which he must go. Chaucer's pilgrims, on the contrary, pass through a landscape that remains almost totally indistinct and unvisualized and thus neither imposes nor reflects a moral-spiritual structure.

Like his counterpart in the Comedy, the poet of The Canterbury Tales is inside his poem as a pilgrim, but he remains peripheral, a mere member of the group, never, like Dante, the virtual centre of the drama. Dante, after all, casts his poem in the form of "spiritual autobiography," where he looks back on his past self from the vantage point of his present self as epic poet reborn in faith. Chaucer, too, casts his poem in the form of a record of a past event in which he participated "with ful devout corage" (I.); for him The Canterbury Tales is also an account of personal spiritual experience, but that experience is presented no longer, as in Dante's case, as somehow outside or separate from the poem, but as an integral part of the poem's fiction. And this point has a number of interesting implications.

It means, in the first place, that with the vivid sense of theater it creates, the poem always insists on its own fictiveness, on the fact that it is after all a transaction, complex but playful, between poet and reader. In The Canterbury Tales, that is, Chaucer the pilgrim and Chaucer the poet-narrator, roles usually kept distinct in the Comedy, are one. And just as Chaucer the poet does not attempt to distance himself from his pilgrim persona, so in the final analysis he does not distance himself from the other pilgrims either. Particularly in their role as tale-tellers, these are so many masks for him, and that is an important reason why we can say that for all its fundamental differences from the Comedy, The Canterbury Tales is still a "spiritual autobiography," a record not so much of the author's past self as of his selfhood imagined in and through others.

A second implication of the idea that it is the fiction which is the autobiography in The Canterbury Tales involves our view of the pilgrimage it describes. In theory this pilgrimage, like Dante's, is a past event now completed. In practice, however, it is not completed at all. I am not referring to the unfinished state in which we have the poem, though that undoubtedly contributes to the effect I have in mind. This is the sense we develop as readers that the pilgrimage is still going on, in the "now" of reading and contemplating the text, and that, in contrast to the apparently perfect closure of Dante's pilgrimage, it will never and can never be completed, for the simple reason that there is always more to be said, further impressions to be revised... In short, I would argue that the fragmentary and unfinished state of The Canterbury Tales might well be regarded as the outward and visible sign of the poem's "inward" condition as "work-in-progress."

Here once again the House of Fame in quite remarkable fashion prepares for The Canterbury Tales even as it defines how that poem will differ from Dante's. Is it entirely accidental, I wonder, that the earlier poem mimics the tripartite organization of the Comedy and still breaks off abruptly, anticipating the seemingly contingent chaos of The Canterbury Tales ? More significant, perhaps, we have seen how the dreamer-poet of the House of Fame begins like a typically Dantean persona only to turn into a peripheral figure, listening, observing, giving others, like the eagle, centre stage on which to reveal themselves.

As visionary poet, furthermore, he has trouble keeping the account of his vision straight; the same apparently applies to his quest, though it is possible that it is the dreamer who can never quite make up his mind or remember what it is he is looking for. Unlike his Dantean counterpart, he experiences no visionary transport but wants to hear "tidings" in a labyrinthine house (–) full of a motley assortment of people, shipmen, pilgrims, pardoners (ff.). These are surely an anticipation of the Canterbury pilgrims, and the whirling house, which stops whirling once the dreamer is inside (–), is perhaps really an inn.

As J. A. W. Bennett suggested a number of years ago, furthermore, what the dreamer is waiting to hear at the house of "Aventure, / That is the moder of tydynges", are in effect the tales to be heard on the way to Canterbury. And in the perspective of the House of Fame, these tales are somehow analogous to the goal of the Pilgrim's quest in the Comedy. In the final cantos of the Paradiso, that is to say, the Christian message, a kind of "tidings," is revealed in the form of symbolic images that have a transfiguring effect on the Pilgrim, so that within the rainbow circles of the Trinity his concluding vision is of the human image, nostra effige (Par. XXXIII.). Like the imagery of the Paradiso, the tales of the Canterbury pilgrims—the tidings awaited by Chaucer's dreamer—will have a revealing and transfiguring power whose ultimate message might well be, once again, the clarified human image.

In this sense, then, the message or "idea" of The Canterbury Tales I am proposing is close to Northrop Frye's idea of "the secular scripture," his collective term for "secular stories" forming "the epic of the creature," in contradistinction to the Bible, "the epic of the creator," whose hero is God. I am not claiming Frye's "secular scripture" as a perfect fit for The Canterbury Tales, but it does strike me as a useful characterization of the inspiration dramatized in the House of Fame, an inspiration combining epic, Dante's Comedy, and tale-telling.

Following Dante, the new epic theme or project that Chaucer envisions will be, precisely, tale-telling, with the implication that there is no tale, however humble or trivial-seeming, that does not deserve to be included because of its potential for illuminating the human condition. That, it seems to me, is the implication of the house of Aventure with its varied clientele and tidings. It is tempting to suggest that the house represents the realm of popular (and essentially oral) literature like the folktale, which Chaucer has discovered as a new source of inspiration, but such an interpretation would nonetheless be too narrow. Instead, I propose that the house signifies a new poetic inclusiveness open to the varied styles, themes, and genres of the oral and popular as well as the learned tradition, and above all open to a varied audience ranging over the entire social spectrum, as implied by the occupants of the house, who, like the Canterbury pilgrims, are at once tellers and audience of the tidings.

By way of summarizing my conclusions about the House of Fame, I can say that it implies two stages in the poet's career, the first associated with the house of Fame, the second with the house of Aventure. In one of its aspects Lady Fame's palace is a satirical portrait of court with its countless attendants and endless crowds of courtiers pressing for royal favor(s). The scene must have been familiar to the younger Chaucer, the poet of the first stage, who, it is generally agreed, wrote the kind of poetry—learned, erotic, French-inspired—calculated to appeal to a court audience, a poetry, furthermore, whose ancestry is on display in Fame's hall of statues.

The house of Aventure, contrariwise, is not familiar to the mature Chaucer, the poet of the second stage, judging by its name, his unorthodox entry by a window with the help of the eagle (–), and his repeated stress on his reclusive, book-centreed existence. As was already indicated, the precise way in which the poetry of this second stage differs from that of the first is not so easy to pinpoint. Looking at the house of Aventure, we can infer that the later poetry will be less conventional because prepared to venture outside the closed world and status quo ante of the house of Fame and into the greater world beyond the court, and the really crucial difference will have to do with the idea of a new audience for which the poet is now writing.

This is the implied or dramatized audience of inn and road in The Canterbury Tales. For all that it is a part of the poet's fiction, it has a decisive effect on the very notion of what a poem is and does. Negatively speaking, this audience makes impossible a "pure" poetry whose intelligibility depends on a knowledge of esoteric symbols or interpretive techniques (as in the case of certain types of allegory). Nor can an author with such an audience in mind rely on stock responses, a favourite recourse, if we follow C. S. Lewis, of the epic poet's style. Given a nonselect, culturally diverse audience, every feature of the poet's literary stock-in-trade is bound to fall under critical scrutiny: one and the same text, line, or word will call forth a whole gamut of interpretations and responses. And this also means that within the context of such an imagined audience must be envisaged the constant possibility of misunderstanding, of the wrong or the altogether irrelevant response, which will somehow insist on its rightness and relevance.

In the heterogeneous audience it postulates for itself and the style it develops as a result, The Canterbury Tales looks ahead to the Elizabethan drama of the public theater and the mass-circulation book once the printing press and widespread literacy have established themselves. The style is what Bakhtin calls "dialogical," always conscious of and responsive to other viewpoints; its frequently artless, innocent appearance allows for, perhaps even invites, the interpretive free-for-all Plato associates with the written word (and that is presumably even more characteristic of the printed word).

It is, to adapt Derrida's entertaining paraphrase of Plato's argument, the phantom, the phantasm, the simulacrum... of living discourse.... This signifier of little, this discourse that doesn't amount to much, is like all ghosts: errant... wandering in the streets, he doesn't even know who he is, what his identity—if he has one—might be, what his name is, what his father's name is.... Uprooted, anonymous, unattached to any house or country, this almost insignificant signifier is at everyone's disposal, can be picked up by both the competent and the incompetent, by those who understand and know what to do with it..., and by those who are completely unconcerned with it, and who, knowing nothing, can inflict all manner of impertinence upon it.

In some ways that also seems a wonderfully apt

description of Chaucer's poetic persona.

It fits the bewildered, wandering dreamer of the House of Fame, twice unceremoniously picked up and transported by the eagle, who also speaks to him with condescension, not to say impertinence. But the dreamer does know his own name, as does the eagle, a "Dante figure," as I suggested earlier, who addresses him as "Geffrey" (; cf.), just as Beatrice calls Dante by his name (Purg. XXX.). In The Canterbury Tales the poet-persona is no longer the slightly dazed dreamer of the House of Fame, or of the Book of the Duchess, for that matter, but a wanderer with a purpose, a pilgrim among pilgrims. Yet he still has the self-effacing, seemingly unfocused manner that tends to elicit an attitude of superiority and impertinence in others. Alongside this persona, evidently anonymous to his fellow pilgrims, Chaucer is, however, careful to inscribe both his name and his career as a poet in The Canterbury Tales.

The shape of that career, furthermore, corresponds perfectly, as we shall see, to that outlined in the House of Fame. I conclude from the foregoing observations that Chaucer, though no post-structuralist, may well have accepted the Nominalist or Ockhamite position that the word, like the poet who uses and depends upon it, is very nearly an "insignificant signifier," almost no more than a breath of air. The word has no inherent authority, no inherently authoritative meaning. Whatever authority and persuasive power it possesses must therefore come from the personality somehow inscribed in it, from the reader's or listener's sense that it is indeed the expression of a person seeking communication, seeking understanding, of his "semblable." For that reason, though not for that reason alone, Chaucer followed Dante in making the poet's self-presentation an integral part of his epic design.

In this connection let us consider the moment (II.ff.) when Chaucer's name is, so to speak, inscribed in The Canterbury Tales by one of the pilgrims, who at the same time provides an ironic and humourous anticipation of what a poet can expect from posterity. In his Introduction the Man of Law cites Chaucer as obviously a well-known writer of love stories who, despite his old-fashioned English and defective craftsmanship, is worthy of comparison with Ovid and significant enough to warrant a brief survey of his career. But when the Man of Law summarizes what he calls the "Seintes Legende of Cupide," his list of heroines is so wildly inaccurate—he mentions eight heroines not even dealt with in the Legend—as to convey the impression that his knowledge of the work is based essentially on hearsay. The degree of his literary sophistication, finally, is indicated by his complaint that he has no story to tell, because Chaucer has already told them all. If posthumous—as well as contemporary—fame depends upon people like this, the poet might well ask himself, who needs it?

Despite such ironies, the Man of Law's opinions deserve our attention, in part because they echo what Chaucer says or implies about his career elsewhere in his poetry. His notion, however simplistic, of Chaucer as an Ovidian love poet from the start corresponds perfectly with Chaucer's self-presentation in the House of Fame as one who has served Venus and Cupid and whose dream about the Aeneid turns that poem almost entirely into a love tragedy. That dream, or rather, the amusingly eccentric synopsis of the Aeneid it gives rise to, could be, as I suggested earlier, a highly indirect allusion to Troilus and Criseyde, another love tragedy with a Trojan setting (which that of the Aeneid is only by extension).

Similarly, there would seem to be another possible (and indirect) allusion to Troilus and Criseyde when the Man of Law mentions "Brixseyde" as one of love's victims in the Legend of Good Women. There is of course no Brixseyde in the Legend, but since she bears the name of the heroine in Benoît de Ste. Maure's Roman de Troie (twelfth century), she almost inevitably brings to mind Boccaccio's Criseida and Chaucer's Criseyde. And these oblique references to the Troilus, I suggest, draw attention to the fact that the "middle" stage of Chaucer's career is absent from the Man of Law's retrospect and from the House of Fame, "middle" not in an exclusively chronological sense but primarily to refer to Troilus and Criseyde as the poetic monument "nel mezzo del cammin" between the early Chaucer of the love visions and the late Chaucer of The Canterbury Tales.

By any standards, Troilus and Criseyde is a masterful achievement. It has been truly said that in it "Chaucer reached the height of his powers," and we saw earlier how in his envoy the poet with proud humility placed it in the line of Virgilian epic. So why, we may ask, is it absent from both the House of Fame and the Introduction to the Man of Law's Tale? Especially since its theme is still love? The reason, I speculate, is that from the perspective of the House of Fame and The Canterbury Tales, the Troilus does not represent the new departure, the epic "breakthrough," that at one time it must have seemed to Chaucer. In spite of its magnificent achievement it looks in retrospect like a continuation of the earlier Ovidian mode, its extension, let us say, into serious tragedy. What I am implying, in other words, is that by the time he was finishing the Troilus and looking ahead to the next project, Chaucer underwent a kind of poetic conversion. That may be a rather hyperbolic, and to some a contradictory, phrase, but poetry is an analogue of religion, and I think that when Chaucer had at length fully absorbed the Dantean poetic it did amount to a real transvaluation of values for him.

The first effect of this transvaluation was the rejection of what might be called Boccaccian antiquarianism, Boccaccio's habit, particularly in the Filostrato and the Teseida, of creating an "antique" world that would serve as a more or less self-contained, edifying object of the reader's contemplation. The Troilus is not an antiquarian poem in that sense, but I believe that in composing it Chaucer became conscious of the risks—of escapism, moralism, excessive irony—that the antiquarian poetic can involve. Certain parallels between Pandarus and Chaucer's own role as poet-narrator, for instance, might recall Francesca's indictment of the romance she and Paolo were reading together: "A Gallehault indeed, that book and he /

who wrote it, too" ("Galeotto fu 'l libro e chi lo scrisse," Inf. V.). Perhaps the most explicit indication of Chaucer's disenchantment with the antiquarian poetic is the awkward, jarring, and yet immensely vigourous recantation that concludes the Troilus.

There is something a trifle absurd in the spectacle of a poet who has to the best of his ability created the sense of a "pagan" past and then recants his fiction because it does not conform ex hypothesi to "Christian" truth. To put it slightly differently, the Boccaccian or antiquarian poet-persona keeps out of his poem, stays in his own world, which is sealed off from the fictive world, except in the theatrical sense that he is its spectator and, Pandarus-or Galeotto-fashion, its "presenter." Once he leaves his pagan theater, how can he do other than acknowledge that, like his readers, he lives under a Christian sky and a Christian sun?

The revolution Dante introduces in this "Boccaccian" scheme will already be apparent to the reader. In the Comedy antiquarianism is, as it were, set on its head, because the past, whether real or fictive, political or literary, is seen entirely in relation to the contemporary world. It is seen through the medium of the poet, who is inside the poem, not as spectator and presenter, but primarily as an active participant who represents or embodies the vital aspects and concerns of the contemporary world.

In the Dantean epic, accordingly, there are no areas that are "off limits": sacred and profane, Christian and pagan, Bible and "secular scripture" mingle and clash from the start, because Dante's poem is both polemical and contemporary from start to finish. Dante's Virgil, once more, can serve as a perfect illustration of this twofold character of the Comedy, which begins with a man in almost complete despair rescued by a poet and a pagan who leads him, furthermore, not back to a real or an imagined past but forward to an understanding of the world as it is and may be.

By this detour we arrive at the second and crucial moment of Chaucer's self-presentation in The Canterbury

Tales, when the poet-pilgrim himself takes centre stage. "What man artow?" the Host demands to know (VII.), underlining once again the anonymity of the pilgrim and the fact that he inspires anything but awe. Like Derrida's "almost insignificant signifier... at everyone's disposal," this man, in the Host's humourous words, "were a popet in an arm t'enbrace / For any womman, smal and fair of face" (–). And when he steps forward to tell his tale it becomes quite simply a distillate of The Canterbury Tales, the phantasm, to quote Derrida's paraphrase of Plato once more, "of living discourse,... signifier of little... [it] can be picked up by those who understand and know what to do with it, and who, knowing nothing, can inflict all manner of impertinence upon it."

As a parody, indeed, the Tale of Sir Thopas could be called the phantasm of a phantasm, so that the Host, not characterized as the possessor of a subtle mind, can perhaps be excused for inflicting his gruff impertinence upon it. He interrupts Chaucer in the middle of a line—"Namoore of this, for Goddes dignitee" —not, as we might think, out of sheer ignorance or unconcern, but precisely because he has some call to consider himself an expert on the genre Chaucer is parodying. According to various scholars who have written on the late-fourteenth-century "popular" romance, this genre evolved when professional minstrels took romances out of their aristocratic milieu and adapted them for recitation to audiences in such places as the courtyards of inns. Though he seems a bit unsure of his terminology—" 'This may wel be rym dogerel,' quod he" —we must for once allow that on his own grounds the Host's critical judgment is justified.

At the point, then, of the Host's interruption, Chaucer's covert poetic autobiography, the trajectory of his career as prophetically adumbrated in the House of Fame, reaches a characteristic climax. With the never-to-be-completed Thopas, Chaucer has triumphantly established the place of The Canterbury Tales in the context of his own poetic development. Together with the Man of Law's retrospect it is his equivalent of the Aeneid 's opening "Ille ego, qui quondam gracili modulatus avena " ("I am he who once turned my song on a slender reed "). The slender reed is now represented by the Ovidian beginnings at court, which he has left to forge a popular epic for a popular audience such as might be found at the Tabard Inn ready for pilgrimage.

This audience encompasses, as was already indicated, high and low, Virgil's men-at-arms as well as his shepherds and farmers, so that "popular" here does not mean quite what it often means in literary histories. There the term is often used as an antonym of "aristocratic" in the sense of "adapted to the understanding, taste, or means of the (common) people." Or, where it is not used in a condescending fashion, the term may carry the opposite implications, derived from nineteenth-century Romantic notions of the folk, of something authentic, real, the "unconscious wisdom of the race." Unavoidable as some of these implications doubtless are, in calling The Canterbury Tales a "popular" epic I intend the idea that its fiction embraces the different social classes of Chaucer's day, plays their perspectives off against one another, and never allows one to emerge as the ultimate or "true" perspective.

The idea of the popular epic is thus connected with the pilgrimage communitas discussed earlier, which, it will be recalled, involves a temporary abandonment of the accustomed social structure and the spontaneous emergence of a new sense of community. In The Canterbury Tales, correspondingly, the pilgrims come to us first like representatives of fourteenth-century society, stamped with names indicating their place and function in that society. But as they start to become individualized in the General Prologue portraits, their names tend to lose force as class or type designations, and as a consequence the whole idea of social structure with its various stratifications insensibly gives way to the fellowship of persons beginning to evolve at the Tabard Inn. With characteristic indirection the poet draws attention to this development near the end of the General Prologue when he concludes his "apologia" to the reader with the request that he may be forgiven for not having "set folk in hir degree / Here in this tale, as they that sholde stonde. / My wit is short, ye may wel understonde" (–). The reader who believes in "degree" is herewith warned to be prepared for surprises.

Once the pilgrimage is under way, it is the tale-telling game that displaces notions of "degree" and social decorum whenever they threaten to obtrude themselves. The important signal here is the "defeat" suffered, near the very beginning of the pilgrimage, by the Host in his role as self-appointed master of ceremonies. Like a typical innkeeper, he is scrupulous about observing the rules of social precedence, so that when he eventually yields to the Miller, who insists on telling his tale next, it can be said without exaggeration that the spirit of play triumphs over principles of social propriety. The triumph is never perfect, but its actuality is shown precisely on those occasions when the pilgrims show themselves anxious to preserve the spirit of play and fellowship in the face of what would disrupt it.

It is in the spirit of play that we must understand Thopas and the role Chaucer the pilgrim adopts in telling it. If that spirit is also, or even preeminently, the spirit of parody in The Canterbury Tales, this should not dismay us. As the House of Fame shows, Chaucerian parody is no simple debunking but the exploration of a style, a mannerism, an attitude, by a process of assimilation that constantly threatens to become total. What saves it as parody, in other words, is the realization that style is not just the expression of an individual consciousness but also a matter of choice; in short, of play. Now, we do not know just what kind of minstrel Chaucer had in mind as the target of his parody in Thopas.

Are we to think of him as a simpleminded hack who caters to his audience's taste for aristocratic entertainment and in the process, out of carelessness or ignorance, gets most of it wrong? Or should we think of him as a shrewd professional who is quite conscious of what he is about in adapting his material to a nonaristocratic audience? Perhaps it does not matter just how we imagine this minstrel. What seems important is that he represents in various possible forms a composite of the author of The Canterbury Tales.

With this we have reached the final stage of Chaucer's self-presentation, beginning with the dreamer in the House of Fame and concluding with the "minstrel" of Thopas as the epic poet. The latter has a recognizable continuity with the past in the form of the pixieish blunderer who is the Chaucerian persona from the very start. The new and "epic" element is less easy to define because in some ways it is no more than an affirmation of his lifelong career as "entertainer" to audiences that never take him quite seriously, never quite accept him as one of them. To this we should add, however, that like the minstrel, the epic poet is also preeminently a transmitter of traditional materials that he has refashioned, and with that, it seems, we have a satisfactory explanation of Chaucer's virtual identification of the roles of epic poet and minstrel in The Canterbury Tales. And that identification, it is somewhat startling to realise, means that the parodist and the target of his parody have become one, as we noted they have a tendency to do. By way of support for this idea we might cite J. A. Burrow's observation that a number of the striking stylistic features parodied in Thopas are in fact Chaucer's own.

Thopas, then, acts as a mirror or speculum in the dual sense current in the Middle Ages of a model and a reflector. What it reflects is an image of some kind of its teller, and in this respect Thopas serves as a model for the rest of the Canterbury tales, all of which, I shall argue later, are mirrors in which the pilgrim-tellers may, but need not, see themselves. At the same time we are bound to recognize that the case of Thopas is rather more complex than the others for the reason that, as I have argued, its narrator brings with him a whole past history demanding to be seen in relation to this tale. Until now our focus has therefore been on the act as well as the manner of its telling, as the climax of that history. But now we must penetrate beyond these "externals" of the presentation to the interior of the tale itself.

That last sentence is misleading to the extent that it

implies a discontinuity between narrative and plot. If we focus for a moment on the tale's hero, "Child" Thopas, it soon becomes apparent that he has a great deal in common with the narrator, whether we think of him as the would-be minstrel or as the pilgrim described by the Host as a "popet" who "semeth elvyssh by his contenaunce". Doll-like, otherworldly, elfin, faintly epicene, the picture conjured up by the Host is a perfect fit for the incongruous Flemish knight "with sydes smale" who rides into fairyland in quest of the elf-queen, with whom he declares himself to have fallen in love in a dream vision.

Sir Thopas is yet another incarnation of the poet, particularly as the world perceives him: a dreamer who boasts of his allegiance to a world beyond the one his fellow human beings can see or inhabit, and who dashes off into this otherworld of his invention at every opportunity, returning with wild stories of exploits like encounters with giants. At the same time this dreamer constantly demonstrates his incompetence in the simplest everyday tasks... We have no difficulty recognizing here numerous features of the Chaucerian persona this chapter has examined. But if we left matters there we would be doing scant justice to Thopas, which, precisely because of the simplicity of its basic plot, seems able to cast a peculiar spell.

Shorn of the comic excesses of its style, Thopas might well stand as an archetype or urtext of Frye's "secular scripture." Its hero in combat with a giant who proves to have three heads could be a god or a semidivine being waging eternal war against the forces of darkness; he could be a fairytale hero destined to marry the queen of fairyland once he has overcome the various obstacles placed in his way; he could be, and in some ways obviously is, the knight of chivalric romance on a quest in the course of which he must prove himself worthy of the ideal represented by the woman he has seen in his dream. Indeed, it seems possible to match Thopas with the protagonists in many of the genres and modes mapped out, say, in Frye's Anatomy of Criticism. Our main concern, though, is with the genre of the epic, and here it gives me considerable satisfaction to recall that Chaucer's most important follower and interpreter among English poets—the true continuator of the Chaucerian epic tradition!—derived from Thopas the seminal plot for his own encyclopedic-allegoric epic of chivalry. Spenser's appropriation of Thopas for the Arthurian plot of his Faerie Queene points at the same time to his understanding that Thopas is likewise at the very basis of Chaucer's epic project.

Rather than attempt to show how Thopas serves as sub- or pretext for the pilgrimage plot of the other Canterbury tales—"endlesse work," indeed, in Spenser's words—I want to approach the matter once more by way of our Dantean theme. Sir Thopas is, I suggest, Chaucer's fictive mirror in the specific sense that he is the poet as hero as he appears above all in the Comedy: inside the otherworld of his poem but always aware of the world beyond that otherworld, this world, an active quester guided by (his love of) the lady of his dream-visions and prepared to encounter, though not without fear and trembling, the monsters in his path. I hope the reader is prepared for yet another parody version of the Comedy, because it seems to me that for all its lighthearted foolery Thopas represents Chaucer's affirmation of his commitment as an epic poet to Dante's example.

In this connection let us examine the episode of Thopas and the giant Olifaunt, who appears to block Thopas's progress into fairyland and calls out to him:

"Child, by Termagaunt! But if thou prike out of myn haunt, Anon I sle thy steede With mace. Heere is the queene of Fayerye, With harpe and pipe and symphonye, Dwellynge in this place."

In response, Thopas promises to return the next day with his armor and to pierce the giant's "maw" as though he were a dragon or a similar monster (ff.). When the giant throws stones at him "out of a fel staf-slynge", like David fighting Goliath, Thopas escapes, "and al it was thurgh Goddes gras, / And thurgh his fair berynge" (–). Back in town Thopas tells his men he must fight "a geaunt with hevedes three, / For paramour and jolitee / Of oon that shoon ful brighte" (–).

In a curious way this entire episode manages to re-create some of the grotesque humour and dreamlike atmosphere of the final cantos of Dante's Inferno. There the travellers' passage through hell seems to be blocked at one point by a whole congregation of giants, though the pilgrim Dante at first mistakes them for the towers of a city (Inf. XXX.–). His error sets the tone for a kind of Swiftian comedy in which the reader is simultaneously impressed with the terror experienced by the Pilgrim and with the narrator's knowledge of the harmlessness of these monsters, the fact that they are, as it were, dinosaurs or extinct volcanoes. The scene increasingly takes on the air of a visit to the zoo where prehistoric animals are kept. The narrator speaks as we might imagine a medieval zookeeper who browsed in the Church Fathers might speak, as when he comments on Nimrod:

Natura certo, quando lasciò l'artedi sí fatti animali, assai fa beneper torre tali essecutori a Marte. E s'ella d'elefanti e di balene non si pente, chi guarda sottilmente più giusta e più discreta la ne tene; chè dove l'argomento della mentes'aggiunge al mal volere ed alla possa, nessun riparo vi può far la gente.
(Inf. XXXI.–)

(Surely when she gave up the art of makingsuch creatures, Nature acted well indeed, depriving Mars of instruments like these. And if she still produces elephants and whales, whoever sees with subtlety holds her—for this—to be more just and prudent; for where the mind's acutest reasoning is joined to evil will and evil power, there human beings can't defend themselves.)

In other words, it is a good thing that elephants (ME olifaunts) are just elephants! And Olifaunt just Olifaunt, thinking he needs a giant-killer's slingshot to fight a puny mortal.

Canto XXXI ends with the comic anticlimax of the giant called Antaeus serving as the pilgrim's conveyance down to the lowest circle of hell (ff.), a scene that looks ahead to their final escape from hell when they climb along Satan's hairy sides and legs. Indeed, the giants of canto XXXI are clearly a prologue to the "emperor of the dolorous kingdom" himself, who is, like them, a combination of terrifying supergiant and absurd impotence, stuck as he is up to his waist in ice and flailing his three sets of wings about like some colossal windmill (Inf. XXXIV. –; ff.). Satan's most startling feature, his three faces, is shared by Olifaunt, at least if we go by Thopas's casual but also startling reference to "a geaunt with hevedes three."

Even as parody, then, Thopas seems remarkably faithful to what I take to be Dante's meaning: What passes for the darkest evil in this—or the other—world is frequently no more than the projection of our fears and feelings of impotence. Accordingly, what at one moment inspired terror can in a flash take on a harmless or even benign aspect. We saw this happening with the giants in the Inferno, who are initially terrifying, at least to the pilgrim hero, but eventually become the means by which he and his companion advance toward their goal of paradise. And so, too, in the comically compressed style of Thopas, the battle with the giant is presented as almost identical with the attainment of the beloved object.

His myrie men comanded he
To make hym bothe game and glee
For nedes moste he fighte
With a geaunt with hevedes three,
For paramour and jolitee
Of oon that shoon ful brighte.

This is not to imply that there is no real evil in the world. Such a view would hardly be compatible with the general tenor of the Inferno. But I think it is a basic implication of the Inferno and of the Comedy generally that at the basis of evil there is what might be called unreality, absence, nothingness, and that this chimerical element must be mastered before the actual evil can be attacked.

The charmed life Sir Thopas leads likewise seems to me in complete harmony with the way we perceive the Pilgrim of the Comedy. The latter, far from being passive, actively explores, questions, and reacts to what is around him, but he is also repeatedly rescued from difficult situations by a timely swoon or the intervention of a benign helper, so that it can also be said about him what was said about Thopas's escape from the giant, "And al it was thurgh Goddes gras / And thurgh his fair berynge". Strictly, the two parts of that statement are incompatible, but in what might be called the dimension of faith they are surely reconciled.

Along with Aeneas, St. Paul, and others, the Pilgrim of the Comedy is doubtless a knight of faith in whose career "Goddes gras" is somehow interchangeable with "his berynge." And Sir Thopas, it need hardly be said, is another such knight, as is all but spelled out just before his story breaks off when we are told that

Hymself drank water of the well,
As dide the knyght sire Percyvell
So worly under wede....

Commentators generally regard this as a reference to the eponymous hero of the Middle English romance Sir Perceval of Galles, which deals with his upbringing by his widowed mother, in the woods, and his eventual knighting by King Arthur. But in fact, as Chaucer and at least some of his audience must have known, Perceval was the one knight of Arthurian romance whose career bears a certain resemblance to that of the Pilgrim in the Comedy. In the earlier Arthurian literature he was the knight of Arthur's court who led the Grail quest and at the climactic conclusion received a vision of Christ.

To be sure, the lines quoted refer only to the simplicity and purity of Perceval's habits, but it is precisely these that set him apart from his fellow knights of the Round Table, making him not only the Grail knight par excellence, but also a type of the "holy fool." This is an important concept in the Middle Ages whose basis is at least partly biblical. In the first Epistle to the Corinthians, Paul describes apostles as "fools for Christ's sake" ("stulti propter Christum," Vulgate.) and develops at length the theme that "God hath chosen the foolish things of the world to confound the wise" ("quae stulta sunt mundi elegit Deus, ut confundat sapientes," Vulgate.). "Let no man deceive himself," Paul warns the Corinthians; "if any man among you seemeth wise in this world, let him become a fool, that he may be wise". Starting from uncourtly, even uncouth, origins—in the Welsh woods and Flanders—Perceval and Thopas appear to the world as foolish knights and by the Pauline logic are therefore well qualified to confound the worldly-wise.

I am not, to be sure, suggesting any direct equation between Perceval and Thopas. The latter belongs, after all, to the realm of pure literary play, whereas Perceval in some ways demands to be taken seriously, even as a knight. The point seems to me, rather, that both characters imply a critique of the tradition of chivalry with its notions of adventure and heroic action, and in that respect, at least, Thopas may be said to represent the more radical perspective. For if, as a Fleming, he begins as that apparent contradiction in terms, a bourgeois knight, he ends by subverting both the chivalric and the bourgeois:

And for he was a knyght auntrous,
He nolde slepen in noon hous,
But liggen in his hoode;
His brighte helm was his wonger,
And by hym baiteth his dextrer
Of herbes fyne and goode.

Thopas's adventurous "houselessness" is altogether consistent, not just with Paul's apostolic "foolishness," but also with a type of unspectacular heroism that we might associate with a St. Francis of Assisi.

Our examination of Thopas leads us to the somewhat surprising conclusion that in the twofold sense mentioned earlier he serves as a mirror for Chaucer's epic persona: reflecting the image of the poet as unworldly bumbler and projecting an image of an individual who in his unlikely, quixotic way is yet prepared to face foes where more conventional heroes fear to tread. Thopas thus shows us

Chaucer as a true follower of Dante, redefining the nature of heroism as involving, not the usual violence of the Homeric and chivalric epic, but a moral and intellectual struggle whose arena is social as well as "interior" and whose outcome is always uncertain, ambiguous. And in this context it is tempting to link Chaucer-Thopas with yet another exemplary figure of Western intellectual history, the ironic, self-mocking, erotically charged and yet supremely self-controlled Socrates, whose uncompromising quest for self-knowledge brought him into conflict with Athenian society.

The connection is all the more tempting because from the start of his career Chaucer's persona bears a striking resemblance to the Socrates of such dialogues as the Phaedo, the Apology, the Phaedrus, and the Symposium. How much of this Socrates could Chaucer have been acquainted with, however? After all, until the fifteenth century, the only dialogues available in the West, in Latin translation, were the Meno, the Phaedo, and a portion of the Timaeus. Now, the first two do in fact provide a very full portrait of the "Platonic" Socrates, and the Phaedo, since it deals with Socrates' final hours and execution, represents, perhaps better than any other single dialogue, a reflection on the meaning of his philosophic career in its personal and public, political dimensions.

Assuming he was acquainted with one or more of these dialogues, therefore, Chaucer would not have had to depend upon the considerable post-Platonic legend of Socrates to arrive at an image not as rich and varied as that afforded by the full range of the Platonic dialogues yet possessing many of their essential features. The chief significance of the surmise that Chaucer might have come to think of his persona in relation to Plato's Socrates would be that it provided him with a model for the view of life as an intellectual quest in which no questions are foreclosed, no answers final.

The persona of The Canterbury Tales differs from that of the earlier poems by the sense of the magnitude and seriousness of the epic quest. Irony and dialogic openness are now in the service of a moral passion that is to be found preeminently in the Platonic dialogues dealing with the collision between Socrates and the Athenian state. A preliminary indication of this moral seriousness, in suitably ironic form, comes from the second tale told by Chaucer the pilgrim after his tale of Thopas has been cut short by the Host. The Tale of Melibee follows its French source very closely, and it is usually assumed that Chaucer simply utilized "this litel tretys heere" out of a habit of thrift, because it was available. Over against this assumption I propose that Chaucer, in looking at Le livre de Mellibee et Prudence, or his translation of it, recognized its character as a dialogue, which at the same time touches upon the central issues of his poem as of Christian morality.

To call this dialogue Socratic or in the Socratic manner may seem like stretching a point, yet I contend that in the context of The Canterbury Tales, Melibee can be seen as dramatizing the victory of dialogue over monologue, of argument over exhortation and legislation. As with a number of Socratic dialogues, the discussion is triggered by an event or situation, in this case the beating of Melibee's wife and the near-killing of his daughter. The intellectual drama that develops is constantly in danger of being swamped by the sheer quantity of authorities cited and the often stilted rhetoric that accompanies the reliance on textual authority. All the same, we never quite forget that the disputants are man and wife who have more than an abstract interest in the issues they are arguing about, and their discussion is genuine in the sense that the conclusions are not given from the outset. However rudimentary the characterization, furthermore, it is by no means totally lacking in psychological interest. For example, Melibee's struggle with himself, at once comic and deeply serious, in gradually yielding to the arguments of his wife, is something the reader can hardly fail to recognize as universally human. And in this struggle we come face to face with what I take to be the real subject of Melibee, the forgiveness of those who have trespassed against us, not as dogma, an article of faith, or a command from on high, but as an intellectual and moral problem with which people must grapple, in Socratic fashion, by weighing and debating the alternatives.

My contention with respect to Melibee is that its character as dialogue is not so much given as realised or achieved by its place in Chaucer's poem, which itself has many of the characteristics of a vast dialogue. In this dialogue, extending over the pilgrimage to Canterbury, entire tales can serve as arguments for their tellers. Accordingly, if we must find allegory in Melibee, I would relate it to the idea of dialogue and of intellectual quest. Chaucer provides an unobtrusive hint, it seems to me, in this direction by giving a name to Melibee's daughter, who in the sources remains anonymous. Her name, Sophie, might suggest the Socratic wisdom, sophia, that Melibee must recover with the help of his wife, Prudence. Melibee's name, Greek, Latin, and now ambiguously English as well, seems to imply that its possessor is a typical European, whereas his wife's name points squarely to the medieval Latin tradition, where prudentia stands for the chief or "mother" of the four cardinal virtues in the Thomistic scheme.

By himself, Melibee is that self-assertive, masculine, socially or tribally oriented spirit that has played such an important part in the Western tradition since Homeric times. Over against it there is the "Latin" spirit of the Church, with its tradition of self-abnegation and a moral and spiritual idealism that is always attentive to the common good. In the history of the West these two have often existed in separation or with one subordinated to the other. Their marriage, the marriage of Melibee and Prudence, is in one sense no more than a partnership in dialogue by which the Socratic sophia is, so to speak, spontaneously brought into being.

By way of conclusion to this chapter I want to suggest that much more emphatically than Dante's Beatricean inspiration, The Canterbury Tales contains a distinctively, and what would nowadays be considered a conventional, marital ideal. This ideal, as Melibee suggests, runs the gamut from the metaphoric and metaphysical, the tension-within-harmony of male and female, "Which two great Sexes animate the World," in Milton's formulation (Paradise Lost VIII.), to the down-to-earth literal partnership of man and woman. Hence the appropriateness of the Host's reaction to Melibee when he contrasts Prudence with his own violent and vengeful wife, ironically named Goodlief. Somewhere in all of this, I feel sure, there also lurks an ironic joke at the expense of Socrates (and his followers) who, as the Wife recalls from Jankyn's "book of wikked wyves," needed all his wisdom to endure the abuse of a shrewish wife or two.

Bibliography

Aers, David. Chaucer, Langland and the Creative Imagination. London: RKP, 1980.

Andrew, Malcolm (critical commentary) and Daniel J. Ransom (textual commentary), eds., with Lynne Hunt Levy and Charles Moorman. A Variorum Edition of the Works of Geoffrey Chaucer, Volume Two [The Canterbury Tales], Part A: The General Prologue. 2 vols. Norman: University of Oklahoma Press, 1993.

Benson, Larry D. and Theodore M. Andersson. The Literary Context of Chaucer's Fabliaux: Texts and Translations. New York: Bobbs-Merrill, 1971.

Bethurum, Dorothy, ed. Critical Approaches to Medieval Literature. New York: Columbia U. P., 1960.

Boenig, Robert. Chaucer and the mystics: the Canterbury tales and the genre of devotional prose. Lewisburg, PA: Bucknell University Press, 1995.

Boitani, Piero. Chaucer and Boccaccio. Oxford: Oxford University Press, 1977.

Chaucer and The Italian Trecento. Cambridge U. P., 1983.

Bowden, Betsy. Chaucer aloud : the varieties of textual interpretation. Philadelphia: University of Pennsylvania Press, 1987.

Bowden, Muriel. Commentary on the General Prologue of The Canterbury Tales. London: Souvenir Press, 1973.

Brewer, Derek, ed. Chaucer and Chaucerians: Critical Studies in Middle English Literature. University, AL: U. of Alabama Press, 1966.

Geoffrey Chaucer: Writers and Their Background. Cambridge: Brewer, 1974.

Chaucer, The Critical Heritage. London: Routledge-Kegan Paul, 1978.

Brown, Peter. Chaucer at work: the making of the Canterbury Tales. London & New York: Longman, 1994.

Brown, Peter. The age of Saturn : literature and history in the CanterburyTales. Oxford, Blackwell, 1991.

Bryan, W. F. and G. Dempster. Sources and Analogues of Chaucer's Canterbury Tales. Chicago, 1941; reprint New York, 1958.

Burrow, John A.. Ricardian Poetry: Chaucer, Gower, Langland, and the Gawain poet. London: Routledge, 1971.

Cooper, Helen. The Structure of the Canterbury Tales. Athens: U. Georgia Press, 1983.

The Canterbury Tales [Oxford guides to Chaucer]. Oxford: Clarendon Press, 1989.

Crane, Susan. Gender and romance in Chaucer's Canterbury Tales. Princeton, N.J.: Princeton University Press, 1994.

Crow, M. M., and C. C. Olson, eds. Chaucer Life-Records. Oxford: Clarendon Press, 1966.

David, Alfred. The Strumpet Muse: Art and Morals in Chaucer's Poetry. Bloomington, IN: Univ. of Indiana Press, 1976.

Davis, Norman. Chaucer Glossary. Oxford: Clarendon Press, 1979.

Dinshaw, Carolyn. Chaucer's Sexual Poetics. Madison, WI: U. of Wisconsin Press, 1989.

Donaldson, E. T. Speaking of Chaucer. London: Athlone Press, 1970.

Evans, Ruth, and Lesley Johnson, eds. Feminist readings in Middle English literature: the Wife of Bath and all her sect. London & New York: Routledge, 1994.

Fein, Susanna Greer, David Raybin, and Peter C. Braeger, eds. Rebels and rivals: the contestive spirit in the Canterbury Tales. Foreword by Derek Pearsall. Kalamazoo, MI: Medieval Institute Publications, 1991.

